From the editors of **diabetic** LIVING®

EAT to
BEAT
diabetes™

A **Better Homes and Gardens**® Book
An Imprint of

△▽○
HMH
www.hmhco.com

For information about permission to reproduce selections from this book, write to trade.permissions@hmhco.com or to Permissions, Houghton Mifflin Harcourt Publishing Company, 3 Park Avenue, 19th Floor, New York, New York 10016.

www.hmhco.com

Library of Congress Cataloging-in-Publication Data is available.

ISBN 978-0-544·58265-1 (spiral bound); ISBN 978-0-544-58266-8 (ebk)

Printed in China

SCP 15 14 13 12 11 10 9 8 7
4500781416

Meredith Corporation
Diabetic Living® Eat to Beat Diabetes™

Creative Director: Michelle Bilyeu

Food and Nutrition Editor: Jessie Shafer, RD

Contributing Project Manager: Shelli McConnell, Purple Pear Publishing, Inc.

Cover Photographer: Blaine Moats

Cover Food Stylist: Dianna Nolin

Houghton Mifflin Harcourt

Publisher: Natalie Chapman

Editorial Director: Cindy Kitchel

Executive Editor: Anne Ficklen

Senior Editor: Adam Kowit

Editorial Associate: Molly Aronica

Managing Editor: Marina Padakis Lowry

Design and Layout: Jill Budden

Illustration: Lucy Engelman, Richard Faust

Production Director: Tom Hyland

FOR PEOPLE WITH TYPE 2 DIABETES

The Look AHEAD Trial (Action for Health in Diabetes), a large study of people diagnosed with type 2 diabetes, echoes this act-early, treat-aggressively mantra.

Research shows that the longer you keep glucose levels under control, the better—even if at times they wander out of control.

Researchers tracking people in these multiyear studies call this the "legacy effect" or "metabolic memory." Translated: The earlier and longer glucose, blood pressure, and lipids are under control, the more you can minimize diabetes complications. And we know the list of complications from chronic elevated glucose levels has grown. It now includes higher rates of some cancers, memory problems, and even frailness. "It's best to not take too many holidays from healthy living," says Dagogo-Jack.

True, there's no cure for type 2 diabetes once you've been diagnosed. But—and this is an important *but*—findings from these studies show that losing even a small amount of weight and being physically active nearly every day are effective ways to slow disease progression and live a longer and healthier life.

NUMBERS
to know

If you have prediabetes, keep an eye on your fasting glucose level and A1C. Make sure neither crosses the diagnostic threshold for diabetes. Those already diagnosed with type 2 diabetes should aim to keep numbers within a healthy range (see management goals, *opposite*).

DIAGNOSING PREDIABETES AND DIABETES

	NO DIABETES	PREDIABETES	DIABETES*
FASTING GLUCOSE TEST	< 100 mg/dl	100–125 mg/dl	≥ 126 mg/dl
RANDOM GLUCOSE TEST	< 140 mg/dl	140–199 mg/dl	≥ 200 mg/dl
A1C TEST**	< 5.6%	5.7–6.4%	≥ 6.5%

Reference: American Diabetes Association, Standards of Medical Care for Diabetes, 2014
*Does not apply to pregnant women with gestational diabetes.
**An A1C lab test (not a home test) has become the preferred test to diagnose prediabetes and diabetes. If the results from one test are not convincingly indicative of a diagnosis, a repeat test should be done another day.

MANAGEMENT GOALS AFTER DIAGNOSIS OF TYPE 2 DIABETES

A1C GOAL	< 7%
GLUCOSE GOAL BEFORE MEALS	70–130 mg/dl
GLUCOSE GOAL 1–2 HOURS AFTER MEALS	< 180 mg/dl
BLOOD PRESSURE GOAL	< 140/80 mmHg
LDL CHOLESTEROL GOAL	< 100 mg/dl
HDL CHOLESTEROL GOAL	> 50 mg/dl
TRIGLYCERIDES GOAL	< 150 mg/dl

CAN MY PREDIABETES OR TYPE 2 DIABETES
be cured?

Diabetes remission, the preferred term, is defined by the American Diabetes Association as achieving blood glucose levels below the range to diagnose diabetes (see *opposite*) without taking any glucose-lowering medications. Remission implies the strong possibility of a relapse if you regain weight and/or if the disease progresses as you age. So even if you put your prediabetes or type 2 into remission, don't erase it from your checklist of health concerns. Get an A1C test once or twice a year to stay aware of your glucose status.

HERE'S WHAT WORKS

Forming a series of healthy habits to beat back diabetes can help you stay healthier longer. Find out how—and why—adopting these habits is a recipe for success.

1 START EACH DAY WITH BREAKFAST

Kick-starting your day with a healthy breakfast can reinforce your resolve to eat healthfully the remainder of the day. Data from the National Weight Control Registry show that people who successfully keep pounds off eat breakfast.

2 PICK BETTER BEVERAGES

Sugar-sweetened beverages are everywhere—and in jumbo sizes. According to the American Diabetes Association, there's sufficient evidence to put sugar-sweetened beverages on your do-not-drink list to reduce both weight gain and diabetes-related risk factors.

3 GET TO KNOW PORTIONS

Obesity experts agree our biggest problem is too much food. Reining in portions can help you trim your calories and your waistline.

4 SWAP IN WHOLE GRAINS

If you're like most Americans, you're shy on getting enough whole grains and fiber. Eating more healthful whole grains can help you feel full and reduce heart disease risk factors.

5 EAT MORE FRUITS & VEGGIES

Fruits and vegetables, whether fresh, canned, or frozen, are nutrient-packed, disease-fighting foods that can help you stay healthy and fight inflammation. The Dietary Guidelines for Americans recommends you eat $2\frac{1}{2}$ cups a day each of fruits and vegetables.

6

COOK AT HOME

When you cook at home, you have ultimate control over how much sugar, salt, butter, and other less-than-healthy chef-favorite ingredients go into your foods. Studies show restaurant meals are notoriously higher in sodium, fat, and calories and light on healthful foods.

7

EAT LESS MEAT

The Adventist Health Study shows vegetarians have lower rates of type 2 diabetes than nonvegetarians. In fact, the more people move toward eating vegan, the more they lower their risk of being overweight and/or having insulin resistance or metabolic syndrome (a precursor to type 2 diabetes).

8

PLAN YOUR MEALS

Here's the weekly drill: Plan your meals, inspect your pantry, stick to your shopping list, prepare your meals, eat, and repeat. Don't worry about putting some meals on autopilot. Some research suggests the fewer decisions you need to make about what and how much to eat, the more successful you'll be with weight control.

9

FIND FLAVOR THE SMART WAY

Two flavor favorites, fat and sodium, do pose some health risks when consumed excessively. To eat healthier, learn to skim and trim your fat grams and the amount of sodium you're eating.

10

MOVE MORE & STRESS LESS

Studies show that losing weight and being physically active at least 30 minutes most days of the week can be powerful medicine to slow the progression of diabetes.

HOW TO FORM
healthy
habits

Now you know the 10 healthy habits to beat diabetes, but do you wonder how to begin forming these healthy habits? Word to the wise: Implement them at tortoise speed—slow and steady. Forming healthy habits takes time, effort, and courage. This is a marathon, not a sprint.

"To reap health benefits, you don't have to completely overhaul your lifestyle," says Jill Weisenberger, M.S., RDN, CDE, author of *The Overworked Person's Guide to Better Nutrition* (American Diabetes Association, 2014).

Over time your successes will lead to more success, and forming healthy habits will get easier. Instead of hard work, it will just be life. And a healthy one at that!

4 JUMP STARTS

Beating diabetes doesn't mean changing everything at once. These tips will help you make changes that will last a lifetime.

1 Select one of the healthy habits in this book that will be the easiest for you to change.

2 Assess your current actions related to this habit and set some goals. For example: You want to eat one more serving of fruits and vegetables each day. Ask yourself: How many fruits and vegetables do I eat now?

"Then take a look at the barriers in your life that may get in your way of forming this habit. Brainstorm realistic goals you can confidently implement to make the new habit a reality," Weisenberger says.

3 Make changes in small steps and incorporate the goals with behaviors you already practice. For example, if you're trying to eat one more serving of fruits and vegetables and you already eat breakfast every day, add sliced banana or blueberries to your morning meal. If you eat a standard lunch of a sandwich and side of chips, choose carrots or grape tomatoes instead of the chips.

4 Be sure to pat yourself on the back for each and every small success you rack up.

SET GOALS THE
the smart way

You'll be closer to forming your healthy habits when you set S-M-A-R-T goals to help you get there.

SPECIFIC
Be exact and detailed. Narrowly define your goal.

MEASURABLE
Choose a frequency. Ask: How often will I do this?

ATTAINABLE
Make your goal challenging but also something you can accomplish.

REALISTIC
Set a goal you can do that fits the realities of your lifestyle and schedule.

TIME FRAME
Stay motivated and on track by setting short-term goals.

SAMPLE GOALS TO GET YOU STARTED

For one week I will plan and portion out the foods for my healthy breakfasts.

For three dinners this week I will make sure half my dinner plate is filled with nonstarchy vegetables.

I will drink at least 64 ounces (8 cups) of water every day this week.

HEALTHY HABIT:
START with BREAKFAST

By starting your day with breakfast, you'll set yourself up for a nutrition-filled noon, afternoon, and evening. Breakfast is a great opportunity to eat more meals at home and to get more of the foods that are hard to fit in, such as whole grains, fruits, and dairy foods, as well as much-needed fiber. Plus, studies show that people who eat breakfast are more successful at keeping off extra pounds.

MY BREAKFAST GOAL

Every day this week I will plan my breakfast the night before.

> **" I lost 130 pounds in 18 months, and my taste buds gravitated to healthy, ungreasy, unprocessed foods. "**

VALERIE SCHROCK | age 39

Starting in adolescence and through college, Valerie developed worsening polycystic ovary syndrome (PCOS). Telltale signs are insulin resistance, excess weight gain, and menstrual irregularities. At 25 years old, she was diagnosed with type 2 diabetes. Her metformin dose ramped up to max, and she needed thyroid medication. Valerie attended college on a softball scholarship, but weight gain narrowed her world. After college, she quit doing anything physical. "I didn't even feel at ease traveling or going to restaurants."

Kick-start into action: "I tried numerous diets over the years, but weight loss was near impossible." After visiting 10 endocrinologists in 20 years and always getting the advice to eat less, Valerie did her own research and pursued gastric bypass surgery. "I lost 130 pounds and my glucose plummeted." Her A1C is now 5.5%.

Words of wisdom: "Even when things are looking grim, embrace change and walk through it with your eyes wide open. See what's on the other side."

MAKE-AHEAD
mornings

Get some of the prep work done early to save time in the morning. All of these recipes can help you meet your goal to start each day the healthy way.

TWO-BRAN
REFRIGERATOR MUFFINS

recipe on *page 24*

Two-Bran Refrigerator Muffins

photo on *page 23*
SERVINGS 12 (1 muffin each)
CARB. PER SERVING 27 g
PREP 15 minutes   CHILL up to 3 days
BAKE 20 minutes

$^2/_3$ cup whole bran cereal
$^1/_3$ cup oat bran
$^2/_3$ cup boiling water
$^1/_2$ cup buttermilk
  2 egg whites, lightly beaten
$^1/_4$ cup unsweetened applesauce
$^1/_4$ cup canola oil
$1^1/_2$ cups all-purpose flour
$^1/_2$ cup packed brown sugar*
$1^1/_2$ teaspoons baking powder
  1 teaspoon ground cinnamon
$^1/_4$ teaspoon baking soda
$^1/_4$ teaspoon salt
  Nonstick cooking spray

1. In a medium bowl stir together whole bran cereal and oat bran. Stir in the boiling water. Stir in buttermilk, egg whites, applesauce, and oil.
2. In a large bowl stir together flour, brown sugar, baking powder, cinnamon, baking soda, and salt. Add cereal mixture all at once to flour mixture, stirring just until moistened. Place plastic wrap over the surface of the batter. Cover tightly; refrigerate up to 3 days (or bake immediately).
3. To bake, preheat oven to 400°F. Coat as many $2^1/_2$-inch muffin cups with cooking spray as needed to bake desired number of muffins. Spoon batter into the prepared muffin cups, filling each two-thirds full. Bake about 20 minutes or until a wooden toothpick inserted near the centers comes out clean. Remove from muffin cups; serve warm.
*SUGAR SUBSTITUTE: We do not recommend using a sugar substitute for this recipe.

PER SERVING: 158 cal., 5 g total fat (0 g sat. fat), 0 mg chol., 168 mg sodium, 27 g carb. (2 g fiber, 11 g sugars), 3 g pro.

Turkey-Sweet Pepper Strata

SERVINGS 8 (1 cup each)
CARB. PER SERVING 17 g
PREP 35 minutes   CHILL 8 to 24 hours
BAKE 50 minutes   STAND 5 minutes

  1 to $1^1/_4$ pounds ground turkey breast
  1 teaspoon onion powder
$^1/_2$ teaspoon dried sage
$^1/_4$ teaspoon ground nutmeg
$^1/_4$ teaspoon crushed red pepper
$^1/_8$ teaspoon dried marjoram
  3 whole grain English muffins, split
  1 cup refrigerated or frozen egg product, thawed, or 4 eggs
  4 eggs
  2 cups fat-free milk
  1 teaspoon dry mustard
$^1/_4$ teaspoon paprika
  2 cups chopped green and/or red sweet peppers
$^1/_4$ cup sliced green onions (2)
  1 cup shredded reduced-fat cheddar cheese

1. In a large bowl combine ground turkey breast, onion powder, $^1/_2$ teaspoon *coarsely ground black pepper,* the dried sage, nutmeg, crushed red pepper, and marjoram; use clean hands to mix well. In large nonstick skillet cook and stir turkey mixture over medium heat until browned.
2. Lightly coat a 3-quart rectangular baking dish with *nonstick cooking spray.* Cut English muffins into quarters; arrange in an even layer in baking dish. Sprinkle with turkey mixture.
3. Whisk together egg product, eggs, milk, dry mustard, $^1/_4$ teaspoon *salt,* and the paprika; pour over turkey mixture. Sprinkle with sweet peppers and green onions. Cover; chill at least 8 hours or up to 24 hours.
4. Preheat oven to 350°F. Bake 45 minutes. Sprinkle with cheese. Bake 5 to 10 minutes more or until a knife inserted in center comes out clean. Let stand 5 minutes before serving. If desired, garnish with *fresh sage leaves.*

PER SERVING: 235 cal., 6 g total fat (3 g sat. fat), 142 mg chol., 448 mg sodium, 17 g carb. (3 g fiber, 7 g sugars), 28 g pro.

TURKEY-SWEET PEPPER
STRATA

FARMER'S CASSEROLE

SERVINGS 6 (1 piece each)
CARB. PER SERVING 24 g
PREP 25 minutes   **BAKE** 40 minutes
STAND 5 minutes

    Nonstick cooking spray
 3 cups frozen shredded hash brown
    potatoes
 ¾ cup shredded Monterey Jack cheese
    with jalapeño peppers or shredded
    cheddar cheese (3 ounces)
 1 cup diced cooked ham, Canadian-style
    bacon, or cooked breakfast sausage
 ¼ cup sliced green onions (2)
 1 cup refrigerated or frozen egg product,
    thawed, or 4 eggs, lightly beaten
 1½ cups fat-free milk
 ⅛ teaspoon salt
 ⅛ teaspoon black pepper

1. Preheat oven to 350°F. Coat a 2-quart square baking dish with cooking spray. Arrange hash brown potatoes evenly in the prepared dish. Sprinkle with cheese, ham, and green onions. In a medium bowl whisk together eggs, milk, salt, and pepper. Pour egg mixture over layers in dish.

2. Bake, uncovered, 40 to 45 minutes or until a knife inserted near the center comes out clean. Let stand 5 minutes before serving.

MAKE-AHEAD DIRECTIONS: Prepare as directed through Step 2. Cover and chill up to 24 hours. Bake as directed 50 to 55 minutes or until a knife inserted near the center comes out clean. Let stand 5 minutes.

PER SERVING: 222 cal., 7 g total fat (4 g sat. fat), 29 mg chol., 527 mg sodium, 24 g carb. (2 g fiber, 4 g sugars), 16 g pro.

Orange-Date Pumpkin Bread

SERVINGS 32 (1 slice each)
CARB. PER SERVING 23 g or 20 g
PREP 25 minutes   BAKE 50 minutes
COOL 10 minutes   STAND overnight

2	cups all-purpose flour
1⅓	cups whole wheat flour
2	teaspoons baking powder
1	teaspoon ground nutmeg
½	teaspoon baking soda
½	teaspoon salt
1	15-ounce can pumpkin
¾	cup sugar*
1	cup refrigerated or frozen egg product, thawed, or 4 eggs, lightly beaten
½	cup honey
⅓	cup canola oil
1	teaspoon finely grated orange peel
⅓	cup orange juice
½	cup chopped walnuts or pecans, toasted
½	cup snipped pitted dates or raisins

ORANGE-DATE PUMPKIN BREAD

1. Preheat oven to 350°F. Grease the bottom and ½ inch up the sides of two 8×4×2-inch loaf pans; set aside. In a large bowl combine flours, baking powder, nutmeg, baking soda, and salt.
2. In a medium bowl stir together pumpkin, sugar, eggs, honey, oil, orange peel, and orange juice. Using a wooden spoon, stir pumpkin mixture into flour mixture just until combined. Stir in walnuts and dates. Divide mixture between prepared loaf pans.
3. Bake about 50 minutes or until a wooden toothpick inserted near the centers comes out clean. Cool in pans on wire racks 10 minutes. Remove from pans. Cool completely on wire racks. Wrap in plastic wrap; store overnight before slicing.
*SUGAR SUBSTITUTE: Choose Splenda Sugar Blend. Follow package directions to use product amount equivalent to ¾ cup sugar.
MAKE-AHEAD DIRECTIONS: Place each cooled loaf of bread in a freezer container or bag. Seal and freeze up to 3 months. To serve, thaw the wrapped bread at room temperature before slicing.

PER SERVING: 130 cal., 4 g total fat (0 g sat. fat), 0 mg chol., 102 mg sodium, 23 g carb. (2 g fiber, 12 g sugars), 3 g pro.

PER SERVING WITH SUBSTITUTE: Same as above, except 123 cal., 20 g carb. (9 g sugars).

ORANGE-BACON BREAKFAST TOASTS: Cut four ½-inch-thick slices from an Orange-Date Pumpkin Bread loaf; set aside. Peel 1 orange; slice crosswise and cut up. Crisp-cook 2 slices bacon; coarsely crumble. Toast the Orange-Date Pumpkin Bread slices until lightly golden brown. Spread 1 tablespoon reduced-fat cream cheese (Neufchâtel) onto each toasted slice. Top with orange pieces and bacon. Serve immediately. Makes 4 servings (1 topped slice each).

PER SERVING: 185 cal., 7 g total fat (2 g sat. fat), 10 mg chol., 195 mg sodium, 27 g carb. (2 g fiber, 15 g sugars), 5 g pro.

OVERNIGHT BLUEBERRY
COFFEE CAKE

Overnight Blueberry Coffee Cake

SERVINGS 12 (1 piece each)
CARB. PER SERVING 25 g or 19 g
PREP 25 minutes   CHILL 8 hours
BAKE 35 minutes

        Nonstick cooking spray
    1   cup whole wheat pastry flour
   ¾   cup yellow cornmeal
   ⅓   cup granulated sugar*
  1½   teaspoons ground cinnamon
    1   teaspoon baking soda
   ½   teaspoon ground ginger
   ¼   teaspoon salt
    1   cup plain fat-free Greek yogurt
   ¾   cup refrigerated or frozen egg product,
        thawed, or 3 eggs, lightly beaten
   ⅓   cup canola oil
   ¼   cup unsweetened applesauce
    1   tablespoon butter flavoring
    2   cups frozen blueberries
    2   tablespoons packed dark brown sugar*
        Frozen light whipped dessert topping,
          thawed (optional)
        Ground ginger (optional)

1. Lightly coat a 2-quart rectangular baking dish with cooking spray; set aside. In a large bowl stir together pastry flour, cornmeal, granulated sugar, 1 teaspoon of the cinnamon, the baking soda, the ½ teaspoon ginger, and the salt.
2. In a medium bowl whisk together yogurt, eggs, oil, applesauce, and butter flavoring until well mixed. Add egg mixture to the flour mixture; stir just until combined. Spread half of the batter into the prepared dish.
3. Sprinkle with 1 cup of the frozen blueberries. Top with the remaining batter; spread evenly. Cover and chill in the refrigerator 8 to 24 hours.
4. Allow coffee cake to stand at room temperature while the oven preheats to 350°F. In a small bowl toss together the remaining 1 cup frozen blueberries, the brown sugar, and the remaining ½ teaspoon cinnamon; sprinkle on top of the batter. Bake, uncovered, about 35 minutes or until a toothpick inserted near the center comes out clean. Serve warm. If desired, serve with whipped topping and sprinkle with additional ginger.
*SUGAR SUBSTITUTES: Choose from Splenda Granular or Sweet'N Low bulk or packets for the granulated sugar. Choose Splenda Brown Sugar Blend for the brown sugar. Follow package directions to use product amounts equivalent to ⅓ cup granulated sugar and 2 tablespoons packed brown sugar.

PER SERVING: 175 cal., 7 g total fat (0 g sat. fat), 0 mg chol., 195 mg sodium, 25 g carb. (2 g fiber, 12 g sugars), 5 g pro.

PER SERVING WITH SUBSTITUTE: same as above, except 152 cal., 19 g carb. (5 g sugars).

EXPERT TIP

"Set your goals high and don't forget to celebrate each and every step you accomplish to keep you motivated and positive on your road to success"

– Kellie Antinori-Lent, M.S.N., RN, CDE, diabetes nurse specialist, University of Pittsburgh Medical Center, Shadyside Hospital

Yogurt Breakfast Pudding

SERVINGS 2 ($^3/_4$ cup each)
CARB. PER SERVING 38 g
PREP 10 minutes
CHILL 8 hours or up to 2 days

- 1 6-ounce carton vanilla
  low-fat yogurt
- $^1/_2$ cup regular rolled oats
- $^1/_2$ cup fat-free milk
- $^1/_4$ cup canned crushed pineapple
  (juice pack)
- 1 tablespoon chia seeds or flaxseed meal
- $^1/_2$ teaspoon vanilla
- $^1/_8$ teaspoon ground cinnamon
- 4 teaspoons sliced almonds, toasted
- $^1/_4$ of a small red apple, chopped

1. In a medium bowl stir together yogurt, oats, milk, pineapple, chia seeds, vanilla, and cinnamon.
2. Transfer to an airtight container. Cover and seal. Chill in the refrigerator at least 8 hours or up to 2 days. Stir well before serving. To serve, sprinkle each serving with 2 teaspoons of the almonds; top with chopped apple.

PER SERVING: 255 cal., 7 g total fat (1 g sat. fat), 5 mg chol., 84 mg sodium, 38 g carb. (5 g fiber, 21 g sugars), 11 g pro.

Cranberry-Almond Cereal Mix

SERVINGS 14 ($^1/_3$ cup each)
CARB. PER SERVING 32 g
PREP 10 minutes   COOK 12 minutes

- 1 cup regular rolled oats
- 1 cup quick-cooking barley
- 1 cup bulgur or cracked wheat
- 1 cup dried cranberries, snipped dried
  apricots, or raisins
- $^1/_2$ cup sliced almonds, toasted
- $^1/_3$ cup sugar*
- 1 tablespoon ground cinnamon
- $^1/_4$ teaspoon salt

1. In a large bowl stir together oats, barley, bulgur, cranberries, almonds, sugar, cinnamon, and salt. Cover tightly. Store at room temperature up to 2 months or freeze up to 6 months (stir or shake mixture before measuring).
2. For two breakfast servings, in a small saucepan bring 1$^1/_3$ cups *water* to boiling. Add $^2/_3$ cup of the oat mixture. Reduce heat. Simmer, covered, 12 to 15 minutes or until desired consistency, stirring occasionally. If desired, serve with *fat-free milk*.
MICROWAVE DIRECTIONS: For one breakfast serving, in a 1-quart microwave-safe bowl combine $^3/_4$ cup *water* and $^1/_3$ cup of the oat mixture. Microwave, uncovered, on 50% power (medium) 8 to 11 minutes or until desired consistency, stirring once. Stir before serving.
*SUGAR SUBSTITUTE: We do not recommend using a sugar substitute for this recipe.

PER SERVING: 158 cal., 2 g total fat (0 g sat. fat), 0 mg chol., 44 mg sodium, 32 g carb. (5 g fiber, 11 g sugars), 4 g pro.

CRANBERRY-ALMOND
CEREAL MIX

PEAR-CRANBERRY BAKED
FRENCH TOAST with
ORANGE-RICOTTA CREAM

Pear-Cranberry Baked French Toast with Orange-Ricotta Cream

SERVINGS 12 (1 portion French toast and 2 tablespoons ricotta cream each)
CARB. PER SERVING 28 g
PREP 45 minutes   **BAKE** 35 minutes
STAND 10 minutes

2	7-ounce loaves whole grain baguette-style bread
1	medium fresh red pear, cored and chopped
½	cup dried cranberries, snipped
5	eggs
1¼	cups fat-free milk
3	tablespoons reduced-calorie maple-flavor syrup
1	tablespoon packed brown sugar*
1	teaspoon pumpkin pie spice
1	teaspoon vanilla
¼	teaspoon salt
1	recipe Orange Ricotta Cream

1. Preheat oven to 350°F. Grease a 2-quart rectangular baking dish; set aside. Trim rounded ends off baguettes and discard. Cut baguettes crosswise into ½-inch slices. To assemble, arrange half of the bread slices in the bottom of the prepared baking dish. Top with half of the pears and half of the cranberries. Repeat layers.
2. In a medium bowl whisk together eggs, milk, maple-flavor syrup, brown sugar, pumpkin pie spice, vanilla, and salt. Slowly pour egg mixture evenly over bread slices.**
3. Bake, uncovered, 35 to 40 minutes or until a knife inserted in center comes out clean. Let stand 10 minutes before serving.
4. To serve, cut French toast into 12 portions. Spoon ricotta cream evenly over French toast. Serve warm.

EXPERT TIP

"In California, we love our huevos (eggs) rancheros. Here's how to make it a fast and healthy breakfast. Warm a corn tortilla in a nonstick frying pan. Add ¼ cup black beans. Crack an egg on top. Cook, covered, over medium heat 4 to 6 minutes. Top with cheese, avocado slices, and/or salsa."

– Debra Lesin Norman, FNP-C, CDE, diabetes educator and advocate, Lanark Medical, Van Nuys, California

ORANGE RICOTTA CREAM: In a small bowl combine one 6-ounce carton plain fat-free or low-fat Greek yogurt, ½ cup light ricotta cheese, 2 tablespoons honey, 1 tablespoon very finely chopped crystallized ginger, and 1 teaspoon finely shredded orange peel. Set aside.

*SUGAR SUBSTITUTE: We do not recommend using a sugar substitute for this recipe.

**MAKE-AHEAD DIRECTIONS: Do not preheat oven in Step 1. Prepare according to directions through Step 2. Cover and chill 2 to 24 hours. Preheat oven to 350°F. Continue with Step 3 as directed.

PER SERVING: 177 cal., 4 g total fat (1 g sat. fat), 81 mg chol., 236 mg sodium, 28 g carb. (2 g fiber, 14 g sugars), 8 g pro.

10-MINUTE
breakfasts

Instead of viewing breakfast as a chore, make mornings fun and flavorful with these quick recipes that leave you plenty of time to get out the door.

QUICK CORNMEAL
SAUSAGE PANCAKE

SOUTHWEST BREAKFAST QUESADILLA

Southwest Breakfast Quesadilla

SERVINGS 1
CARB. PER SERVING 25 g
START TO FINISH 10 minutes

Nonstick cooking spray
¼ cup refrigerated or frozen egg product, thawed
⅛ to ¼ teaspoon salt-free Southwest chipotle seasoning blend
1 whole wheat flour tortilla
2 tablespoons shredded part-skim mozzarella cheese
2 tablespoons canned no-salt-added black beans, rinsed and drained
2 tablespoons refrigerated fresh pico de gallo or chopped tomato
Refrigerated fresh pico de gallo or chopped tomato (optional)

1. Coat a medium nonstick skillet with cooking spray. Preheat skillet over medium heat. Add egg to hot skillet; sprinkle with seasoning blend. Cook over medium heat, without stirring, until egg begins to set on the bottom and around edge. Using a spatula or a large spoon, lift and fold the partially cooked egg so that the uncooked portion flows underneath. Continue cooking over medium heat 30 to 60 seconds or until egg is cooked through but is still glossy and moist.
2. Immediately spoon cooked egg onto one side of the tortilla. Top with cheese, beans, and the 2 tablespoons pico de gallo. Fold tortilla over filling to cover; press gently.
3. Wipe out the same skillet with a paper towel. Coat skillet with cooking spray. Preheat skillet over medium heat. Cook filled tortilla in hot skillet about 2 minutes or until tortilla is browned and filling is heated through, turning once. If desired, top with additional pico de gallo.

PER SERVING: 175 cal., 5 g total fat (1 g sat. fat), 9 mg chol., 507 mg sodium, 25 g carb. (14 g fiber, 2 g sugars), 19 g pro.

Quick Cornmeal Sausage Pancake

SERVINGS 1
CARB. PER SERVING 31 g
START TO FINISH 10 minutes

Nonstick cooking spray
1 link country-style chicken breakfast sausage, such as Al Fresco All Natural brand, cut into bite-size pieces
1 egg
2 tablespoons cornmeal
1 teaspoon honey
2 tablespoons sugar-free maple-flavor syrup
2 teaspoons chopped pecans

1. Lightly coat a small nonstick skillet with cooking spray. Heat over medium-high heat. Add sausage pieces and cook until browned.
2. Meanwhile, in a small bowl whisk together egg, cornmeal, and honey. Pour egg mixture over hot sausage. Cook 1 to 2 minutes or until bottom is set and golden brown. Flip pancake over. Cook 1 to 2 minutes more or until second side is golden brown. Drizzle with syrup and sprinkle with pecans.

PER SERVING: 273 cal., 12 g total fat (3 g sat. fat), 211 mg chol., 283 mg sodium, 31 g carb. (1 g fiber, 10 g sugars), 14 g pro.

QUICK BREAKFAST PIZZAS

SERVINGS 1
CARB. PER SERVING 23 g
START TO FINISH 10 minutes

Nonstick cooking spray
4   slices turkey pepperoni, quartered
2   tablespoons chopped green sweet
     pepper
2   tablespoons sliced fresh mushrooms
2   egg whites
1   tablespoon milk
1   deli flat 7-grain thin roll, split
2   teaspoons pizza sauce
1   slice mozzarella cheese,
     cut diagonally into quarters
4   slices roma tomato

1. Coat a small nonstick skillet with cooking spray. Heat over medium heat. Add pepperoni, sweet pepper, and mushrooms to skillet; cook and stir 2 minutes.

2. In a small bowl whisk together egg whites and milk; pour over pepperoni mixture in skillet. Cook until egg white mixture begins to set. Using a spatula, fold the partially cooked egg white mixture over; cook about 2 minutes more or until cooked through.

3. Meanwhile, toast the roll halves. While still warm, spread each half with 1 teaspoon of the pizza sauce; place two of the cheese quarters on each half.

4. Spoon half of the egg mixture over each of the prepared roll halves. Top with tomato slices.

PER SERVING: 218 cal., 6 g total fat
(3 g sat. fat), 23 mg chol.,
563 mg sodium, 23 g carb.
(6 g fiber, 5 g sugars), 21 g pro.

PEANUT BUTTER BANANA
BREAKFAST SANDWICH

Peanut Butter Banana Breakfast Sandwich

SERVINGS 1
CARB. PER SERVING 35 g
START TO FINISH 10 minutes

2 slices 100% whole wheat with honey bread (45 calories per slice), such as Sara Lee Delightful brand
4 teaspoons reduced-fat natural-style creamy peanut butter, such as Smucker's brand
1 very small banana or ½ of a medium banana, sliced

1. Toast bread. While toast is still warm, spread 2 teaspoons of the peanut butter on each slice. Arrange banana slices on one of the slices of peanut butter toast. Top with the other slice, peanut butter side down, to make a sandwich.

PER SERVING: 269 cal., 9 g total fat (1 g sat. fat), 0 mg chol., 237 mg sodium, 35 g carb. (8 g fiber, 11 g sugars), 12 g pro.

MAPLE BERRY-TOPPED
WAFFLES

Maple Berry-Topped Waffles

SERVINGS 2 (1 waffle each)
CARB. PER SERVING 26 g
START TO FINISH 10 minutes

- 2 frozen 7-grain waffles, such as Kashi brand
- ½ cup fresh blueberries, blackberries, and/or raspberries
- 6 tablespoons plain fat-free Greek yogurt
- 2 tablespoons light pancake syrup

1. Toast the frozen waffles according to package directions.
2. Meanwhile, in a small bowl combine half of the berries, the yogurt, and syrup. Divide the yogurt mixture between the toasted waffles; sprinkle with the remaining berries.

PER SERVING: 143 cal., 3 g total fat (0 g sat. fat), 0 mg chol., 239 mg sodium, 26 g carb. (5 g fiber, 13 g sugars), 6 g pro.

Chocolate-Strawberry Breakfast Parfaits

SERVINGS 2 (1 parfait each)
CARB. PER SERVING 30 g
START TO FINISH 10 minutes

- 1 4-ounce carton chocolate fat-free Greek yogurt, such as Oikos brand
- ½ cup sliced fresh strawberries
- 2 chocolate-flavor breakfast biscuits, such as belVita brand, crushed (half of one package)
- 1 6-ounce carton strawberry fat-free Greek yogurt

1. Layer chocolate yogurt, sliced strawberries, crushed biscuits, and strawberry yogurt in two parfait glasses.

PER SERVING: 189 cal., 2 g total fat (0 g sat. fat), 0 mg chol., 98 mg sodium, 30 g carb. (2 g fiber, 22 g sugars), 13 g pro.

CHOCOLATE-STRAWBERRY
BREAKFAST PARFAITS

COCOA ALMOND FRENCH TOAST

SERVINGS 2 (2 slices bread, 1 tablespoon chocolate-flavor syrup, and 2 a fresh raspberries each)
CARB. PER SERVING 29 g
START TO FINISH 10 minutes

- ½ cup unsweetened almond milk, such as Almond Breeze brand
- ⅓ cup refrigerated or frozen egg product, thawed
- ½ teaspoon ground cinnamon
- ½ teaspoon ground nutmeg
- ¼ cup dark chocolate-flavor almonds, finely chopped (1½ ounces)
  Nonstick cooking spray
- 4 slices light whole wheat bread, such as Village Hearth or Sara Lee brand
- 2 tablespoons sugar-free chocolate-flavor syrup
- ¼ cup fresh raspberries

1. In a shallow dish beat together almond milk, eggs, cinnamon, and nutmeg. Set aside ½ tablespoon of the almonds. Place the remaining almonds in another shallow dish.

2. Coat a griddle* with cooking spray. Heat griddle over medium heat. Meanwhile, dip each bread slice into the egg mixture, turning to coat both sides (let bread soak in egg mixture about 10 seconds per side). Dip soaked bread in the almonds, turning to coat both sides.

3. Cook almond-coated bread slices on hot griddle 4 to 6 minutes or until golden brown, turning once. Cut slices in half diagonally. Arrange on two plates. Drizzle with chocolate syrup; top with raspberries and reserved almonds.

***TEST KITCHEN TIP:** If you do not have a griddle, coat a large skillet with nonstick cooking spray; continue as directed, except cook half of the bread slices at a time.

PER SERVING: 250 cal., 12 g total fat (1 g sat. fat), 0 mg chol., 391 mg sodium, 29 g carb. (8 g fiber, 4 g sugars), 15 g pro.

HEALTHY HABIT:
PICK BETTER BEVERAGES

From sodas and energy drinks to teas and juices, sugar-sweetened beverages line the aisles of supermarkets, convenience stores, and coffee shops. They're also available in unreasonably large portions. Cutting back on these beverages can help you drop pounds and reduce your diabetes-related risk factors, such as high blood glucose and weight gain.

MY BEVERAGE GOAL

I will drink at least 64 ounces (8 cups) of water a day at least five days this week.

BETTER BEVERAGES

" Within 6 months, I felt better mentally and was no longer ashamed of myself. "

DARLENE MAALO | age 74

In 2000, Darlene was hit with a triple whammy—her husband died, she lost her job, and she was diagnosed with breast cancer. "I went into a mental tailspin. I ate a lot and got depressed." By 2006, she weighed 300 pounds and was diagnosed with type 2 diabetes, high blood pressure, and abnormal lipids.

Kick-start into action: Darlene knew she had to do something, so she joined Curves with a friend who had a buddy plan. "I remember saying, 'If I see one bit of Spandex, I'm outta here!'" Darlene recalls her first day at the gym, when the instructors had to help her in and out of the machines. Regardless, they cheered her on. She also met with a dietitian who helped her learn what and how much to eat. Darlene has now lost more than 100 pounds, and, after working out at Curves for two years, she became an instructor. "The members call me The Sarge," she says with a laugh.

Words of wisdom: "It's not just the weight loss. It's about how I feel good about myself and inspire others."

HOW BEVERAGES stack up

When it comes to managing diabetes, beware of beverages. They go down fast, and the calories and carbohydrate add up quickly.

+ medium caramel latte
240 cal.
34 g carb.

+ 12 oz. orange juice
160 cal.
37 g carb.

+ 20 oz. regular cola
250 cal.
65 g carb.

+ 16 oz. sports drink
106 cal.
28 g carb.

+ 8 oz. coffee with 1 tsp. sugar
16 cal.
4 g carb.

WOW!

= **772** calories
168 g carb.

SIPPING
calories

Americans take in an average of 21 teaspoons of added sugars per day—and many of those added sugars (which are a carbohydrate) come from liquids. Unfortunately, those drinks add calories and carbohydrate without making us feel full. Sugar-sweetened beverages aren't our only source of added sugars, but they lead the pack by supplying more than one-third of added sugars consumed worldwide. You can see how calories and carbohydrate from beverages add up fast.

Beverages of all types and sizes line supermarket aisles and convenience stores. Restaurants and coffee shops love to serve them bigger than ever.

Many of these drinks are high in calories and carbohydrate from sucrose, high-fructose corn syrup, or other caloric sweeteners. Consuming sweetened drinks in vast quantities has become a health concern. Most beverage choices, other than 100-percent fruit juice and milk, provide very little nutrition. Research now shows that beyond packing on the pounds, these empty calories may be worsening diabetes risk factors, such as those related to cardiovascular disease.

Picking better beverages may be one big key to a healthier you. Even better, it may be a painless way to trim calories and pounds. For Joe Dragon (see his story on *page 162*), the simple change of giving up regular soda helped him put his type 2 diabetes in reverse. Now he drinks diet soda, iced tea, and water. Like Joe, you can pick better beverages to help control your diabetes.

BETTER BEVERAGES

- Water
- Diet soda, punch, or flavored tea
- Club soda
- Plain or flavored seltzer, mineral, or sparkling water
- Diet tonic water
- Fat-free (skim) or 1% milk
- Hot or iced coffee*
- Hot or iced tea*
- 100-percent fruit juice**

*Flavor with reduced-fat milk and/or a low-calorie sweetener if desired.
**Drink small quantities or, better yet, eat whole fruits instead.

ARE SUGAR SUBSTITUTES safe?

Health rumors related to artificial sweeteners have some people choosing sugar-sweetened beverages over those sweetened with sugar substitutes. If perceived health risks are holding you back from switching to diet drinks, have no fear: Sugar substitutes are approved by the U.S. Food and Drug Administration for essentially the whole population, including people with diabetes. In addition, the American Diabetes Association concludes these sweeteners don't raise blood glucose levels unless the food or beverage contains other ingredients with calories.

Do sugar substitutes cause hunger and weight gain?

You might be familiar with headlines accusing diet drinks sweetened with sugar substitutes of causing weight gain, sugar cravings, and blood glucose spikes and warning that these beverages could thwart weight loss efforts.

To the contrary, two recent clinical studies, each with about 300 overweight participants, showed people in the group who drank diet beverages lost more weight than the people who were told not to drink them. One study showed a decrease in hunger among diet beverage drinkers.

The other study showed that diet beverage drinkers reduced their dessert consumption more. Perhaps diet drinks helped people satisfy their sweet tooth.

Is it safe to consume sugar substitutes when pregnant?

It is natural to be concerned about what is safe to eat for healthy development of a baby. It is especially important for women with diabetes to control how much sugar they consume to avoid fetal and neonatal complications from high blood sugar.

Using sugar substitutes can help curb sugar intake. According the Academy of Nutrition and Dietetics and the American Diabetes Association, using sugar substitutes is acceptable during pregnancy. The acceptable daily limit for sugar substitutes, set by the FDA, does include pregnant and lactating women, and it is nearly impossible to consume more than this limit on a daily basis.

WHAT COUNTS AS ONE SERVING?

One drink of alcohol is **5 ounces** of wine, **12 ounces** of beer, or **1½ ounces** of distilled liquor.

ALCOHOL & diabetes

You may be wondering if it's safe or smart to drink alcohol with diabetes. Research shows there are some benefits to drinking a moderate amount. If you choose to do so, keep your intake in line with safe limits.

CAN PEOPLE WITH DIABETES DRINK ALCOHOL?

Yes, if you want to. But do bear in mind safety concerns and the fact that all alcoholic beverages contain calories.

Pregnant women and people with a history of alcohol abuse, liver disease, pancreatitis, or elevated triglycerides should not drink alcohol. People who take prescription or over-the-counter medications that can interact with alcohol should not drink. To practice caution, ask your health care provider if drinking alcohol is wise for you.

WHAT IS A SAFE AMOUNT OF ALCOHOL?

Women can safely drink up to one drink per day and no more than three. For men, it's two drinks per day and no more than four. Don't save up or average this amount over a few days.

ARE THERE HEALTH BENEFITS OF DRINKING ALCOHOL?

In fact, there are. Studies show light to moderate alcohol intake can increase insulin sensitivity and decrease insulin resistance over time. This is due to alcohol's anti-inflammatory effects and is exactly the response you want to slow your prediabetes or type 2. It results in lower fasting glucose, lower risk of heart disease and strokes, and lower risk of death. If you don't currently drink, however, don't start just to gain the health benefits.

Excess alcohol intake, on the other hand, produces the opposite response and wipes away any benefit.

"Moderate amounts of alcohol have little short- or long-term effects on glucose levels in people with diabetes. But more than three drinks per day over time can make glucose control a challenge," says Marion Franz, M.S., RD, CDE, a member of *Diabetic Living*'s advisory board.

Although alcoholic beverages are made from grains or fruits (which contain starches and sugars), through the process of fermentation and distillation, alcohol cannot be changed into glucose.

WHAT ABOUT ALCOHOL AND MY DIABETES MEDICATIONS?

If you take insulin and/or a glucose-lowering medication that can cause hypoglycemia, such as a pill in the category of sulfonylureas, eat some food when you drink alcohol and always carry a treatment for low blood sugar, such as glucose tabs. Keep in mind that hypoglycemia may occur many hours after you drink.

IS RED WINE THE BEST CHOICE?

Despite what you may have heard, research doesn't show one type of alcohol has more benefits than another. The benefit is the anti-inflammatory effects of alcohol in general.

SPLITTING
strategies

At a party where the alcohol is flowing? Stretch your volume of alcoholic drinks by mixing wine or beer with a zero-calorie beverage, such as diet ginger ale or diet lemonade. That way, when others are reaching for another glass, you can do the same without doubling your calorie and alcohol intake.

LIGHT LEMON SHANDY

Combine
12 ounces light beer
with
6 ounces light lemonade

Get two drinks for a total
106 calories and 7 g carb

RED WINE SPRITZER

Combine
5 ounces red wine
with
6 ounces diet ginger ale

Get two drinks for a total
120 calories and 4 g carb

PEAR-APPLE CIDER

CITRUS GREEN TEA

HOT & COLD
quenchers

Whether you want something warm and comforting or cool and refreshing, sip on these lighter, flavor-filled beverages.

Warm Pear-Apple Cider

SERVINGS 4 (10 ounces each)
CARB. PER SERVING 8 g or 5 g
PREP 20 minutes **COOK** 20 minutes

- 6 cups water
- 2 medium ripe pears, quartered, cored, and thinly sliced
- 2 medium red-skin cooking apples, quartered, cored, and thinly sliced
- 2 3- to 4-inch sticks cinnamon
- 1 1-inch piece fresh ginger, peeled and thinly sliced
- 1 teaspoon whole cloves
- 2 tablespoons sugar*
- ¼ teaspoon ground cinnamon
- ¼ teaspoon ground ginger
- Pear and apple slices (optional)
- Cinnamon sticks (optional)

1. In a 4- to 5-quart Dutch oven combine the water, pears, and apples. Cut an 8-inch square of double-thickness cheesecloth. Place the 2 cinnamon sticks, the ginger slices, and whole cloves in the center of the cheesecloth. Pull up corners around the spices; tie with kitchen string. Add the spice bag to the Dutch oven. Stir in sugar, ground cinnamon, and ground ginger.
2. Bring mixture to boiling; reduce heat. Simmer, covered, 20 to 25 minutes or until pear and apple slices are very tender. Remove the spice bag from the fruit mixture and discard.
3. Place a fine-mesh sieve on top of a large heatproof bowl. Pour fruit mixture into the sieve. Using a large spoon, press on the fruit to remove as much juice as possible.
4. Pour the strained spiced cider into a clean saucepan and heat through. Serve in mugs; if desired, garnish with additional pear and apple slices and cinnamon sticks.
*SUGAR SUBSTITUTES: Choose from Splenda Sugar Blend or C&H Light Sugar Blend. Follow package directions to use product amount equivalent to 2 tablespoons sugar.

PER SERVING: 31 cal., 0 g total fat, 0 mg chol., 11 mg sodium, 8 g carb. (0 g fiber, 7 g sugars), 0 g pro.
PER SERVING WITH SUBSTITUTE: Same as above, except 21 cal., 5 g carb. (4 g sugars).

EXPERT TIP

"Take charge. Turn the table on your provider by knowing your ABC's—**A**1c and glucose, **B**lood pressure, and **C**holesterol and the target goals. If your numbers aren't hitting their targets, ask why not and what you can both do to achieve them."

– Kathy Gold, RN, CDE, Director of Education and Wellness for the Diabetes Research and Wellness Foundation based in Washington, D.C.

Citrus Green Tea

SERVINGS 1 (7 ounces)
CARB. PER SERVING 5 g
START TO FINISH 20 minutes

- 1 cup water
- 1 lemon peel strip (2½ × 1 inches)
- 1 orange peel strip (2½ × 1 inches)
- 1 green tea bag
- ½ teaspoon honey
- 1 lemon slice

1. In a small saucepan combine the water, lemon peel strip, and orange peel strip. Bring to boiling; reduce heat. Simmer, uncovered, 10 minutes. Using a slotted spoon, remove lemon and orange peel strips; discard.
2. Place tea bag in a heatproof mug or cup; immediately add the simmering water. Cover and let steep according to package directions (1 to 3 minutes). Remove tea bag, squeezing gently, and discard. Stir in honey. Garnish with lemon slice.

PER SERVING: 15 cal., 0 g total fat, 0 mg chol., 6 mg sodium, 5 g carb. (1 g fiber, 3 g sugars), 0 g pro.

MINT-BERRY SPRITZER

Mint-Berry Spritzer

SERVINGS 4 (8 ounces each)
CARB. PER SERVING 10 g
PREP 10 minutes
CHILL 2 hours

- 3 tablespoons fresh mint leaves
- 3 cups light cranberry-raspberry juice or light cranberry juice
- 1 cup berry-flavor sparkling water
- Ice cubes
- 16 fresh raspberries
- Fresh mint sprigs

1. Place the 3 tablespoons mint leaves in a pitcher. Use the back of a large spoon to lightly bruise the leaves. Stir in cranberry-raspberry juice. Cover and chill 2 to 4 hours.

2. Strain mint from juice and discard the mint. Slowly pour in sparkling water; stir gently. Divide among ice-filled glasses. Add 4 raspberries to each glass. Garnish with additional fresh mint sprigs.

PER SERVING: 41 cal., 0 g total fat, 0 mg chol., 67 mg sodium, 10 g carb. (1 g fiber, 8 g sugars), 0 g pro.

STRAWBERRY-LIME COOLER

Strawberry-Lime Cooler

SERVINGS 4 (6 ounces each)
CARB. PER SERVING 16 g
START TO FINISH 15 minutes

- 2 cups chopped fresh strawberries
- 1 cup coconut water
- 1½ tablespoons honey
- 1 tablespoon lime juice
- 1 cup carbonated water
- Ice
- Lime slices and/or strawberry halves

1. In a blender combine strawberries, coconut water, honey, and lime juice. Cover and blend until smooth. Slowly pour in carbonated water; stir gently.

2. Divide among ice-filled glasses. Garnish with lime slices and/or strawberry halves.

PER SERVING: 64 cal., 0 g total fat, 0 mg chol., 77 mg sodium, 16 g carb. (3 g fiber, 12 g sugars), 1 g pro.

Lemonade Shake-Ups

SERVINGS 1
CARB. PER SERVING 7 g
START TO FINISH 10 minutes

> 1 lemon, cut into 4 wedges
> Sugar substitute*
> 1 cup ice
> ½ cup cold water

1. Squeeze lemon wedges into a tall 16-ounce glass. Add lemon wedges to glass. Sprinkle sugar substitute over lemon wedges. Using a fork or the end of a wooden spoon, lightly mash lemon and sugar substitute together. Add the ice cubes and the water. Stir gently to combine.

*SUGAR SUBSTITUTES: Choose from Splenda Granular, Equal Spoonful or packets, or Sweet'N Low bulk or packets. Follow package directions to use product amount equivalent to 2 tablespoons sugar.

PER SERVING: 25 cal., 0 g total fat, 0 mg chol., 8 mg sodium, 7 g carb. (5 g fiber, 5 g sugars), 1 g pro.

LEMONADE
SHAKE-UPS

HEALTHY HABIT: GET TO KNOW PORTIONS

Eating too much food results in excess calories and packs on the pounds. But when you're used to seeing restaurant-size portions, it can be hard to retrain your eyes. Dust off those measuring tools in your cupboards and drawers and keep them on your kitchen counter. Use them often until you get a feel for what healthy portions look like.

MY PORTION GOAL

Twice this week I will use measuring cups and spoons to check that my dinner portions are sized right.

> " I feel better and have more energy than I've had in ages. "

JOHNNY HEWITT | age 87

Johnny's previous doctor, whom he saw for 40 years, would tell him that his "sugar" was creeping up. After retiring at the age of 84, Johnny went to a new doctor, who started from scratch. The results of Johnny's A1C test revealed that he had more than just a touch of sugar—his numbers showed that he clearly had prediabetes and was headed toward type 2 diabetes.

Kick-start into action: Johnny enrolled in a prediabetes education program at his local hospital, where he learned what to eat and, more important, how much to eat. "I've cut down on portions, switched to 2-percent milk and unsweetened tea, and I limit sweets." The program included a free three-month membership to the hospital's wellness center. "I went from not exercising at all to visiting the wellness center five days a week. I walk two miles per visit and work out on strength-training equipment." Johnny's fasting blood glucose is now around 104, and he doesn't take any glucose, blood pressure, or lipid medications.

Words of wisdom: "Go see a dietitian and get exercising. It's that simple."

PORTION
control

Monitoring portions is critical when you have diabetes. You need to know how many carbs and calories are in the foods you eat so you know how the amounts affect your blood sugar. Follow these tips to rein in portions.

USE SMALLER PLATES

Portion control is easier when your plate is no more than 9 inches wide. If your dinnerware's plate size is larger than 9 inches, fill just inside the rim.

LOAD UP on VEGGIES

Buffets are usually loaded with highly pleasurable foods. Eating even a small portion of each of your favorite foods on a buffet table can cause calories to add up quickly. When a buffet is your only option, fill your plate with vegetables first so you won't load up on other foods.

BUDDY UP

When dining out, share an appetizer or entrée. Even a small plating charge saves in the long run. Or plan to take half of your meal home.

SIZING UP portions

There's no doubt about it: Serving sizes have increased over time. And because of that, you may be eating more than you realize. Follow a few portion and serving tips to help you avoid overeating or gaining weight.

Dish up plates from the kitchen counter instead of the dinner table. When you keep serving dishes farther away, where it's harder to go back for more, studies show you'll eat less. When a big serving dish of pasta is on the table, men will typically eat 29 percent more and women will eat 10 percent more than if the bowl isn't nearby.

Choose thin options for pizza crusts, breads, bagels, tortillas, and buns whenever possible. You'll cut your calorie and carb intake by as much as half by eating thinner versions of these foods. Additionally, thin crusts and buns often allow you to enjoy the flavor of toppings and fillings more.

TRAIN YOUR eyes

It's important to learn what a standard serving size looks like so you can start to recognize when the food you're served is more than that amount. Here are healthful portion sizes of foods that are often served in larger-than-necessary amounts.

ICE CREAM

½ cup
150 calories
15–20 g carb.

NUTS

¼ cup
160 calories
4–8 g carb.

POTATOES

½ cup
80 calories
16 g carb.

PEANUT BUTTER

1 tablespoon
95 calories
5 g carb.

PASTA

⅓ cup cooked
75 calories
15 g carb.

SHREDDED CHEESE

2 tablespoons
60 calories
1 g carb.

BUTTER

1 teaspoon
35 calories
0 g carb.

ORANGE JUICE

½ cup
55 calories
13 g carb.

REDUCED-FAT DRESSING

2 tablespoons
60 calories
7–10 g carb.

how to
STRETCH PORTIONS

Do you ever feel underwhelmed by typical "diabetic" portions? Learn creative tricks to get full plates and satisfying servings without adding a ton of calories and carbs.

STANDARD PORTION
½ cup mashed potatoes and 3 ounces cooked steak

STRETCHED PORTION

Steak and Mushrooms with Parsley Mashed Potatoes

SERVINGS 4 (3 ounces cooked steak, 1 cup potatoes, and ⅓ cup gravy each)
CARB. PER SERVING 31 g
PREP 40 minutes **GRILL** 10 minutes

- 4 4-ounce boneless beef top sirloin steaks, cut 1 inch thick
- 1¼ cups 50%-less-sodium beef broth
- 1 clove garlic, minced
- 2 cups sliced fresh mushrooms
- 4 teaspoons cornstarch
- 1 recipe Parsley Mashed Potatoes

1. Sprinkle steaks with ¼ teaspoon *salt*. For a gas or charcoal grill, grill steaks on the rack of a covered grill over medium heat to desired doneness, turning once halfway through grilling time. Allow 10 to 12 minutes for medium rare (145°F).
2. Meanwhile, for mushroom gravy, lightly coat a medium nonstick skillet with *nonstick cooking spray*. Add ¼ cup of the broth and the garlic. Heat broth just until simmering; add mushrooms.

Cook 3 minutes. Stir cornstarch into the remaining 1 cup broth. Add to the mushroom mixture. Cook and stir until thickened and bubbly. Cook and stir 2 minutes more.
3. Thinly slice steak across the grain. Serve over Parsley Mashed Potatoes. Top with gravy.

PARSLEY MASHED POTAOTES: In a Dutch oven cook 12 ounces Yukon gold potatoes, peeled and cubed; 6 cups cauliflower florets; and ½ cup chopped onion in boiling water about 25 minutes or until very tender. Drain. Beat with an electric mixer on medium speed until nearly smooth. Beat in 1 tablespoon butter, ½ teaspoon salt, and ¼ teaspoon black pepper. Stir in 2 tablespoons snipped fresh parsley.

PER SERVING: 293 cal., 8 g total fat (4 g sat. fat), 68 mg chol., 623 mg sodium, 31 g carb. (5 g fiber, 6 g sugars), 27 g pro.

make it STRETCH

Double a standard serving of mashed potatoes by stirring in nonstarchy cauliflower. To help the meat fill the plate, cut it into thin slices and top with a low-calorie mushroom sauce.

STANDARD PORTION

2 thin slices bread, 2 slices bacon, 2 tomato slices, 1 lettuce leaf, and 1 tablespoon mayonnaise

STRETCHED PORTION

BLT Salad

SERVINGS 1
CARB. PER SERVING 36 g
START TO FINISH 25 minutes

- 2 tablespoons plain fat-free Greek yogurt
- 2 tablespoons fat-free milk
- 1 tablespoon light mayonnaise
- ¼ teaspoon dried minced garlic
- 2 cups coarsely chopped romaine lettuce
- 1 cup coarsely chopped tomatoes (2 medium)
- ½ cup coarsely chopped cucumber
- 2 teaspoons balsamic vinegar
- 1 slice light Italian bread, toasted and cubed
- 2 slices bacon, crisp-cooked, drained, and crumbled

1. For dressing, in a small bowl whisk together yogurt, milk, mayonnaise, ¼ teaspoon *black pepper*, and the dried garlic; set aside.

2. In a large bowl combine lettuce, tomatoes, and cucumber. Drizzle lettuce mixture with balsamic vinegar; toss well to combine. Add toasted bread cubes; toss again. Drizzle with the dressing. If desired, sprinkle with additional pepper. Top with bacon.

PER SERVING: 297 cal., 11 g total fat (2 g sat. fat), 23 mg chol., 680 mg sodium, 36 g carb. (9 g fiber, 14 g sugars), 18 g pro.

Spicy Chicken Kabobs with Vegetable Rice

SERVINGS 4 (3 skewers and ³/₄ cup vegetable-rice mixture each)
CARB. PER SERVING 33 g
PREP 25 minutes **GRILL** 8 minutes

make it STRETCH

No more plates of boring chicken breasts! Make the standard serving stretch by skewering chicken with nonstarchy vegetables and tossing a standard portion of rice with kale and flavorful seasonings.

- 2   tablespoons olive oil
- 4   teaspoons lemon juice
- ¼   teaspoon crushed red pepper
- ⅛   teaspoon dried thyme
- 1   medium zucchini
- 1   pound skinless, boneless chicken breast, cut into 1-inch pieces
- 1   medium red onion, cut into ½-inch-thick wedges
- 24 red and/or yellow cherry tomatoes
- ¾   cup chopped red sweet pepper (1 medium)
- 2   cloves garlic, minced
- 4   cups chopped kale
- ¼   cup reduced-sodium chicken broth
- ¾   teaspoon Cajun seasoning
- 1⅓ cups cooked brown rice

STANDARD PORTION

⅓ cup cooked brown rice and 3 ounces cooked chicken breast

1. Whisk together oil, lemon juice, crushed red pepper, thyme, ⅛ teaspoon *salt*, and ⅛ teaspoon *black pepper*; set aside. Cut zucchini in half crosswise. Chop half of the zucchini; cut the remaining zucchini lengthwise into thin slices. Add zucchini slices, chicken, onion, and tomatoes to oil mixture; toss. On twelve 8-inch skewers* alternately thread chicken pieces, zucchini slices, onion wedges, and tomatoes.

2. For a charcoal or gas grill, grill skewers on the rack of a covered grill directly over medium heat 8 to 10 minutes or until chicken is no longer pink, turning occasionally.

3. Meanwhile, coat a large skillet with *nonstick cooking spray*. Heat skillet over medium heat. Add chopped zucchini, sweet pepper, and garlic. Cook and stir 3 minutes. Add kale, broth, and Cajun seasoning. Simmer, covered, 5 minutes or until kale is tender. Stir in rice; heat. Serve with skewers.

*****TEST KITCHEN TIP:** If using wooden skewers, soak in enough water to cover 30 minutes.

PER SERVING: 300 cal., 10 g total fat (2 g sat. fat), 47 mg chol., 264 mg sodium, 33 g carb. (5 g fiber, 8 g sugars), 22 g pro.

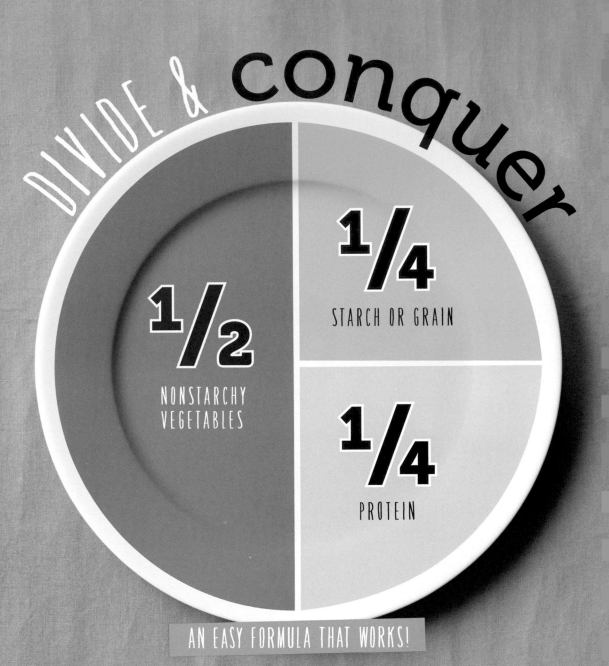

DIVIDE & conquer

1/2
NONSTARCHY VEGETABLES

1/4
STARCH OR GRAIN

1/4
PROTEIN

AN EASY FORMULA THAT WORKS!

One of the easiest ways to control portions doesn't even require the use of measuring cups or carb-counting books. Instead, all you have to do is fill your plate! Divide your plate into the three sections shown *above*, filling half the plate with nonstarchy vegetables and the remaining two quadrants with protein and a starch or grain. That's the simple formula for making a healthful meal. Not sure what counts as a nonstarchy vegetable or starch? Turn to the lists on *page 82*.

½ plate

NONSTARCHY VEGGIES
yellow summer
squash, zucchini

¼ plate

STARCH OR GRAIN
garlic toast

¼ plate

PROTEIN
chicken,
cheese

BALSAMIC ROASTED CHICKEN and SQUASH

recipe on *page 68*

Balsamic Roasted Chicken and Squash

photo on *page 67*

SERVINGS 4 (1 chicken breast half,
$^3/_4$ cup squash, and 1 ounce bread each)
CARB. PER SERVING 22 g
PREP 20 minutes   ROAST 20 minutes

- 4 small skinless, boneless chicken breast halves (1$^1/_4$ pounds total)
- $^1/_4$ cup balsamic vinegar
- 2 tablespoons olive oil
- 3 cups sliced zucchini
- 3 cups sliced yellow summer squash and/or zucchini
- 2 cloves garlic, minced
- $^1/_4$ cup snipped fresh basil
- 3 tablespoons grated Parmesan cheese
- 1 recipe Easy Garlic Toast

1. Preheat oven to 425°F. Place chicken breast halves in a 2-quart baking dish. Drizzle with 2 tablespoons of the balsamic vinegar and 1 tablespoon of the oil. Sprinkle all sides of chicken evenly with $^1/_4$ teaspoon *salt* and $^1/_4$ teaspoon *black pepper*. Place zucchini, summer squash, and garlic in a large shallow baking pan. Drizzle with the remaining 2 tablespoons balsamic vinegar and the remaining 1 tablespoon oil; toss to coat. Spread vegetables in an even layer.

2. Roast chicken and vegetables about 20 minutes or until chicken is no longer pink (165°F) and vegetables are tender, stirring vegetables halfway through roasting time. To serve, divide chicken and vegetables among four plates. Sprinkle vegetables with basil and Parmesan. Serve with Easy Garlic Toast.

EASY GARLIC TOAST: Thinly slice 4 ounces crusty whole grain bread; toast bread. Halve 1 clove garlic. Rub toast slices lightly with the cut sides of the garlic.

PER SERVING: 285 cal., 11 g total fat (2 g sat. fat), 50 mg chol., 403 mg sodium, 22 g carb. (4 g fiber, 10 g sugars), 23 g pro.

Mediterranean Cod with Roasted Tomatoes

SERVINGS 4 (1 fish portion,
$^1/_2$ cup tomato mixture, and
$^1/_3$ cup couscous each)
CARB. PER SERVING 25 g
PREP 30 minutes   BAKE 8 minutes
COOK 12 minutes (couscous)

- 4 4-ounce fresh or frozen skinless cod fillets, $^3/_4$ to 1 inch thick
- 2 teaspoons snipped fresh oregano
- 1 teaspoon snipped fresh thyme
- $^1/_4$ teaspoon garlic powder
- $^1/_4$ teaspoon paprika
- 3 cups cherry tomatoes
- 2 cloves garlic, sliced
- 1 tablespoon olive oil
- 2 tablespoons sliced black olives
- 2 teaspoons capers
- 1 recipe Israeli Couscous

1. Preheat oven to 450°F. Thaw fish, if frozen. Rinse fish; pat dry with paper towels. In a small bowl combine oregano, thyme, $^1/_2$ teaspoon *salt*, garlic powder, paprika, and $^1/_4$ teaspoon *black pepper*. Sprinkle half of the herb mixture over all sides of fish.

2. Line a 15×10×1-inch baking pan with foil. Coat foil with *nonstick cooking spray*. Place fish on one side of the pan. Add tomatoes and garlic slices to the other side of the pan. Stir oil into the remaining herb mixture. Drizzle oil mixture over tomatoes and garlic; toss to coat. Bake 8 to 12 minutes or until fish flakes easily when tested with a fork, stirring tomato mixture once. Stir olives and capers into cooked tomato mixture.

3. Divide fish, cooked Israeli Couscous, and roasted tomato mixture among four plates. If desired, sprinkle with *fresh oregano and/or thyme leaves*.

ISRAELI COUSCOUS: In a small saucepan combine 1 cup water and $^2/_3$ cup Israeli (large pearl) couscous. Bring to boiling; reduce heat. Simmer, covered, 12 to 15 minutes or until tender.

PER SERVING: 243 cal., 5 g total fat (1 g sat. fat), 49 mg chol., 428 mg sodium, 25 g carb. (3 g fiber, 4 g sugars), 24 g pro.

½ plate

NONSTARCHY VEGGIES
tomatoes

¼ plate

STARCH OR GRAIN
Israeli
couscous

¼ plate

PROTEIN
cod

MEDITERRANEAN COD
with ROASTED TOMATOES

½ plate

NONSTARCHY VEGGIES
cauliflower,
carrots,
green onions

¼ plate

STARCH, GRAIN, OR
OTHER CARB
fettuccine,
orange juice

¼ plate

PROTEIN
pork,
peanuts

CURRY-GLAZED PORK KABOBS
and PEANUT FETTUCCINE
with ROASTED CAULIFLOWER

Curry-Glazed Pork Kabobs

SERVINGS 4 (1 kabob each)
CARB. PER SERVING 2 g
PREP 15 minutes
MARINATE 4 to 24 hours
BAKE 12 minutes

  1 pound pork tenderloin, cut into
    1½-inch pieces
  3 tablespoons orange juice
  2 tablespoons yellow curry paste

1. Place pork in a large resealable plastic bag. Combine juice and curry paste; add to pork. Seal bag; turn bag to coat pork. Marinate in refrigerator at least 4 hours or up to 24 hours, turning bag twice.
2. Preheat oven to 425°F. Drain pork, discarding marinade. Thread pork pieces onto four 8- to 10-inch skewers,* leaving ¼ inch between pieces. Place kabobs on a lightly greased baking sheet.
3. Bake kabobs 12 to 15 minutes or until pork pieces are slightly pink in the centers, turning once halfway through baking time. Serve with Peanut Fettuccine with Roasted Cauliflower.
*TEST KITCHEN TIP: If using wooden skewers, soak in water 30 minutes; drain before using.

PER SERVING: 128 cal., 2 g total fat (1 g sat. fat), 72 mg chol., 368 mg sodium, 2 g carb. (0 g fiber, 1 g sugars), 23 g pro.

Peanut Fettuccine with Roasted Cauliflower

SERVINGS 4 (1½ cups each)
CARB. PER SERVING 38 g
PREP 20 minutes   ROAST 20 minutes

  6 cups bite-size cauliflower florets
  1 tablespoon olive oil
  4 ounces dried whole grain fettuccine
  1 cup packaged jullienned carrots
  ½ cup thinly sliced green onions (4)
  2 tablespoons coarse ground mustard
  2 tablespoons honey
  ¼ cup snipped fresh cilantro
  ¼ cup chopped unsalted peanuts

1. Preheat oven to 425°F. Place cauliflower in a shallow baking pan; drizzle with olive oil and sprinkle with ⅛ teaspoon *black pepper*. Toss to coat. Roast 20 to 30 minutes or just until cauliflower is tender and lightly browned, stirring twice.
2. Meanwhile, cook fettuccine according to package directions, adding carrots for the last 2 minutes of cooking. Drain pasta mixture, reserving ½ cup of the pasta cooking liquid. Transfer pasta mixture to a large bowl. Add green onions and roasted cauliflower to pasta mixture; toss to combine.
3. In a small bowl combine the reserved pasta cooking liquid, the mustard, and honey. Add to pasta mixture; toss to coat. Divide among four plates. Sprinkle with cilantro and peanuts.

PER SERVING: 244 cal., 9 g total fat (1 g sat. fat), 0 mg chol., 143 mg sodium, 38 g carb. (5 g fiber, 13 g sugars), 8 g pro.

Crisp Chicken Parmesan

SERVINGS 4 (2 to 3 chicken pieces,
$1/2$ cup sauce, and $1/2$ cup pasta each)
CARB. PER SERVING 38 g
PREP 25 minutes BAKE 15 minutes

Olive oil nonstick cooking spray
- $1/4$ cup refrigerated or frozen egg product, thawed, or 2 egg whites, lightly beaten
- 1 tablespoon water
- 1 clove garlic, minced
- 1 cup bran cereal flakes, crushed (about $1/2$ cup crushed)
- $1/4$ cup grated Parmesan cheese
- 1 teaspoon dried Italian seasoning, crushed
- 1 pound chicken breast tenderloins
- 4 ounces dried multigrain or whole grain spaghetti
- 1 cup coarsely chopped yellow sweet pepper or 1-inch pieces cubed eggplant, peeled if desired
- $1^{1}/2$ cups purchased light tomato-basil pasta sauce
- 1 cup torn fresh spinach
- $1/2$ cup chopped roma tomatoes

1. Preheat oven to 425°F. Line a 15×10×1-inch baking pan with foil; lightly coat foil with cooking spray. Set aside. In a shallow dish combine egg, the water, and garlic. In another shallow dish combine bran flakes, Parmesan cheese, and Italian seasoning.

2. Dip chicken pieces, one at a time, in egg mixture, turning to coat evenly and allowing excess to drip off. Dip chicken pieces in cereal mixture, turning to coat evenly. Place chicken pieces in a single layer in the prepared baking pan. Coat tops of chicken pieces with cooking spray. Bake 15 to 20 minutes or until chicken is no longer pink (170°F).

3. Meanwhile, cook spaghetti according to package directions; drain and keep warm. Coat an unheated medium saucepan with cooking spray. Heat saucepan over medium heat. Add sweet pepper and cook about 5 minutes or until tender, stirring occasionally. Add pasta sauce; heat through. Stir in spinach and tomatoes.

4. Divide spaghetti among four plates. Top with sauce mixture and chicken pieces.

PER SERVING: 300 cal., 5 g total fat (1 g sat. fat), 51 mg chol., 518 mg sodium, 38 g carb. (7 g fiber, 7 g sugars), 26 g pro.

Spinach Salad

SERVINGS 4 (2 cups each)
CARB. PER SERVING 13 g
START TO FINISH 15 minutes

- 8 cups fresh baby spinach or torn fresh spinach (5 ounces)
- $1/2$ cup red onion slivers
- $1/4$ cup dried cranberries
- 3 tablespoons bottled reduced-calorie Italian salad dressing

1. In a large bowl toss together spinach, onion, and dried cranberries. Drizzle dressing over the salad and toss to coat. Divide among plates.

PER SERVING: 69 cal., 1 g total fat (0 g sat. fat), 0 mg chol., 215 mg sodium, 13 g carb. (3 g fiber, 6 g sugars), 3 g pro.

¼ plate

PROTEIN

chicken, egg, cheese

½ plate

NONSTARCHY VEGGIES

spinach, onion, sweet pepper, tomatoes

¼ plate

STARCH, GRAIN, OR OTHER CARB

spaghetti, cereal flakes, dried cranberries

CRISP CHICKEN PARMESAN
with SPINACH SALAD

73

¼ plate

PROTEIN
beef, almonds

¼ plate

STARCH, GRAIN, OR
OTHER CARB
corn, beets,
apple

½ plate

NONSTARCHY VEGGIES
watercress,
celeriac

STEAK with WATERCRESS PESTO
and FRESH BEET SLAW

Steak with Watercress Pesto

SERVINGS 4 (1 steak and 1 tablespoon pesto each)
CARB. PER SERVING 3 g
PREP 20 minutes GRILL 7 minutes

- 1 cup lightly packed fresh watercress, tough stems removed
- ½ cup lightly packed fresh mint
- 3 tablespoons slivered almonds, toasted
- 2 cloves garlic, minced
- 2 tablespoons water
- 1 tablespoon olive oil
- 4 4-ounce beef chuck top blade (flat iron) steaks, cut ¾ inch thick

1. For pesto, in a food processor or blender combine watercress, mint, almonds, garlic, and ¼ teaspoon *salt*. Cover and pulse with several on-off turns to chop the watercress and mint. With the processor or blender running, gradually add water and oil through the feed tube until mixture is well combined, scraping sides of bowl as needed.
2. Sprinkle steaks evenly with ⅛ teaspoon *salt* and ⅛ teaspoon *black pepper.* For a gas or charcoal grill, place steaks on the greased grill rack of a covered grill directly over medium heat. Grill, covered, to desired doneness, turning once halfway through grilling. Allow 7 to 9 minutes for medium rare (145°F) or 10 to 12 minutes for medium (160°F). Divide steaks among four plates and top with the pesto.

PER SERVING: 200 cal., 12 g total fat (3 g sat. fat), 56 mg chol., 248 mg sodium, 3 g carb. (1 g fiber, 0 g sugars), 20 g pro.

Sweet Corn

Remove husks and silks from 2 fresh ears of corn. Break each ear in half. Cook, covered, in enough boiling lightly salted water to cover for 5 to 7 minutes or until kernels are tender. Or to grill the corn, soak corn in the husks 1 hour; drain. Grill over medium heat about 25 minutes or until kernels are tender. Remove husks and silks; cut cobs in half for serving. Makes 4 servings (½ ear each).

PER SERVING: 39 cal., 1 g total fat (0 g sat. fat), 0 mg chol., 7 mg sodium, 8 g carb. (1 g fiber, 3 g sugars), 1 g pro.

Fresh Beet Slaw

SERVINGS 4 (¾ cup each)
CARB. PER SERVING 26 g
PREP 20 minutes

- 12 ounces fresh beets (without greens), trimmed, peeled, and coarsely shredded*
- 12 ounces celeriac, trimmed, peeled, and coarsely shredded, or 2 medium parsnips, peeled and coarsely shredded*
- 1 cup fresh watercress, tough stems removed
- 1 large apple, cored and chopped
- ⅓ cup light mayonnaise
- ¼ cup cider vinegar
- 2 tablespoons snipped fresh basil
- ¼ teaspoon kosher salt
- ⅛ teaspoon black pepper

1. In a large bowl combine beets, celeriac, watercress, and apple. Set aside.
2. In a small bowl combine mayonnaise, vinegar, basil, salt, and pepper until well combined. Add to beet mixture; toss to coat. Serve immediately or cover and chill up to 8 hours. Divide among plates.
*TEST KITCHEN TIP: Use a food processor fitted with a coarse shredder to easily shred the beets and celeriac or parsnips.

PER SERVING: 173 cal., 7 g total fat (1 g sat. fat), 7 mg chol., 414 mg sodium, 26 g carb. (5 g fiber, 14 g sugars), 3 g pro.

Pork Empanadas

SERVINGS 6 (2 empanadas each)
CARB. PER SERVING 46 g
PREP 40 minutes BAKE 20 minutes

- ¼ cup cornmeal
- 1 16-ounce loaf frozen whole wheat bread dough, thawed
- 12 ounces lean ground pork
- 1 medium onion, chopped
- 1 medium red, yellow, or green sweet pepper, chopped
- 2 cloves garlic, minced
- 1 14.5-ounce can no-salt-added diced tomatoes, drained
- ¼ cup frozen whole kernel corn
- 1 teaspoon finely chopped chipotle pepper in adobo sauce (tip, *page 252*)
- ½ teaspoon ground cumin
- ⅛ teaspoon salt
- ½ cup shredded Monterey Jack cheese (2 ounces)

1. Preheat oven to 375°F. Lightly grease a baking sheet. Sprinkle baking sheet with cornmeal; set aside. On a lightly floured surface let thawed bread dough stand, covered, while preparing filling.

2. For filling, in a large skillet cook pork, onion, sweet pepper, and garlic over medium heat until meat is browned. Drain off fat. Stir in tomatoes, corn, chipotle pepper, cumin, and salt until well combined. Remove from heat. Stir in cheese. Set aside.

3. Divide bread dough into 12 equal portions. On the lightly floured surface roll each dough portion into a 5-inch circle. Divide filling evenly among dough rounds, spooning filling onto center of each dough round. Brush edge of each dough round lightly with water; fold dough round in half, pinching edge to seal. If desired, press edge with tines of a fork. Place filled empanadas on the prepared baking sheet. Prick tops with tines of a fork.

4. Bake 20 to 25 minutes or until empanadas are golden brown and heated through. Place two empanadas on each of six plates.

PER SERVING: 402 cal., 15 g total fat (5 g sat. fat), 45 mg chol., 590 mg sodium, 46 g carb. (5 g fiber, 4 g sugars), 23 g pro.

Jicama Slaw

SERVINGS 6 (⅔ cup each)
CARB. PER SERVING 9 g
PREP 25 minutes CHILL 6 hours

- 2 cups very thin jicama strips
- 2 large red and/or green sweet peppers, chopped
- ½ cup thinly sliced green onions (4)
- ¼ cup chopped fresh cilantro
- ½ cup light sour cream
- ½ teaspoon finely shredded lime peel
- 2 tablespoons lime juice
- 1 teaspoon sugar*
- ½ teaspoon ground cumin
- ¼ teaspoon salt
- ⅛ teaspoon cayenne pepper

1. In a large bowl toss together jicama, sweet peppers, green onions, and cilantro. In a small bowl combine sour cream, lime peel, lime juice, sugar, cumin, salt, and cayenne pepper. Add sour cream mixture to jicama mixture; stir until well combined. Serve immediately or cover and chill up to 6 hours before serving. Divide among plates.

*SUGAR SUBSTITUTES: Choose from Splenda Granular, Equal Spoonful or packets, Sweet'N Low bulk or packets, or Truvia Spoonable or packets. Follow package directions to use product amount equivalent to 1 teaspoon sugar.

PER SERVING: 58 cal., 2 g total fat (1 g sat. fat), 6 mg chol., 114 mg sodium, 9 g carb. (3 g fiber, 3 g sugars), 2 g pro.
PER SERVING WITH SUBSTITUTE: Same as above, except 56 cal., 2 g sugars.

¼ plate

STARCH OR GRAIN

whole wheat
bread, corn

½ plate

NONSTARCHY VEGGIES

onion,
sweet pepper,
green onion,
tomatoes

¼ plate

PROTEIN

pork,
cheese

PORK EMPANADAS
with JICAMA SLAW

¼ plate

STARCH OR GRAIN
corn tortillas

¼ plate

PROTEIN
tilapia, yogurt

½ plate

NONSTARCHY VEGGIES
cucumber, carrots, onion

CHIPOTLE CILANTRO TILAPIA
and CARROT-CUCUMBER SALAD

Chipotle-Cilantro Tilapia

SERVINGS 4 (2 tortillas, 1 fillet, and about 2 tablespoons sauce each)
CARB. PER SERVING 15 g
START TO FINISH 25 minutes

- 4 4-ounce fresh or frozen skinless tilapia fillets
- ¼ teaspoon salt
- ¼ teaspoon ground cumin
- ⅛ teaspoon chipotle chile powder
- ⅛ teaspoon black pepper
- 2 teaspoons canola oil
- ½ cup plain fat-free yogurt
- 2 tablespoons snipped fresh cilantro
- ½ to 1 teaspoon chipotle chile peppers in adobo sauce, minced (tip, *page 252*)
- 8 6-inch corn tortillas, warmed

1. Thaw fish, if frozen. Rinse fish and pat dry with paper towels. Sprinkle with salt, cumin, chile powder, and black pepper.

2. In an extra-large nonstick skillet heat oil over medium heat. Add fish fillets. Cook 6 to 8 minutes or until fish flakes easily when tested with a fork, turning once halfway through cooking.

3. Meanwhile, for yogurt sauce, in a small bowl combine yogurt, cilantro, and chipotle peppers in adobo sauce. To serve, place 1 fish fillet, 2 warmed tortillas, and about 2 tablespoons yogurt sauce on each of four plates.

PER SERVING: 207 cal., 5 g total fat (1 g sat. fat), 57 mg chol., 235 mg sodium, 15 g carb. (1 g fiber, 2 g sugars), 26 g pro.

Carrot-Cucumber Salad

SERVINGS 4 (1 cup each)
CARB. PER SERVING 8 g
PREP 20 minutes   CHILL 2 hours

- ¼ cup rice vinegar
- 2 tablespoons snipped fresh cilantro
- 1 tablespoon toasted sesame oil
- ¼ teaspoon salt
- ⅛ teaspoon chipotle chile powder
- ⅛ teaspoon black pepper
- 1 medium cucumber, halved lengthwise and cut into ¼-inch slices (12 ounces)
- 2 medium carrots, cut into matchstick-size pieces (1 cup)
- ½ of a small red onion, thinly sliced (½ cup)

1. In a large bowl whisk together vinegar, cilantro, oil, salt, chile powder, and black pepper. Stir in cucumber, carrots, and red onion. Toss to coat. Cover and chill 2 to 4 hours before serving. Divide salad among plates.

PER SERVING: 60 cal., 4 g total fat (1 g sat. fat), 0 mg chol., 200 mg sodium, 8 g carb. (1 g fiber, 3 g sugars), 1 g pro.

EXPERT TIP

"Each day blood glucose levels remain elevated, you increase your risk of developing complications down the road. Don't resist glucose-lowering medications if your provider thinks you need them. The medications work in partnership with lifestyle changes, which are harder to put into action and slower to take effect. If you lose weight and no longer need the medication, talk to your provider about stopping." – *Evan M. Sisson, Pharm.D., CDE, VCU School of Pharmacy, Richmond, Virginia*

Broccoli Cheese Tortellini Soup

SERVINGS 6 (1⅓ cups each)
CARB. PER SERVING 33 g
PREP 20 minutes   COOK 20 minutes

- 2 cups thinly sliced fresh mushrooms, such as button, cremini, or stemmed shiitake
- ½ cup chopped onion
- 3 cloves garlic, minced
- 1 tablespoon olive oil
- 1½ cups low-sodium vegetable broth or stock
- 1 cup water
- 1 9-ounce package refrigerated whole wheat three-cheese tortellini
- 1 tablespoon snipped fresh sage or 1 teaspoon dried sage, crushed
- 1½ cups small fresh broccoli florets
- 1 cup fresh sugar snap peas, trimmed
- 3 cups low-fat (1%) milk
- 2 tablespoons cornstarch
- 6 ounces reduced-fat cream cheese (Neufchâtel), cut into cubes and softened
- Fresh sugar snap peas, very thinly sliced lengthwise (optional)

1. In a 4-quart Dutch oven cook mushrooms, onion, and garlic in hot oil over medium heat 5 minutes, stirring occasionally. Carefully add broth, water, tortellini, and dried sage (if using). Bring to boiling; reduce heat. Simmer, covered, 4 minutes.

2. Add broccoli; return to simmering. Cook, covered, 2 minutes. Add 1 cup peas; cook 2 to 3 minutes more or until tortellini is just tender.

3. In a medium bowl whisk together milk and cornstarch until smooth. Add all at once to the soup. Cook and stir until thickened and bubbly.

4. Place cream cheese in a small bowl; microwave on 100 percent power (high) 30 seconds or until melted. Stir until smooth. Add melted cream cheese and fresh sage (if using) to the soup. Cook and stir until soup is smooth. Ladle into six warm serving bowls. If desired, garnish with thinly sliced peas.

PER SERVING: 321 cal., 15 g total fat (6 g sat. fat), 53 mg chol., 412 mg sodium, 33 g carb. (5 g fiber, 11 g sugars), 15 g pro.

Kohlrabi Chopped Salad

SERVINGS 6 (1¼ cups each)
CARB. PER SERVING 7 g
START TO FINISH 15 minutes

- 6 cups chopped romaine lettuce
- ¾ cup coarsely shredded, peeled kohlrabi or carrots
- ½ cup bite-size red sweet pepper strips
- 1 ounce Parmesan cheese, shaved
- 6 tablespoons bottled light honey-Dijon salad dressing

1. Divide romaine among six plates. Top with kohlrabi, sweet pepper, and cheese. Drizzle with dressing.

PER SERVING: 71 cal., 4 g total fat (1 g sat. fat), 6 mg chol., 208 mg sodium, 7 g carb. (2 g fiber, 4 g sugars), 3 g pro.

¼ plate

NONSTARCHY VEGGIES
romaine,
kohlrabi,
sweet pepper,
mushrooms,
onion, broccoli,
sugar snap peas

½ plate

PROTEIN
cheese,
cream cheese

¼ plate

**STARCH, GRAIN, OR
OTHER CARB**
tortellini,
salad dressing

BROCCOLI CHEESE TORTELLINI SOUP
and KOHLRABI CHOPPED SALAD

PICK YOUR plate

Mix and match one food per section to compose a healthful plate.

¼ PLATE: STARCH OR GRAIN

- ½ cup potatoes
- 1¾-inch piece corn bread
- ⅓ cup cooked brown rice
- ½ cup corn
- ½ cup green peas
- ½ whole wheat English muffin
- 2 slices reduced-cal whole grain bread
- 5 whole wheat crackers

½ PLATE: NONSTARCHY VEGGIES

- Asparagus
- Green beans
- Sweet pepper strips
- Mixed salad greens
- Sugar snap peas
- Cauliflower
- Celery sticks and radishes
- Brussels sprouts

¼ PLATE: PROTEIN

- 3 oz. pork loin chop
- 3 oz. skinless chicken breast half
- 3 oz. skinless turkey breast cutlet
- 3 oz. beef sirloin or round steak
- 3 oz. 95% lean beef patty
- ¾ cup egg product, scrambled
- 3 oz. tuna canned in water
- 3 oz. fish fillet
- ¾ cup low-fat cottage cheese

HEALTHY PLATE tips

- Use a 9-inch plate for meals.
- Pile foods ½ inch to 1 inch high.
- Add sides of 1 cup low-fat dairy and ½ cup fruit at least twice a day as your calorie and carb counts permit.
- Limit extras such as sauces, dressings, and spreads to 1 tablespoon.

HEALTHY HABIT: SWAP IN WHOLE GRAINS

Reduce your heart disease risk factors by eating whole grains. Studies show that Americans already eat plenty of grains, so the key is to swap in more whole grain versions of the foods you're already eating. Eating more whole grains also helps you increase your fiber intake, which lowers your risk of many diseases, including cancer, and helps you feel full.

MY WHOLE GRAIN GOAL

The next time I buy groceries, I'll look for whole grain breads, pastas, and dry cereals to try.

> " After a cruise, I hit my highest weight. My lab work revealed prediabetes. No surprise; nearly everyone on my mother's side has or had type 2 diabetes. "

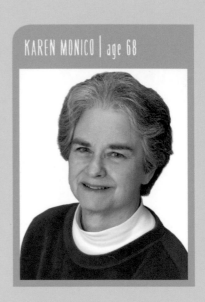

KAREN MONICO | age 68

The diabetes center at the hospital where Karen works was offering a yearlong diabetes prevention program. She joined. Being competitive, she met the 7 percent weight loss goal by week 11. Due to hip and back problems, that was without much physical activity. Karen reversed her prediabetes and improved her lipids. She no longer takes a statin drug and has cut her blood pressure medication in half.

Kick-start into action: "Knowing the damage diabetes can cause, the diagnosis of prediabetes and this convenient program kicked me into gear." Through the program Karen became acutely aware of the fat grams and calories in foods. She faithfully kept food logs, used her food scale, and planned meals.

Words of wisdom: "Take that diagnosis seriously. Realize you have the power to change your habits. Read food labels and look up restaurant nutrition information to open your eyes to the calories and fat in foods. Keep your plan in gear and weight off with ongoing support." Karen now attends a hospital-based weight control program.

WHY YOU NEED
whole
grains

Americans eat, on average, less than one serving of whole grains a day. And more than 40 percent of Americans never eat any whole grains. Here's why you need them.

GO WITH THE GRAIN

Y ou've likely heard you should eat more whole grains. But do you know why? Choosing whole grains over refined grains offers you more nutrition bang for your calories and carbohydrate grams. "While the nutrition attributes of whole grains vary, they generally provide essential vitamins and minerals like magnesium, manganese, phosphorus, B vitamins, plus other phytochemicals," says Hillary Wright, M.Ed., RD, LD, author of *The Prediabetes Diet Plan* (Ten Speed Press, 2013). Plus, whole grains are a plant source of protein, and many contain fiber. Additionally, research shows that eating a sufficient amount of whole grains can protect against cardiovascular disease and help control your weight.

What's exciting for people with insulin resistance and prediabetes is new research that indicates eating enough whole grains can reduce the incidence of insulin resistance and the progression to type 2 diabetes.

A recent study compared a whole grain diet and a refined-grain diet (with equal calories) for eight weeks in a small number of adults with prediabetes. The study, conducted by John Kirwan, director of the Metabolic Translational Research Center at the Cleveland Clinic's Lerner Research Institute, showed that those who ate the whole grain diet had lower blood glucose due to improved insulin sensitivity and insulin production in the pancreas. "This study shows these benefits are most likely due to a component of whole grains, perhaps polyphenol or a change in the gut environment," Kirwan says.

finding foods

1 The Dietary Guidelines for Americans recommends you eat 48 grams of whole grains a day. A serving of whole grains contains 8 or 16 grams, depending on whether the food is an intact whole grain or contains whole grain ingredients. Is more better? Yes, if you have the calories to spare.

2 Look for the grams of whole grains per serving on the package label. It's likely to be on foods that brag about whole grain content with phrases like "15 grams of whole grains per serving" or "contains 100% whole grains."

3 Spot the whole grain stamp, which can can appear on the package of a food that contains at least 8 grams of whole grains per serving (many contain more). The 100% banner indicates all the grains in the food are whole grains. Food companies that are members of the Whole Grains Council can use the stamp.

EASY WAYS TO EAT more whole grains

- **Make swaps in the foods you already eat.**
  At home and at restaurants, choose brown rice, whole grain bread and crackers, and whole grain pasta whenever available. Order or make pizza with whole grain crust.

- **Select whole grain (and high-fiber) cereals.**
  For hot cereal, opt for oatmeal, oat bran, and quinoa. For dry cereal, look for a whole grain cereal that also contains at least 3 grams of fiber per serving.

- **Purchase whole grain breads, rolls, buns, tortillas, pita pockets, and pizza crusts.**
  If there's no whole grain stamp or claim on the package, check the ingredients. It should list at least one of the following: whole grain [name of grain], whole [wheat or other grain], or stone-ground whole [grain].

- **Work whole grains into your recipes.**
  Add $\frac{1}{2}$ cup cooked whole grains to your favorite canned or homemade soup, side salad, and casserole. Add $\frac{3}{4}$ cup uncooked oats for each pound of ground meat when making meatballs, meat loaf, and burgers. And use whole cornmeal to make corn muffins and corn bread.

TRY A NEW
whole grain

Think of whole grains as you do any other food group—eat a variety of them for maximum taste and health benefits.

TABBOULEH
with EDAMAME
recipe on *page 90*

BULGUR

AMARANTH

QUINOA

9 GREAT GRAINS

Grains in all their forms fill you up, provide fiber and other nutrients, and are a satisfying element in many delicious dishes.

FARRO

ROLLED OATS

BUCKWHEAT

STEEL-CUT OATS

BROWN RICE

BARLEY

BULGUR

Because bulgur is precooked and dried, it cooks in about the same time as pasta, making it a great option for fast meals.

Tabbouleh with Edamame

photo on *page 88*

SERVINGS 6 (1 cup each)
CARB. PER SERVING 32 g
START TO FINISH 30 minutes

- 1¼ cups bulgur
- ¼ cup lemon juice
- 3 tablespoons basil pesto
- 2 cups fresh or frozen shelled sweet soybeans (edamame), thawed
- 2 cups cherry tomatoes, halved
- ⅓ cup thinly sliced green onions
- 2 tablespoons snipped fresh parsley
- ⅓ cup crumbled feta cheese

1. In a medium saucepan bring 2½ cups *water* to boiling; stir in bulgur. Return to boiling; reduce heat. Simmer, covered, about 15 minutes or until the water is absorbed. Transfer to a large bowl.
2. In a small bowl whisk together lemon juice and pesto; drizzle over cooked bulgur. Let bulgur mixture cool to room temperature. Gently stir in edamame, cherry tomatoes, green onions, parsley, and ¼ teaspoon *black pepper*. Sprinkle with feta. If desired, cover and refrigerate up to 4 hours. If desired, garnish with additional snipped fresh parsley and/or *lemon wedges*.

PER SERVING: 239 cal., 9 g total fat (2 g sat. fat), 10 mg chol., 176 mg sodium, 32 g carb. (9 g fiber, 4 g sugars), 12 g pro.

Rosemary Roasted Chicken with Tangerine-Walnut Bulgur Pilaf

SERVINGS 6 (4 ounces chicken and ⅔ cup pilaf each)
CARB. PER SERVING 31 g
PREP 20 minutes **ROAST** 1 hour 15 minutes
STAND 10 minutes

- 4 cloves garlic, minced
- 1 tablespoon snipped fresh rosemary
- ½ teaspoon salt
- ½ teaspoon black pepper
- 1 3½- to 4-pound broiler-fryer chicken
- 1 recipe Tangerine-Walnut Bulgur Pilaf (recipe, *page 91*)

1. Preheat oven to 375°F. In a small bowl stir together the garlic, rosemary, salt, and pepper; set aside. Rinse the inside of chicken; pat dry with paper towels. Using kitchen shears, cut the skin along the side of the breast, cutting along the full length of each side of the breast. Use your fingers to gently loosen and pull the skin away from the breast meat, leaving the skin attached at the top end of the breast and exposing the meat. Use your fingers to loosen the skin from the top of each drumstick and thigh. Rub the breast meat evenly with some of the garlic mixture. Rub the remaining garlic mixture evenly under the skin and on top of the drumstick and thigh meat. Lay the skin of the breast back down over the seasonings and meat.
2. Skewer neck skin of chicken to back; tie legs to tail. Twist wing tips under back. Place chicken, breast side up, on a rack in a shallow roasting pan. If desired, insert a meat thermometer into center of an inside thigh muscle. (The thermometer should not touch bone.)
3. Roast, uncovered, 45 minutes. Cut the string that ties the legs together. Roast 30 to 45 minutes more or until at least 170°F in the thigh. Remove chicken from oven. Cover; let stand 10 minutes before carving.
4. Remove skin from chicken before serving. Serve with Tangerine-Walnut Bulgur Pilaf.

PER SERVING: 351 cal., 11 g total fat (2 g sat. fat), 89 mg chol., 531 mg sodium, 31 g carb. (7 g fiber, 7 g sugars), 34 g pro.

ROSEMARY ROASTED CHICKEN
with TANGERINE-WALNUT
BULGUR PILAF

TANGERINE-WALNUT BULGUR PILAF: Juice 1 tangerine. Peel and section 2 tangerines. Set juice and sections aside. In a large skillet cook 4 cups chopped fresh kale and $\frac{1}{2}$ cup chopped onion in 1 tablespoon hot olive oil over medium heat 5 minutes, stirring occasionally. Add 1 cup uncooked bulgur; cook and stir 2 minutes. Add $1\frac{1}{2}$ cups reduced-sodium chicken broth and $\frac{1}{4}$ teaspoon salt; bring to boiling. Cover; remove from heat. Let stand 15 to 20 minutes or until liquid is absorbed. Fluff with a fork. Stir in tangerine sections and juice and $\frac{1}{3}$ cup chopped toasted walnuts.

GREEK PORK and
FARRO SALAD

FARRO

Farro, the oldest cultivated grain in the world, puffs like rice when cooked but is still slightly chewy.

Greek Pork and Farro Salad

SERVINGS 5 (1 cup spinach, about 1¼ cups salad mixture, and about 2 tablespoons dressing each)

CARB. PER SERVING 26 g

PREP 20 minutes **COOK** 25 minutes

- ¾ cup farro*
- 3 cups water
- 12 ounces pork tenderloin, trimmed
- 1 teaspoon Greek seasoning
- Nonstick cooking spray
- 1 cup chopped tomato (1 large)
- 1 cup halved lengthwise and sliced cucumber
- ¾ cup chopped yellow sweet pepper (1 medium)
- ¼ cup red wine vinegar
- 3 tablespoons olive oil
- 2 tablespoons snipped fresh oregano
- 1 teaspoon Dijon-style mustard
- ¼ teaspoon black pepper
- 1 clove garlic, minced
- 5 cups fresh baby spinach
- 2 ounces reduced-fat feta cheese, crumbled

1. In a medium saucepan combine farro and water. Bring to boiling; reduce heat. Simmer, uncovered, 15 to 20 minutes or until farro is desired tenderness; drain. Place farro in a large bowl.

2. Meanwhile, cut pork into 1-inch pieces. Toss pork with Greek seasoning. Coat an unheated large nonstick skillet with cooking spray. Heat skillet over medium heat. Add pork and cook 5 to 6 minutes or until no longer pink. Add to farro. Cool slightly. Add tomato, cucumber, and sweet pepper to farro mixture. Toss to combine.

3. For dressing, in a screw-top jar combine vinegar, olive oil, oregano, mustard, black pepper, and garlic; shake well. Toss with farro mixture. Serve at room temperature or chilled. To serve, arrange spinach on five plates. Spoon farro salad over spinach and sprinkle with feta cheese.

*TEST KITCHEN TIP: If you prefer, use 2 cups of packaged cooked farro, such as Archer Farms brand.

PER SERVING: 299 cal., 11 g total fat (3 g sat. fat), 45 mg chol., 275 mg sodium, 26 g carb. (4 g fiber, 2 g sugars), 22 g pro.

FARRO

Farro and Vegetable Chicken Chili

SERVINGS 8 (1¹⁄₂ cups and 2 tablespoons cheese each)
CARB. PER SERVING 31 g
PREP 50 minutes   **COOK** 20 minutes

"Always pinched for time? Try one of these whole grains that cook up fast: brown rice, bulgur, semipearled farro, or quinoa."

– Sarah Neil Pilkinton, RD, CDE, Diabetes Prevention Program Coordinator at Williamson Medical Center in Tennessee

1	cup semipearled farro
1¹⁄₄	pounds skinless, boneless chicken breast halves
2	cups chopped onions (2 large)
2	cups chopped zucchini (2 small)
1	cup chopped carrots (2 medium)
1	fresh jalapeño chile pepper, seeded (if desired) and finely chopped (tip, *page 252*)
2	teaspoons olive oil
2	tablespoons chili powder
2	teaspoons ground cumin
¹⁄₂	teaspoon crushed red pepper
2	14.5-ounce cans reduced-sodium chicken broth
1	14.5-ounce can no-salt-added diced tomatoes, undrained
1	6-ounce can tomato paste
1	cup shredded cheddar cheese (4 ounces)

1. Rinse farro. In a medium saucepan bring 2 cups *water* to boiling. Stir in farro. Return to boiling; reduce heat. Simmer, covered, 20 to 25 minutes or until farro is tender. Drain off excess water.

2. In a large skillet bring 2 cups *water* to boiling. Add chicken breasts; reduce heat. Simmer, covered, 12 to 15 minutes or until no longer pink (165°F). Using a slotted spoon, transfer chicken to a cutting board. Cool slightly. Coarsely chop or shred chicken. Set aside.

3. Meanwhile, in a 4-quart Dutch oven cook onions, zucchini, carrots, and chile pepper in hot oil about 5 minutes or until tender. Stir in chili powder, cumin, and crushed red pepper. Stir in broth, tomatoes, tomato paste, and another 2 cups *water*. Bring to boiling; reduce heat. Simmer, covered, 20 minutes. Stir in cooked farro and chicken. Cook and stir until heated through. Ladle soup into eight bowls. Top each serving with 2 tablespoons of the cheese.

SERVING SUGGESTION: If your meal plan allows, serve this dish with crisp whole grain sesame crackers.

PER SERVING: 305 cal., 8 g total fat (4 g sat. fat), 60 mg chol., 504 mg sodium, 31 g carb. (5 g fiber, 7 g sugars), 26 g pro.

FARRO and VEGETABLE
CHICKEN CHILI

QUINOA

Use this high-protein grain in the same ways you use rice.

Vegetable, Bacon, and Quinoa Quiche

SERVINGS 6 (1 wedge each)
CARB. PER SERVING 15 g
PREP 25 minutes **BAKE** 55 minutes

- ½ cup quinoa, rinsed and drained
- 8 ounces sliced fresh mushrooms
- 1 cup loosely packed coarsely chopped fresh spinach
- ½ cup sliced, halved leeks
- 4 ½-ounce slices applewood smoked bacon, crisp-cooked and coarsely crumbled (32 slices per pound)
- 4 eggs, lightly beaten
- 1 cup refrigerated or frozen egg product, thawed
- 1 12-ounce can evaporated fat-free milk
- 2 ounces Gruyère or Havarti cheese, shredded (½ cup)
- ½ teaspoon salt
- ⅛ teaspoon black pepper

1. Preheat oven to 350°F. Coat a deep 10-inch pie plate with *nonstick cooking spray.*
2. Using a rubber spatula, spread quinoa as evenly as possible over the bottom of the prepared pie plate.
3. In a medium bowl stir together mushrooms, spinach, leeks, and bacon. Spread mushroom mixture evenly over the quinoa.
4. In a large bowl whisk together the eggs, egg product, evaporated milk, cheese, salt, and pepper. Pour into the pie plate (it will be full).
5. Bake 55 to 60 minutes or until set in the center and browned on top. Cut into wedges.

PER SERVING: 288 cal., 12 g total fat (4 g sat. fat), 163 mg chol., 571 mg sodium, 15 g carb. (1 g fiber, 4 g sugars), 20 g pro.

Seared Scallops with Citrus-Ginger Quinoa

photo on *page 98*
SERVINGS 4 (3 to 4 scallops, ⅓ cup quinoa, and 1 tablespoon sauce each)
CARB. PER SERVING 17 g
PREP 20 minutes **COOK** 15 minutes

- 1 pound fresh or frozen sea scallops
- 1 cup water
- ½ cup quinoa, rinsed and drained
- 1 teaspoon grated fresh ginger
- ¾ teaspoon finely shredded orange peel
- ½ teaspoon finely shredded lemon peel
- ¼ teaspoon salt
- ¼ teaspoon crushed red pepper
- 2 tablespoons snipped fresh basil
- 4 teaspoons butter
- ½ cup reduced-sodium chicken broth
  Fresh basil (optional)

1. Thaw scallops, if frozen. Rinse scallops; pat dry with paper towels. Set aside.
2. In a small saucepan combine the water, quinoa, ginger, ½ teaspoon of the shredded orange peel, ¼ teaspoon of the shredded lemon peel, the salt, and crushed red pepper. Bring to boiling; reduce heat. Simmer, covered, about 15 minutes or until liquid is absorbed. Stir in snipped basil.
3. Meanwhile, in a large skillet melt butter over medium-high heat. Add scallops to skillet. Cook 2 to 3 minutes or until scallops are nearly opaque, turning once. Remove scallops from skillet; keep warm. Add broth, the remaining ¼ teaspoon shredded orange peel, and the remaining ¼ teaspoon shredded lemon peel to skillet. Bring to boiling. Boil, uncovered, 2 minutes.
4. Serve scallops and broth mixture with quinoa mixture. If desired, garnish with basil.

PER SERVING: 215 cal., 6 g total fat (3 g sat. fat), 48 mg chol., 434 mg sodium, 17 g carb. (2 g fiber, 0 g sugars), 23 g pro.

VEGETABLE, BACON,
and QUINOA QUICHE

SEARED SCALLOPS with
CITRUS-GINGER QUINOA

recipe on *page 96*

BASIL QUINOA SALAD

QUINOA

Basil Quinoa Salad

SERVINGS 6 (³/₄ cup quinoa mixture and ²/₃ cup lettuce each)
CARB. PER SERVING 24 g
START TO FINISH 30 minutes

- 1 cup fresh basil
- 2 tablespoons grated Parmesan cheese
- 2 tablespoons lemon juice
- 2 tablespoons olive oil
- 4 cloves garlic, minced
- ¼ teaspoon salt
- ¼ teaspoon black pepper
- 2 cups cooked quinoa*
- 1 15-ounce can no-salt-added red kidney beans, rinsed and drained, or 1³/₄ cups cooked red kidney beans
- 1 cup chopped yellow sweet pepper (1 large)
- ½ cup chopped, seeded tomato (1 medium)
- ½ cup sliced green onions (4)
- 4 cups baby spinach or arugula

1. Place basil in a food processor. Add Parmesan cheese, lemon juice, olive oil, garlic, salt, and black pepper. Cover and process until nearly smooth, stopping to scrape down sides of processor bowl as needed. Set aside.

2. In a medium bowl stir together cooked quinoa, beans, sweet pepper, tomato, and green onions. Add basil mixture; stir to coat. Serve quinoa mixture over baby spinach.

*TEST KITCHEN TIP: To make 2 cups cooked quinoa, in a fine strainer rinse ½ cup quinoa under cold running water; drain. In a small saucepan combine 1¼ cups water, the quinoa, and ¼ teaspoon salt. Bring to boiling; reduce heat. Simmer, covered, for 15 minutes. Let stand to cool slightly. Drain off any excess liquid.

PER SERVING: 177 cal., 6 g total fat (1 g sat. fat), 1 mg chol., 235 mg sodium, 24 g carb. (8 g fiber, 1 g sugars), 8 g pro.

OAT PILAF with TOMATOES,
CHILE, GINGER, and HERBS

STEEL-CUT OATS

This form of oats is relatively unprocessed. It consists of whole oat kernels that have been sliced two or three times so that they cook faster.

Oat Pilaf with Tomatoes, Chile, Ginger, and Herbs

SERVINGS 10 ($\frac{1}{2}$ cup each)
CARB. PER SERVING 18 g
PREP 15 minutes **COOK** 25 minutes
STAND 5 minutes

- 1 tablespoon canola oil
- $\frac{1}{2}$ cup chopped onion (1 medium)
- 1 tablespoon grated fresh ginger
- 2 teaspoons minced garlic
- 1 fresh jalapeño chile pepper, halved, seeded, and finely chopped (tip, *page 252*)
- 1 cinnamon stick
- 5 whole cloves
- $1\frac{1}{2}$ cups steel-cut oats, rinsed and drained
- $2\frac{1}{2}$ cups reduced-sodium chicken broth or vegetable broth
- 1 cup grape or cherry tomatoes, halved
- $\frac{1}{2}$ cup finely snipped fresh cilantro and/or finely snipped fresh mint
- $\frac{1}{4}$ cup thinly sliced green onions (2)
  Dash salt

1. In a large skillet with a tight-fitting lid heat oil over medium heat. Add the onion, ginger, chile pepper, garlic, cinnamon stick, and cloves. Cook and stir about 10 minutes or until onion is softened and starting to brown.
2. Stir in oats. Cook and stir about 2 minutes until lightly toasted. Stir in the broth. Bring to boiling; reduce heat. Simmer, covered, about 12 minutes or until nearly all the liquid has been absorbed. Remove from heat. Stir in tomatoes; let stand, covered, 5 minutes.
3. Before serving, stir in cilantro, green onions, and salt.

PER SERVING: 109 cal., 3 g total fat (0 g sat. fat), 0 mg chol., 155 mg sodium, 18 g carb. (3 g fiber, 1 g sugars), 5 g pro.

ROLLED OATS

Rolled oats are steamed and flattened kernels. They rarely have their bran and germ removed in processing, so they are a whole grain in nearly all forms.

Crispy Chicken-Bacon Sandwiches

SERVINGS 4 ($^1/_2$ of a chicken breast, 1 sandwich thin, 1 lettuce leaf, 1 tomato slice, and 2 slices bacon each)
CARB. PER SERVING 36 g or 35 g
PREP 30 minutes **BAKE** 15 minutes

2 tablespoons light mayonnaise
$^1/_2$ teaspoon finely chopped canned chipotle chile peppers in adobo sauce (tip, *page 252*)
$^1/_2$ teaspoon sugar*
$^1/_2$ teaspoon lime juice
Nonstick cooking spray
2 skinless, boneless chicken breast halves (about 1 pound total)
$^1/_4$ cup plain fat-free Greek yogurt
1 tablespoon water
$^1/_2$ cup soft whole wheat bread crumbs
$^1/_4$ cup regular rolled oats
3 tablespoons finely chopped dried cherries
4 whole wheat sandwich thins, such as Oroweat brand, toasted
4 to 8 lettuce leaves
4 slices tomato
8 slices lower-sodium, less-fat bacon, cooked

1. In a small bowl combine mayonnaise, chile peppers, sugar, and lime juice; set aside.
2. Preheat oven to 425°F. Line a baking sheet with foil; coat foil with cooking spray and set aside. Cut chicken breasts in half lengthwise. In a shallow dish combine yogurt and the water. In another shallow dish combine bread crumbs, oats, and dried cherries. Dip chicken pieces in yogurt mixture, turning to coat. Dip in bread crumb mixture, turning to coat evenly.
3. Place chicken on prepared baking sheet. Bake 15 to 18 minutes or until chicken is no longer pink (165°F) and outside is golden brown.
4. To serve, spread mayonnaise mixture on cut sides of sandwich thin tops. Place lettuce on sandwich thin bottoms; top with chicken, tomato, and bacon. Add tops of sandwich thins, mayonnaise sides down.

*****SUGAR SUBSTITUTES:** Choose from Splenda Granular, Truvia Spoonable or packets, or Sweet'N Low bulk or packets. Follow package directions to use product amount equivalent to $^1/_2$ teaspoon sugar.

PER SERVING: 361 cal., 9 g total fat (2 g sat. fat), 80 mg chol., 567 mg sodium, 36 g carb. (7 g fiber, 9 g sugars), 36 g pro.
PER SERVING WITH SUBSTITUTE: Same as above, except 359 cal., 35 g carb. (8 g sugars)

CRISPY CHICKEN-BACON
SANDWICHES

BUCKWHEAT

Also known as soba or kasha, buckwheat is high in antioxidants. The whole grains are called groats.

Brussels Sprouts and Buckwheat Hash

SERVINGS 6 (1 cup each)
CARB. PER SERVING 35 g
START TO FINISH 50 minutes

- ¾ cup dried whole buckwheat groats
- 1 egg white
- 2 teaspoons canola oil
- 1½ cups water
- ½ teaspoon salt
- 10 strips lower-sodium, less-fat bacon, chopped
- 1 pound fresh Brussels sprouts
- 2 medium leeks, trimmed, halved, and cut crosswise into ½-inch-thick slices
- 2 medium cooking apples, quartered, cored, and thinly sliced
- 1 tablespoon snipped fresh sage or thyme
- 1 tablespoon honey
- 2 tablespoons cider vinegar

1. In a large dry nonstick skillet cook buckwheat groats over medium-high heat 4 to 5 minutes or until browned and fragrant, stirring occasionally. Cool slightly. In a small bowl beat egg white and oil until foamy. Add toasted buckwheat; stir until well coated. Add buckwheat mixture back to the same skillet. Cook over medium-high heat about 3 minutes or until buckwheat groats have separated and browned, stirring often. Remove skillet from the heat; add water and ¼ teaspoon of the salt. Return to the heat; bring to boiling. Reduce heat; simmer, covered, 10 to 12 minutes or until buckwheat is tender and liquid is absorbed.

2. Meanwhile, in an extra-large skillet cook bacon over medium heat until crisp, stirring occasionally. Using a slotted spoon, transfer bacon to a medium bowl; set aside. Reserve 2 tablespoons of the bacon droppings in skillet.

3. Trim stems and remove any wilted outer leaves from Brussels sprouts; wash sprouts. Drain well; cut in half. Add sprouts to bacon drippings in skillet. Add leeks and remaining ¼ teaspoon salt. Cook, covered, over medium heat 5 minutes. Add apples; cook, uncovered, 5 to 10 minutes more or until sprouts are tender and golden brown, stirring occasionally.

4. Add cooked buckwheat to the Brussels sprouts mixture. Sprinkle with sage and drizzle with honey. Cook and stir 1 to 2 minutes or until heated through. Remove from the heat. Drizzle with vinegar; toss to coat. Top evenly with bacon.

PER SERVING: 208 cal., 5 g total fat (1 g sat. fat), 6 mg chol., 346 mg sodium, 35 g carb. (7 g fiber, 12 g sugars), 9 g pro.

BRUSSELS SPROUTS
and BUCKWHEAT HASH

BUCKWHEAT-PEA FALAFELS
with ZUCCHINI NOODLES

Buckwheat-Pea Falafels with Zucchini Noodles

SERVINGS 4 (3 falafels and 1 cup noodles each)
CARB. PER SERVING 34 g
START TO FINISH 1 hour

- $2/3$ cup dried whole buckwheat groats
- $1\frac{1}{2}$ cups water
- $1/2$ cup frozen shelled green peas
- $1/3$ cup coarsely shredded carrot
- 3 tablespoons whole wheat flour
- 2 tablespoons refrigerated or frozen egg product, thawed
- 6 cloves garlic, minced
- $1/2$ teaspoon salt
- $1/2$ teaspoon ground coriander
- $1/2$ teaspoon ground cumin
- $1/8$ teaspoon ground nutmeg
- 2 tablespoons olive oil
- 2 medium zucchini (about 10 ounces each)
- $1/4$ teaspoon salt
- Light sour cream or fat-free plain Greek yogurt (optional)
- $1/4$ cup chopped fresh mint

1. In a large dry nonstick skillet cook buckwheat groats over medium-high heat 4 to 5 minutes or until browned and fragrant, stirring occasionally. Transfer groats to a medium saucepan; set skillet aside for later. Add water to the buckwheat. Bring to boiling; reduce heat. Simmer, covered, 10 to 12 minutes or until buckwheat is tender and most of the liquid is absorbed. If necessary, drain off excess liquid. Cool slightly.

2. In a food processor combine peas, carrot, flour, egg, three cloves of the garlic, $1/2$ teaspoon salt, the coriander, cumin, and nutmeg. Cover and pulse until peas are coarsely chopped and mixture is combined. Add cooked buckwheat. Cover and pulse just until combined (should have some visible pieces of peas and carrots).

3. Divide mixture into 12 equal portions (mixture will be a little sticky). Using moist hands, shape each portion into a ball. Pat each ball into a 2-inch patty. Heat oil in the large skillet over medium-high heat. Add half of the patties to the hot oil. Cook 5 to 6 minutes or until browned and heated through, turning once. Remove falafels from the skillet; cover to keep warm. Repeat with remaining patties, reserving any oil in the skillet; cover to keep warm.

4. Meanwhile, use a spiral vegetable slicer to cut zucchini into long thin strands (or use a julienne-style vegetable peeler to cut into long julienne strips). Snip zucchini strands so they are easier to serve.

5. Add the remaining three cloves garlic to the large skillet. Add zucchini and sprinkle with $1/4$ teaspoon salt. Cook and toss with tongs 1 to 2 minutes or until noodles are crisp-tender.

6. Divide zucchini among four plates. Place three falafels on each plate. If desired, serve with light sour cream or fat-free plain Greek yogurt. Sprinkle with mint.

PER SERVING: 224 cal., 8 g total fat (1 g sat. fat), 0 mg chol., 494 mg sodium, 34 g carb. (6 g fiber, 5 g sugars), 8 g pro.

MEXICAN RICE and
BEAN PATTIES

BROWN RICE

Make the swap from white rice to versatile whole grain brown rice to increase your intake of fiber, B vitamins, and minerals.

Mexican Rice and Bean Patties

SERVINGS 4 (1 patty, 2 cups greens, and ¹/₄ cup sauce each)
CARB. PER SERVING 32 g
PREP 25 minutes   **CHILL** 15 minutes
COOK 6 minutes

- 4 teaspoons olive oil
- ½ cup chopped red sweet pepper (1 small)
- ⅓ cup chopped red onion (1 small)
- 2 tablespoons reduced-sodium taco seasoning
- ⅔ cup cooked brown rice
- 1 14.5-ounce can no-salt-added black beans, rinsed and drained
- ½ of a 4-ounce can diced green chile peppers
- ½ cup light sour cream
- ½ cup pico de gallo
- 8 cups mixed salad greens

1. In a medium skillet heat 1 teaspoon of the oil over medium heat. Add sweet pepper and onion; cook 4 to 5 minutes or until tender. Stir in 1 tablespoon of the taco seasoning (mixture will be dry). Remove from heat. Stir in rice. Set aside to cool.

2. Use a fork to mash beans slightly. Add rice mixture, chile peppers, and the remaining 1 tablespoon taco seasoning to the beans; stir and mash until the mixture holds together.

3. Divide bean mixture into four equal portions. Shape each portion into a patty about 3½ inches in diameter. Carefully place patties on a platter. Cover and chill 15 minutes.

4. In an extra-large nonstick skillet heat the remaining 3 teaspoons oil over medium-high heat. Cook the patties in hot oil 6 to 8 minutes or until heated through, turning once halfway through cooking. (If patties brown too quickly, reduce heat to medium.)

5. In a small bowl stir together sour cream and pico de gallo. Divide greens among four plates; place patties on top of greens. Serve sour cream mixture with patties.

PER SERVING: 228 cal., 7 g total fat (2 g sat. fat), 8 mg chol., 596 mg sodium, 32 g carb. (5 g fiber, 4 g sugars), 8 g pro.

BROWN RICE

BROWN RICE-STUFFED PEPPERS

Brown Rice-Stuffed Peppers

SERVINGS 4 (2 stuffed pepper halves each)
CARB. PER SERVING 38 g
PREP 30 minutes   **COOK** 40 minutes
BAKE 45 minutes

- ½ cup chopped onion (1 medium)
- 2 cloves garlic, minced
- 2 teaspoons olive oil
- 1½ cups unsalted chicken stock
- ½ cup uncooked regular brown rice
- ½ teaspoon dried oregano, crushed
- ½ teaspoon black pepper
- ¼ teaspoon salt
- ⅛ teaspoon paprika
- 1 14.5-ounce can no-salt-added diced tomatoes, drained
- 1 cup frozen whole kernel corn, thawed
- ¼ cup snipped fresh cilantro
- 8 ounces bulk Italian turkey sausage
- 4 green, yellow, and/or red sweet peppers
- ¼ cup water
- ½ cup shredded cheddar cheese (2 ounces) (optional)

1. In a medium saucepan cook onion and garlic in hot oil over medium heat about 5 minutes or until onion is tender. Stir in chicken stock. Bring to boiling; stir in brown rice, oregano, black pepper, salt, and paprika. Simmer, covered, about 40 minutes or until rice is tender. Remove from heat. Stir in tomatoes, corn, and cilantro. Meanwhile, in a large skillet cook the sausage until browned, using a spoon to break up meat as it cooks. Drain off fat. Stir cooked sausage into rice mixture.

2. Preheat oven to 400°F. Cut sweet peppers in half lengthwise; remove and discard seeds and membranes from pepper halves. Arrange sweet pepper halves in a 3-quart rectangular baking dish. Divide rice mixture among pepper halves, spooning evenly into pepper halves. Pour the water into the dish around the stuffed peppers.

3. Bake, covered, about 45 minutes or until peppers are tender and rice mixture is heated through. If desired, sprinkle cheese over peppers; bake, uncovered, 5 minutes more.

PER SERVING: 293 cal., 10 g total fat (2 g sat. fat), 34 mg chol., 599 mg sodium, 38 g carb. (5 g fiber, 7 g sugars), 16 g pro.

Creamy Basil-Rosemary Chicken and Rice

SERVINGS 4 (1 cup each)
CARB. PER SERVING 21 g
PREP 25 minutes   **COOK** 30 minutes

- 1   teaspoon canola oil
- 1½ cups chopped onions (3 medium)
- 1   cup thinly sliced celery (2 stalks)
- 1   14.5-ounce can reduced-sodium chicken broth
- 1   cup instant brown rice
- 2   cups chopped cooked chicken breast
- 4   ounces light semisoft cheese with garlic and fine herbs
- ¼   cup water
- 1   clove garlic, minced
- ¼   cup snipped fresh basil
- 1   tablespoon snipped fresh rosemary
- ⅛   teaspoon salt
- Snipped fresh basil (optional)
- Snipped fresh rosemary (optional)

1. In a medium nonstick skillet heat oil over medium-low heat. Add onions; cook about 15 minutes or until golden brown. Stir in celery; cook about 4 minutes more or until celery is tender. Stir in broth and rice. Bring to boiling; reduce heat. Simmer, covered, about 10 minutes or until liquid is absorbed.

2. Stir in chicken, cheese, the water, and garlic; heat through, stirring occasionally. Stir in the ¼ cup basil, the 1 tablespoon rosemary, and the salt. If desired, sprinkle with additional basil and/or rosemary.

PER SERVING: 294 cal., 10 g total fat (5 g sat. fat), 80 mg chol., 559 mg sodium, 21 g carb. (3 g fiber, 4 g sugars), 29 g pro.

CREAMY
BASIL-ROSEMARY
CHICKEN and RICE

AMARANTH

Amaranth is actually a tiny seed. It has a peppery flavor, is high in protein, and is gluten-free.

Pork Stew with Amaranth Biscuit Topper

SERVINGS 8 (about ⅔ cup stew and 1 biscuit each)
CARB. PER SERVING 40 g
PREP 40 minutes **STAND** 1 hour
BAKE 42 minutes

½   cup whole grain amaranth
    Nonstick cooking spray
1½ pounds lean pork shoulder, trimmed of fat and cut into 1-inch pieces
1   teaspoon dried sage, crushed
1   teaspoon olive oil
8   ounces fresh mushrooms, sliced
1   cup chopped onion (1 large)
2   cloves garlic, minced
2   cups cubed, peeled sweet potato
1   tablespoon cornstarch
½   teaspoon salt
1½ cups all-purpose flour
¼   cup yellow cornmeal
2   teaspoons baking powder
1   teaspoon dried thyme, crushed
½   teaspoon black pepper
½   cup light butter

1. Place amaranth in a small bowl. Stir in 1 cup boiling water. Cover and let stand at least 1 hour.
2. Preheat oven to 375°F. Lightly coat a 3-quart rectangular baking dish with cooking spray.

Sprinkle pork with sage; toss to coat. In a large nonstick skillet brown pork in hot oil over medium-high heat. Transfer pork to the prepared baking dish.
3. Add mushrooms, onion, and garlic to the same skillet. Cook and stir about 5 minutes or until the onion is tender. Stir in sweet potato cubes and 1 cup water. Bring to boiling. In a small bowl stir together ¼ cup cold water, the cornstarch, and ¼ teaspoon of the salt; stir into mixture in skillet. Cook and stir until mixture thickens. Pour into baking dish over pork. (Sweet potatoes will not be done yet.) Bake 30 minutes. Remove from oven. Increase oven temperature to 450°F.
4. For biscuit topper, in a large bowl combine flour, cornmeal, baking powder, thyme, pepper, and the remaining ¼ teaspoon salt. Using a pastry blender, cut in light butter until mixture resembles coarse crumbs. Add soaked amaranth and any liquid remaining in the bowl. Stir until combined.
5. Using a large spoon, drop biscuit topper into eight mounds (about ¼ cup each) onto pork stew. Bake in the 450°F oven 12 to 15 minutes or until biscuits are browned and a wooden toothpick inserted in centers comes out clean.

PER SERVING: 363 cal., 13 g total fat (6 g sat. fat), 66 mg chol., 447 mg sodium, 40 g carb. (3 g fiber, 3 g sugars), 22 g pro.

CURIED SWEET POTATO
and AMARANTH SOUP

Curried Sweet Potato and Amaranth Soup

SERVINGS 6 (1 cup each)
CARB. PER SERVING 31 g
PREP 20 minutes   **COOK** 30 minutes

- 1   medium onion, chopped (¹/₂ cup)
- ¹/₄   cup chopped carrot
- ¹/₄   cup chopped celery
- 1   tablespoon minced fresh ginger
- 2   teaspoons minced garlic (4 cloves)
- 1   bay leaf
- ¹/₈   teaspoon crushed red pepper
- 1   tablespoon olive oil
- 1¹/₂   cups cubed, peeled sweet potato
- 1   to 2 teaspoons curry powder
- ¹/₄   cup dry white wine
- 1   32-ounce carton reduced-sodium chicken or vegetable broth
- 1   15-ounce can no-salt-added black beans, rinsed and drained
- 1   medium tomato, chopped (¹/₂ cup)
- ¹/₂   cup amaranth, rinsed
- ¹/₂   cup finely snipped fresh cilantro
- 2   tablespoons lemon juice
- ¹/₂   teaspoon salt
- ¹/₂   teaspoon black pepper
  Plain low-fat yogurt

1. In a large saucepan cook onion, carrot, celery, ginger, garlic, bay leaf, and crushed red pepper in hot oil over medium heat about 8 minutes or until tender, stirring occasionally.

2. Add sweet potato and curry powder; cook and stir about 1 minute or until fragrant. Add wine. Bring to boiling; reduce heat. Simmer, uncovered, until liquid is nearly evaporated. Add broth, beans, tomato, and amaranth. Return to boiling; reduce heat. Simmer, covered, about 20 minutes or until vegetables are tender and amaranth is cooked (it will still be slightly crunchy when done).

3. Remove from heat; remove bay leaf. Stir in cilantro, lemon juice, salt, and black pepper. Ladle into bowls and serve with a spoonful of yogurt on top.

PER SERVING: 197 cal., 4 g total fat (1 g sat. fat), 0 mg chol., 583 mg sodium, 31 g carb. (6 g fiber, 4 g sugars), 9 g pro.

EXPERT TIP

"Cook a bunch of whole grains at a time. Use them as side dishes, main courses with roasted vegetables and herbs, and tossed on a salad or in a casserole. Quinoa and farro also double as a hot cereal."

– Melissa Joy Dobbins, RD, CDE, dietitian, diabetes educator, and president of Sound Bites, Inc., a nutrition communications company

BARLEY

Barley may be better than oats in reducing cholesterol.

Italian Beef and Barley Cups

SERVINGS 4 (3 meat cups and 3 tablespoons sauce each)
CARB. PER SERVING 26 g
PREP 20 minutes **COOK** 12 minutes
BAKE 13 minutes **COOL** 5 minutes

2/3 cup water
1/3 cup quick-cooking barley
2 cups chopped fennel
1/2 cup chopped red sweet pepper
1/2 cup chopped onion
2 egg whites
1/2 cup finely shredded Parmesan cheese
1/4 cup fine dry bread crumbs
2 tablespoons snipped fresh Italian (flat-leaf) parsley
1 teaspoon dried Italian seasoning, crushed
1/4 teaspoon black pepper
1 pound 95% lean ground beef
Nonstick cooking spray
3/4 cup bottled marinara sauce, warmed

1. Preheat oven to 350°F. In a medium saucepan bring water and barley to boiling; reduce heat. Simmer, covered, 8 minutes. Stir in fennel, sweet pepper, and onion. Cover and cook about 4 minutes more or until barley and vegetables are just tender. Remove from heat; cover and set aside.

2. In a medium bowl whisk egg whites until lightly beaten. Stir in 1/4 cup of the Parmesan cheese, the bread crumbs, parsley, Italian seasoning, and black pepper. Add beef and mix well.

3. Lightly coat twelve 2 1/2-inch muffin cups with cooking spray. Divide beef mixture evenly among prepared cups. Press mixture on the bottom and up the sides of each cup, making a well in the center of each cup.

4. Drain barley mixture if needed. Spoon evenly into the wells in the beef cups. Cover top of pan with foil.

5. Bake 10 minutes. Uncover and sprinkle tops with remaining Parmesan cheese. Bake, uncovered, 3 to 5 minutes until the cups are heated through (160°F).* Let cups cool on a wire rack 5 minutes.

6. Run a thin sharp knife around the edge of each beef cup. Carefully remove cups from the pan. Divide cups among four plates. To serve, top with marinara sauce.

*TEST KITCHEN TIP: Very lean ground beef (95% lean) may have a pink color even when it is cooked and has a temperature of 160°F. It is safe to eat.

PER SERVING: 331 cal., 10 g total fat (5 g sat. fat), 78 mg chol., 554 mg sodium, 26 g carb. (5 g fiber, 5 g sugars), 34 g pro.

BARLEY

Curried Chicken, Barley, and Vegetables

SERVINGS 8 (1 chicken thigh and $^3/_4$ cup barley mixture each)
CARB. PER SERVING 34 g
PREP 25 minutes **SLOW COOK** 8 hours (low) or 4 hours (high)

2 cups packaged peeled fresh baby carrots
1 cup regular pearled barley
$1^1/_2$ teaspoons minced garlic
3 cups coarsely shredded cabbage
8 bone-in chicken thighs, skin removed (about 3 pounds total)
2 tablespoons orange marmalade
5 teaspoons curry powder
$^1/_2$ teaspoon salt
$^1/_4$ teaspoon black pepper
$3^1/_2$ cups reduced-sodium chicken broth
$^1/_2$ cup unsalted peanuts, coarsely chopped
$^1/_4$ cup raisins
$^1/_4$ cup sliced green onions (2)

1. In a 5- to 6-quart slow cooker combine carrots, barley, and garlic. Top with cabbage and chicken thighs.
2. In a small bowl whisk together orange marmalade, curry powder, salt, and pepper. Spread over chicken. Pour broth over mixture in slow cooker. Cover and cook on low-heat setting 8 hours or on high-heat setting 4 hours.
3. Garnish each serving with peanuts, raisins, and green onions.

PER SERVING: 282 cal., 8 g total fat (1 g sat. fat), 66 mg chol., 482 mg sodium, 34 g carb. (6 g fiber, 9 g sugars), 20 g pro.

Barley Waldorf Salad

SERVINGS 8 (³/₄ cup each)
CARB. PER SERVING 23 g
PREP 20 minutes **COOK** 40 minutes

- ³/₄ cup regular pearled barley or quinoa
- 3³/₄ cups water
- ³/₄ teaspoon salt
- ¹/₄ cup plain low-fat yogurt
- 3 tablespoons light mayonnaise or salad dressing
- ¹/₄ teaspoon finely shredded lemon peel
- 1 tablespoon lemon juice
- ¹/₄ teaspoon sugar
- 1¹/₂ cups seedless red and/or green grapes, halved
- ²/₃ cup coarsely chopped apple (1 medium)
- ¹/₂ cup sliced celery (1 stalk)
- 8 leaves butterhead (Boston or Bibb) lettuce
- ¹/₄ cup coarsely chopped walnuts, toasted
- Coarsely shredded lemon peel (optional)

1. In a large saucepan toast barley over medium-low heat 4 to 5 minutes or until golden brown, stirring occasionally. Add the water and ¹/₄ teaspoon of the salt. Bring to boiling; reduce heat. Simmer, covered, about 40 minutes (15 minutes for quinoa) or until tender; drain. Rinse with cold water to cool; drain.

2. Meanwhile, in a large bowl combine yogurt, mayonnaise, the finely shredded lemon peel, the lemon juice, sugar, and the remaining ¹/₂ teaspoon salt. Stir in cooked barley, grapes, apple, and celery.

3. To serve, spoon barley mixture onto lettuce leaves. Sprinkle with walnuts. If desired, garnish with coarsely shredded lemon peel.

MAKE-AHEAD DIRECTIONS: Prepare Barley Waldorf Salad as directed through Step 2. Cover and refrigerate up to 24 hours. If necessary, stir a little milk into salad to moisten. Serve as directed.

PER SERVING: 135 cal., 4 g total fat (1 g sat. fat), 1 mg chol., 276 mg sodium, 23 g carb. (4 g fiber, 7 g sugars), 3 g pro.

¼ cup nuts
4 g fiber

¾ cup fresh raspberries
6 g fiber

1 Tbsp. seeds
2 g fiber

WHAT'S THE DEAL with fiber?

Learn why you need to eat fiber and how it benefits you the most.

½ cup cooked beans
7–9 g fiber

½ cup oatmeal
6 g fiber

½ cup cooked spinach
2 g fiber

½ cup cooked whole grain pasta
3 g fiber

¾ cup whole grain cereal
5–10 g fiber

½ cup cooked squash
3–5 g fiber

Fitting in plenty of fiber every day results in both short- and long-term health benefits, similar to those from eating whole grains—reducing the risk factor for heart disease and high blood pressure, excess weight, and type 2 diabetes.

One reason it's been a challenge for researchers to identify the distinct health benefits of whole grains and fiber is because many foods with whole grains contain other fiber. But still, the evidence is clear enough to encourage you to eat more whole grains AND more dietary fiber.

One immediate benefit of upping your fiber intake is fiber's role in digestive health by minimizing constipation. Fiber's role in moving food through your gastrointestinal tract is one reason eating more fiber has the potential to decrease your risk of heart disease and colon cancer.

People have the notion that fiber dramatically lowers glucose levels, particularly after eating. However, research doesn't support that unless your fiber intake tops out at nearly 50 grams per day, which is twice the recommended amount of 25 grams—and way more fiber than most people eat.

Bottom line: You should eat more fiber and whole grains because of their digestive and disease-preventing effects, not because of their glucose lowering power.

FIBER defined

Dietary fiber is the nondigested portion of plant-based foods. You'll find fiber in legumes (beans and peas), fruits, vegetables, and most whole grains.

You hear the term "dietary fiber" used as if it's a singular nutrient. But foods contain hundreds of different types of fibers. Various fibers perform different functions in the body that go well beyond the gastrointestinal tract. You need to eat all types of fibers to stay healthy and get the following benefits.

1 DIGESTION & REGULARITY

Get this benefit from the fiber in fruits, vegetables, and whole grains.

2 IMPROVED CHOLESTEROL

Get this benefit from the fiber in barley, lentils, and flaxseed.

3 WEIGHT CONTROL & FEELING FULL

Get this benefit from the resistant starches in beans, peas, and underripe bananas.

EASY WAYS TO GET MORE FIBER

LEARN THE LABEL LINGO
The "good source of fiber" nutrition claim can be used if a serving contains between 10 percent (2.5 grams) and 19 percent (5 grams) of the 25 grams per day that women need. A food can claim it's an "excellent source of fiber" if a serving has 20 percent or more (5 grams or more) of the daily fiber requirement for women.

ADD SMALL AMOUNTS
Sprinkle ground flax, chia seeds, wheat germ, sesame seeds, or chopped nuts over hot or dry cereal, yogurt, and fruit to up your intake of fiber. But keep an eye on the calorie counts in these foods. They add up quickly, and you only need one or two tablespoons to get more fiber.

ENJOY MORE NUTRIENT-PACKED LEGUMES
Use dried, frozen, and canned legumes (beans and peas). Eat them in soups, omelets, and casseroles or as a side dish. Toss them into salads, mix up some corn and black beans for a side dish, and blend chickpeas or white beans with garlic and lemon juice for a quick bean dip to eat with veggies or whole grain crackers.

EAT MORE BERRIES
Snack on a handful of berries, add them to dry or cooked cereal, and mix them into yogurt and cottage cheese.

HEALTHY HABIT:
EAT MORE FRUITS & VEGGIES

Nature's bounty of fruits and vegetables supplies many of the nutrients you need to thrive and stay free of diseases that are caused or worsened by inflammation. Plus, fruits and veggies can add a spectrum of textures, flavors, and colors to your day's meals and snacks. Aim to eat $2\frac{1}{2}$ cups of fruits and $2\frac{1}{2}$ cups of veggies every day.

MY FRUIT & VEGGIE GOAL

For three dinners this week I will make sure that half of my dinner plate is filled with nonstarchy vegetables.

SUCCESS STORY

> ❝ I eat on smaller plates now and no longer feel the need to be part of the clean-plate club. ❞

LINDA DAVIS | age 48

A public health nurse with two parents who have diabetes, Linda has seen enough pain and suffering due to the disease. Being Native American, she knew she was at greater risk for developing type 2 diabetes. So with her blood sugar readings putting her in the prediabetes range, Linda enrolled in a group diabetes-prevention program offered through the health department where she works.

Kick-start into action: "I wear my pedometer. It motivates me to get up and get moving. And eating at night was a problem for me. I learned that if I brushed my teeth after dinner, I wouldn't eat again until morning." With her lifestyle changes, losing 25 pounds, and starting metformin, Linda's A1C dropped from 6.4% to 5.9%.

Words of wisdom: "Be realistic. Lose the first five pounds, then the next. Remember to make your life the best it can be. You only get one shot at it."

FRUIT & VEGGIE
smoothies

One of the easiest
ways to up your intake
of fruits and veggies
is to blend them into
a delicious smoothie.
You'll love these
nutrition-packed blends.

PINK BLUSH

recipe on page 127

125

LEAN & GREEN

CHERRY-BERRY
BANANA

CARROT-MANGO
GREEN TEA

PINK BLUSH

photo on *page 125*

SERVINGS 4 (³/₄ cup each)

CARB. PER SERVING 33 g

START TO FINISH 15 minutes

2 medium red grapefruit
1½ cups frozen unsweetened raspberries
1 cup frozen unsweetened mango chunks
1 6-ounce carton light strawberry-flavor yogurt
½ cup reduced-calorie cranberry juice

1. Using a sharp knife, cut the peel off the grapefruit, making sure to remove all the white pith. Working over a blender, section the grapefruit, allowing the sections and any juice to fall into the blender. After sectioning the grapefruit, squeeze excess juice into the blender from the membranes. Discard membranes.

2. Add raspberries, mango, yogurt, and cranberry juice to blender. Cover and blend until smooth, stopping and scraping sides as needed. Pour into glasses to serve.

PER SERVING: 139 cal., 0 g total fat, 1 mg chol., 26 mg sodium, 33 g carb. (4 g fiber, 23 g sugars), 3 g pro.

LEAN & GREEN

SERVINGS 4 (³/₄ cup each)

CARB. PER SERVING 19 g

START TO FINISH 10 minutes

2½ cups stemmed kale leaves
1 cup cubed pineapple
¾ cup apple juice, chilled
½ cup seedless green grapes, frozen
½ cup chopped Granny Smith apple

1. Place kale, pineapple, apple juice, frozen grapes, and apple in a blender. Cover and blend until smooth. If desired, chill smoothies 1 to 2 hours. Stir before serving. Pour into glasses to serve.

PER SERVING: 81 cal., 1 g total fat (0 g sat. fat), 0 mg chol., 19 mg sodium, 19 g carb. (2 g fiber, 14 g sugars), 2 g pro.

CHERRY-BERRY BANANA

SERVINGS 4 (³/₄ cup each)

CARB. PER SERVING 20 g

START TO FINISH 10 minutes

1½ cups frozen unsweetened pitted dark sweet or sour cherries
1 cup unsweetened vanilla-flavor almond milk
1 6-ounce carton blueberry-flavor Greek nonfat yogurt
½ cup fresh or frozen unsweetened blueberries
1 small banana, peeled

1. In a blender combine cherries, milk, yogurt, blueberries, and banana. Cover and blend until smooth. Pour into glasses to serve.

PER SERVING: 104 cal., 1 g total fat (0 g sat. fat), 0 mg chol., 62 mg sodium, 20 g carb. (3 g fiber, 16 g sugars), 5 g pro.

CARROT-MANGO GREEN TEA

SERVINGS 4 (³/₄ cup each)

CARB. PER SERVING 17 g

PREP 10 minutes COOK 10 minutes

STAND 4 minutes CHILL 10 minutes

3 cups water
1 cup sliced carrots
1 inch fresh ginger, thinly sliced
4 green tea bags
2 cups frozen mango chunks
1 teaspoon honey

1. In a saucepan bring water to boiling. Add carrots; cover and cook 10 to 15 minutes or until tender; add ginger the last 2 minutes. Remove from heat; add tea bags. Cover; steep 4 minutes.

2. Remove tea bags, squeezing out tea. Remove ginger. Set pan on a hot pad in refrigerator 10 minutes. Transfer mixture to a blender. Add mango and honey. Cover and blend until smooth. Pour into glasses to serve.

PER SERVING: 69 cal., 0 g total fat, 0 mg chol., 27 mg sodium, 17 g carb. (2 g fiber, 14 g sugars), 1 g pro.

PB & J

CUCUMBER, MINT & MELON

ALMOND-CHOCOLATE BANANA

PB & J

SERVINGS 4 ($^3/_4$ cup each)
CARB. PER SERVING 11 g
START TO FINISH 10 minutes

      6 ounces soft, silken-style tofu
         (fresh bean curd)
  1$^1/_4$ cups unsweetened vanilla-flavor
         almond milk, chilled
    $^2/_3$ cup frozen blueberries
    $^1/_2$ cup grape juice, chilled
      2 tablespoons creamy peanut butter
    $^1/_2$ cup small ice cubes or crushed ice
         Fresh blueberries (optional)

1. In a blender combine tofu, almond milk, the $^2/_3$ cup frozen blueberries, the grape juice, and peanut butter. Cover and blend until smooth. Gradually add ice through hole in lid, blending until almost smooth. Pour into glasses to serve. If desired, garnish with fresh blueberries.

PER SERVING: 112 cal., 6 g total fat (1 g sat. fat), 0 mg chol., 97 mg sodium, 11 g carb. (2 g fiber, 8 g sugars), 5 g pro.

CUCUMBER, MINT & MELON

SERVINGS 4 (1 cup each)
CARB. PER SERVING 21 g
PREP 10 minutes   **COOK** 10 minutes

      1 cup coarsely chopped fresh cauliflower
      2 cups 1-inch cubes honeydew melon
      2 cups 1-inch pieces cucumber
    $^1/_2$ cup lightly packed fresh mint
    $^1/_4$ cup water
      2 to 3 tablespoons honey
      1 cup ice cubes

1. In a small saucepan cook cauliflower, uncovered, in enough boiling water to cover 10 to 12 minutes or until very tender; drain. Rinse with cold water to cool quickly; drain again.

2. In a blender add honeydew melon, cauliflower, cucumber, mint, water, and honey. Cover and blend until very smooth, stopping and scraping sides of blender as needed. Add ice cubes. Cover and blend until smooth. Pour into glasses to serve.

PER SERVING: 83 cal., 0 g total fat, 0 mg chol., 29 mg sodium, 21 g carb. (2 g fiber, 17 g sugars), 2 g pro.

ALMOND-CHOCOLATE BANANA

SERVINGS 4 ($^3/_4$ cup each)
CARB. PER SERVING 12 g
PREP 10 minutes   **FREEZE** 1 hour

      2 small bananas
      2 cups unsweetened vanilla-flavor
         almond milk
      3 tablespoons sugar-free chocolate-flavor
         syrup
      1 tablespoon almond butter

1. Peel and slice bananas. Place banana slices on a waxed paper-lined tray. Cover and freeze 1 to 2 hours or until firm.

2. Transfer frozen banana slices to a blender. Add half of the milk, the chocolate syrup, and almond butter. Cover and blend until smooth. With the blender running, gradually add the remaining milk through hole in the lid, blending until combined. Pour into glasses to serve.

PER SERVING: 83 cal., 4 g total fat (0 g sat. fat), 0 mg chol., 103 mg sodium, 12 g carb. (2 g fiber, 5 g sugars), 2 g pro.

CREAMY
GREEN

COCONUT-ORANGE
BANANA BLAST

STRAWBERRIES
& CREAM

130

CREAMY GREEN

SERVINGS 4 (1 cup each)
CARB. PER SERVING 30 g
START TO FINISH 15 minutes

> 3   ripe green kiwifruits, peeled and chopped
> 2   cups chopped, trimmed fresh Swiss chard or spinach
> 1½ cups frozen unsweetened sliced peaches
> 1   medium avocado, halved, pitted, peeled, and chopped
> ½   cup unsweetened pineapple juice
> 2   tablespoons lime juice (optional)
> 1   cup ice cubes

1. In a blender combine kiwi, chard, peach slices, avocado, pineapple juice, lime juice (if using), and ice. Cover and blend until very smooth, stopping and scraping sides as needed. Pour into glasses to serve.

PER SERVING: 167 cal., 6 g total fat (1 g sat. fat), 0 mg chol., 43 mg sodium, 30 g carb. (5 g fiber, 21 g sugars), 2 g pro.

COCONUT-ORANGE BANANA BLAST

SERVINGS 4 (about ¾ cup each)
CARB. PER SERVING 28 g
PREP 25 minutes   FREEZE 1 hour
COOK 10 minutes

> 1   medium banana, peeled and sliced
> 1   cup small fresh cauliflower florets
> 1   medium orange
> 1½ cups fresh pineapple chunks
> 1   cup refrigerated unsweetened coconut milk beverage
> 2   tablespoons honey

1. Line a tray with waxed paper. Arrange banana slices in a single layer on waxed paper. Cover loosely with plastic wrap; freeze 1 to 2 hours or until completely firm.

2. In a small saucepan cook cauliflower, uncovered, in enough boiling water to cover 10 to 12 minutes or until very tender. Drain; cool.

3. Finely zest 1 teaspoon of orange peel from orange; add to blender. Using a sharp knife, cut the peel off the orange, making sure to remove all the white pith. Working over the blender, section the orange, allowing the sections and any juice to fall into the blender. After sectioning the orange, squeeze any excess juice into the blender from the membranes.

4. Add frozen banana slices, cooled cauliflower, pineapple, coconut milk, and honey to blender. Cover and blend until very smooth, stopping and scraping sides of blender as needed. Pour into four glasses to serve.

PER SERVING: 121 cal., 2 g total fat (1 g sat. fat), 0 mg chol., 13 mg sodium, 28 g carb. (3 g fiber, 21 g sugars), 2 g pro.

STRAWBERRIES & CREAM

SERVINGS 4 (1 cup each)
CARB. PER SERVING 18 g
START TO FINISH 15 minutes

> 1   6-ounce carton light lemon-flavor yogurt
> ¼   cup light cream cheese spread, softened
> ¼   cup pomegranate juice
> 3   cups fresh or frozen* unsweetened strawberries
> 1   cup small ice cubes

1. In a blender combine yogurt, cream cheese, and pomegranate juice. Cover and blend until very well combined. Add strawberries; cover and blend until smooth. With blender running, gradually add ice cubes through hole in the lid; blend until smooth. Pour into four glasses to serve.

*TEST KITCHEN TIP: If using frozen strawberries, let stand at room temperature 30 to 60 minutes or until slightly thawed before blending.

PER SERVING: 113 cal., 3 g total fat (2 g sat. fat), 11 mg chol., 103 mg sodium, 18 g carb. (3 g fiber, 14 g sugars), 3 g pro.

PRODUCE-PACKED
lunches

Make a goal to eat more fruits and veggies in the midday. Each of these filling lunch options includes a full serving of both!

CHICKEN and ARTICHOKE SPINACH SALAD

recipe on
page 143

TUNA and FENNEL
SANDWICH

recipe on *page 143*

CUCUMBER-FETA
PITA SANDWICH

recipe on *page 143*

EXPERT TIP

"Fitting your workouts in is the hardest part of exercise. One of my no-brainer multitasking workouts is to put on a phone headset and take a walk, garden, or dust while I catch up with a friend or loved one."

– *Molly McElwee-Malloy, RN, CDE, Diabetes Education & Management Program, University of Virginia Health System, Charlottesville, and person with diabetes.*

133

CHILI-CILANTRO TURKEY
SANDWICHES

recipe on *page 136*

Shrimp and Broccoli Noodle Bowl

SERVINGS 1
CARB. PER SERVING 37 g
START TO FINISH 10 minutes

- ⅓ cup cooked whole grain spaghetti
- 2 ounces cooked shrimp
- ¾ cup packaged broccoli slaw
- ⅓ cup snow peas
- 2 tablespoons green onion
- 2 teaspoons raisins
- 1 teaspoon toasted sesame seeds
- 1 tablespoon low-fat sesame-ginger salad dressing
- 1 tablespoon orange juice
- ½ of a small orange

1. In a serving container layer spaghetti, shrimp, broccoli slaw, snow peas, green onion, raisins, and sesame seeds. Stir together salad dressing and orange juice; drizzle over all. Serve with orange.

PER SERVING: 260 cal., 5 g total fat (1 g sat. fat), 107 mg chol., 236 mg sodium, 37 g carb. (7 g fiber, 17 g sugars), 20 g pro.

Meatless Taco Salad

SERVINGS 1
CARB. PER SERVING 50 g
START TO FINISH 10 minutes

- 1½ cups torn romaine lettuce
- ½ cup reduced-sodium black beans, rinsed and drained
- ½ cup red sweet pepper strips
- ¼ cup grape tomatoes, halved
- 2 tablespoons shredded reduced-fat Mexican four-cheese blend
- 2 tablespoons light creamy salad dressing
- ¾ cup fresh pineapple pieces

1. In a serving container layer lettuce, beans, sweet pepper, tomatoes, and cheese Drizzle with salad dressing. Serve with pineapple.

PER SERVING: 323 cal., 11 g total fat (2 g sat. fat), 17 mg chol., 665 mg sodium, 50 g carb. (11 g fiber, 19 g sugars), 13 g pro.

MEATLESS
TACO SALAD

SHRIMP and BROCCOLI
NOODLE BOWL

Chili-Cilantro Turkey Sandwiches

photo on *page 134*
SERVINGS 4 (1 sandwich
and 1 cup berries each)
CARB. PER SERVING 33 g
START TO FINISH 25 minutes

- 3 tablespoons light mayonnaise
- 2 tablespoons snipped fresh cilantro
- 1 teaspoon hot or mild chili powder
- 8 slices very thinly sliced whole wheat bread
- 4 ounces thinly sliced lower-sodium cooked turkey
- 4 slices reduced-fat cheddar cheese (3 ounces total)
- 1 medium fresh poblano chile pepper, stemmed, seeded, and thinly sliced crosswise (tip, *page 252*)
- 1 medium fresh tomato, thinly sliced
- 4 cups mixed fresh berries

1. In a small bowl combine mayonnaise, cilantro, and chili powder. Spread evenly on one side of each slice of bread.

2. Layer the turkey, cheese, pepper slices, and tomato slices on top of the mayonnaise on four of the bread slices. Place remaining bread slices, mayonnaise sides down, on tomato slices. Cut sandwiches in half.

3. Serve sandwiches with berries.

PER SERVING: 302 cal., 13 g total fat (5 g sat. fat), 39 mg chol., 557 mg sodium, 33 g carb. (8 g fiber, 12 g sugars), 15 g pro.

Miso-Marinated Tofu and Cabbage Wraps

SERVINGS 6 (1 wrap and 1 kiwifruit each)
CARB. PER SERVING 32 g
PREP 25 minutes   MARINATE 2 hours

- 1 18-ounce package firm tofu (fresh bean curd)
- ⅓ cup rice vinegar
- ¼ cup snipped fresh mint
- 2 tablespoons honey
- 2 tablespoons white miso paste
- ¼ teaspoon crushed red pepper
- 6 8-inch low-carb, high-fiber tortillas
- 6 napa cabbage leaves
- 2 medium carrots, julienned or coarsely shredded
- 6 medium radishes, trimmed and very thinly sliced (about 1 cup)
- ¾ cup thinly sliced cucumber
- 2 small shallots, thinly sliced
- 6 medium fresh kiwifruits, peeled and sliced

1. Drain tofu and pat dry with paper towels. Cut tofu into 1-inch cubes. Place tofu in a resealable plastic bag set in a shallow dish. In a small bowl whisk together vinegar, mint, honey, miso paste, and crushed red pepper. Pour over tofu. Seal bag; turn to coat. Marinate in the refrigerator at least 2 hours or up to 8 hours, turning bag occasionally.

2. Drain tofu, discarding marinade. Place a cabbage leaf on each tortilla. Layer drained tofu, carrot, radishes, cucumber, and shallots evenly on the cabbage leaves. Roll up tortillas; cut in half crosswise. Serve immediately or wrap in plastic wrap and chill up to 8 hours before serving.

3. Serve the wraps with kiwifruit.

PER SERVING: 197 cal., 5 g total fat (0 g sat. fat), 0 mg chol., 240 mg sodium, 32 g carb. (11 g fiber, 13 g sugars), 14 g pro.

MISO-MARINATED TOFU
and CABBAGE WRAPS

CHICKEN-EGG SALAD

Chicken-Egg Salad

SERVINGS 1
CARB. PER SERVING 31 g
START TO FINISH 15 minutes

- 1½ cups torn romaine lettuce
- ½ cup yellow sweet pepper strips
- ¼ cup sliced fresh strawberries
- 2 tablespoons light olive oil and vinegar salad dressing
- 1 hard-cooked egg, chopped
- ¼ cup chopped cooked chicken breast
- 2 tablespoons sliced green onion (1)
- 2 tablespoons cucumber-dill Greek yogurt dip
- 1 ounce whole grain baguette-style bread

1. In a serving container layer lettuce, sweet pepper, and strawberries. Drizzle with salad dressing. In a small bowl stir together chicken, green onion, and yogurt dip; spoon over lettuce mixture. Serve with the bread.

PER SERVING: 337 cal., 13 g total fat (3 g sat. fat), 219 mg chol., 664 mg sodium, 31 g carb. (6 g fiber, 12 g sugars), 23 g pro.

Kale-Lentil and Squash Salad

SERVINGS 1
CARB. PER SERVING 45 g
START TO FINISH 10 minutes

- 1 cup chopped kale
- ¼ cup packaged ready-to-eat lentils
- ½ cup coarsely chopped cooked butternut squash
- ½ cup sliced cooked chicken breast
- ½ cup grape tomatoes, halved
- 1 ounce semisoft goat cheese
- 2 tablespoons light balsamic vinaigrette
- 3 thin slices cantaloupe

1. In a serving container layer kale, lentils, squash, chicken, tomatoes, and goat cheese. Drizzle vinaigrette over all. Serve with cantaloupe.

PER SERVING: 443 cal., 13 g total fat (7 g sat. fat), 82 mg chol., 582 mg sodium, 45 g carb. (11 g fiber, 22 g sugars), 38 g pro.

KALE-LENTIL and SQUASH SALAD

Chicken Avocado BLT Wrap

SERVINGS 1
CARB. PER SERVING 43 g
START TO FINISH 10 minutes

- 1 100-calorie cup guacamole
- 1 8-inch low-carb whole wheat tortilla
- ²⁄₃ cup fresh spinach
- 2 ounces cooked chicken breast, shredded
- 1 slice reduced-fat, reduced-sodium bacon, cooked and drained
- ½ cup cherry tomatoes, halved
- 17 grapes

1. Spread guacamole on tortilla. Top with spinach, chicken, bacon, and tomatoes. Roll up. Serve with grapes.

PER SERVING: 381 cal., 16 g total fat (3 g sat. fat), 52 mg chol., 647 mg sodium, 43 g carb. (18 g fiber, 17 g sugars), 31 g pro.

Beef and Blue Wrap

SERVINGS 1
CARB. PER SERVING 40 g
START TO FINISH 10 minutes

- 1 8-inch low-carb whole wheat tortilla
- ½ cup fresh spinach
- ¼ cup fresh basi
- 2 ounces lower-sodium deli-sliced roast beef
- 3 thin tomato slices
- ½ cup cut-up sugar snap peas
- 1 tablespoon crumbled reduced-fat blue cheese
- 2 teaspoons balsamic vinegar
- 1 teaspoon light mayonnaise
- ½ cup unsweetened applesauce

1. On the tortilla layer spinach, basil, roast beef, tomato, and sugar snap peas; sprinkle with blue cheese. Stir together balsamic vinegar and mayonnaise; drizzle over all. Roll up tortilla. Serve with applesauce.

PER SERVING: 300 cal., 9 g total fat (2 g sat. fat), 41 mg chol., 538 mg sodium, 40 g carb. (16 g fiber, 17 g sugars), 27 g pro.

CHICKEN AVOCADO
BLT WRAP

BEEF and BLUE WRAP

HAM and DOUBLE SWISS
SALAD

Ham and Double Swiss Salad

SERVINGS 4 (2 cups salad, 2 tablespoons dressing, and 1 apple each)
CARB. PER SERVING 30 g
START TO FINISH 25 minutes

- 3 cups torn fresh romaine lettuce
- 2 cups torn, trimmed fresh Swiss chard
- 1 cup coarsely chopped cucumber
- 1 cup coarsely shredded carrots
- 4 ounces reduced-sodium deli-sliced ham, chopped (about ¾ cup)
- ½ cup shredded reduced-fat Swiss cheese (2 ounces)
- 1 recipe Creamy Honey-Sage Dressing
- 4 small apples

1. In four serving containers layer romaine, Swiss chard, cucumber, carrots, ham, and cheese. Store Creamy Honey-Sage Dressing in a separate container. Cover and chill until ready to serve. When ready to serve, drizzle dressing over all. Serve with apples.

CREAMY HONEY-SAGE DRESSING: In a small bowl whisk together ⅓ cup light mayonnaise; 1 tablespoon Dijon-style mustard; 1 tablespoon honey; 1 tablespoon fat-free milk; 2 teaspoons snipped fresh sage; ¼ to ½ teaspoon caraway seeds, finely crushed; and ¼ teaspoon freshly ground black pepper until smooth.

PER SERVING: 261 cal., 12 g total fat (3 g sat. fat), 33 mg chol., 574 mg sodium, 30 g carb. (5 g fiber, 20 g sugars), 13 g pro.

Chicken and Artichoke Spinach Salad

photo on *page 132*
SERVINGS 4 (2 cups salad and about ¹/₂ cup grapes each)
CARB. PER SERVING 35 g
START TO FINISH 45 minutes

¹/₄   cup dried quinoa
¹/₂   cup water
2   tablespoons olive oil
2   tablespoons balsamic vinegar
2   teaspoons snipped fresh oregano
¹/₄   teaspoon salt
¹/₈   teaspoon black pepper
4   cups fresh baby spinach
¹/₃   cup torn fresh basil
1   14-ounce can quartered artichoke hearts, drained and coarsely chopped
8   ounces cooked chicken breast or turkey breast, chopped
³/₄   cup grape tomatoes, halved
³/₄   cup quartered, thinly sliced red onion
4   teaspoons shredded Parmesan cheese
2¹/₂ cups grapes

1. Rinse quinoa using a fine-mesh sieve. Drain well. In a small saucepan combine quinoa and water. Bring to boiling; reduce heat. Simmer, covered, 12 to 15 minutes or until quinoa is tender and most of the liquid is absorbed. Drain if necessary. Set aside to cool slightly.
2. In a small bowl whisk together the olive oil, vinegar, oregano, salt, and pepper.
3. In four serving containers layer spinach, basil, cooked quinoa, artichoke hearts, chicken, tomatoes, onion, and cheese. Cover and chill until ready to serve. When ready to serve, drizzle dressing over all. Serve with grapes.

PER SERVING: 321 cal., 10 g total fat (2 g sat. fat), 49 mg chol., 468 mg sodium, 35 g carb. (6 g fiber, 18 g sugars), 23 g pro.

Tuna and Fennel Sandwich

photo on *page 133*
SERVINGS 1
CARB. PER SERVING 31 g
START TO FINISH 10 minutes

1   2.6-ounce pouch low-sodium chunk light tuna in water
2   tablespoons sliced green onion (1)
1   tablespoon light mayonnaise
2   teaspoons tomato paste
2   very thin slices whole wheat bread
2   very thin slices fennel
¹/₂   cup fresh spinach
¹/₃   cup shredded carrot
¹/₂   cup fresh raspberries

1. Combine tuna, green onion, mayonnaise, and tomato paste; spread on one slice of bread. Top with fennel, spinach, and carrot. Add the remaining slice of bread. Serve with raspberries.

PER SERVING: 260 cal., 8 g total fat (1 g sat. fat), 38 mg chol., 510 mg sodium, 31 g carb. (9 g fiber, 9 g sugars), 20 g pro.

Cucumber-Feta Pita Sandwich

photo on *page 133*
SERVINGS 1
CARB. PER SERVING 41 g
START TO FINISH 10 minutes

¹/₂   cup cucumber slices
2   tablespoons plain fat-free yogurt
2   teaspoons rice vinegar
¹/₄   teaspoon sugar
¹/₂   of a whole grain pita bread
2   tablespoons olive tapenade-flavor hummus
¹/₂   cup fresh spinach
2   tablespoons jarred roasted red pepper and caramelized onion
1   tablespoon reduced-fat feta cheese
1   kiwifruit

1. Combine cucumber, yogurt, vinegar, sugar, and dash *black pepper*. In pita layer cucumber mixture, hummus, spinach, red pepper and onion, and cheese. Serve with kiwifruit.

PER SERVING: 249 cal., 7 g total fat (1 g sat. fat), 3 mg chol., 646 mg sodium, 41 g carb. (6 g fiber, 15 g sugars), 11 g pro.

1 CHICKEN-BROCCOLI SALAD with BUTTERMILK DRESSING

recipe on page 154

supersize
SALADS

Bring fresh color and crunch to the table with these salads brimming with delicious, disease-fighting fruits and vegetables.

2 SHRIMP and EDAMAME SALAD with GINGER DRESSING

recipe on *page 154*

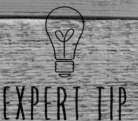

EXPERT TIP

"Use this formula to make a hearty and satisfying meatless pasta dish for one: $\frac{1}{3}$ cup dry multigrain pasta, cooked; 1 cup chopped fresh or frozen veggies; 2 tablespoons quality oil or oil-based sauce; 2 tablespoons hard cheese; and 1 tablespoon nuts."

— *Regan Jones, RD, blogger, The Professional Palate*

SEARED TUNA with FENNEL-APPLE SLAW

recipe on *page 155*

3

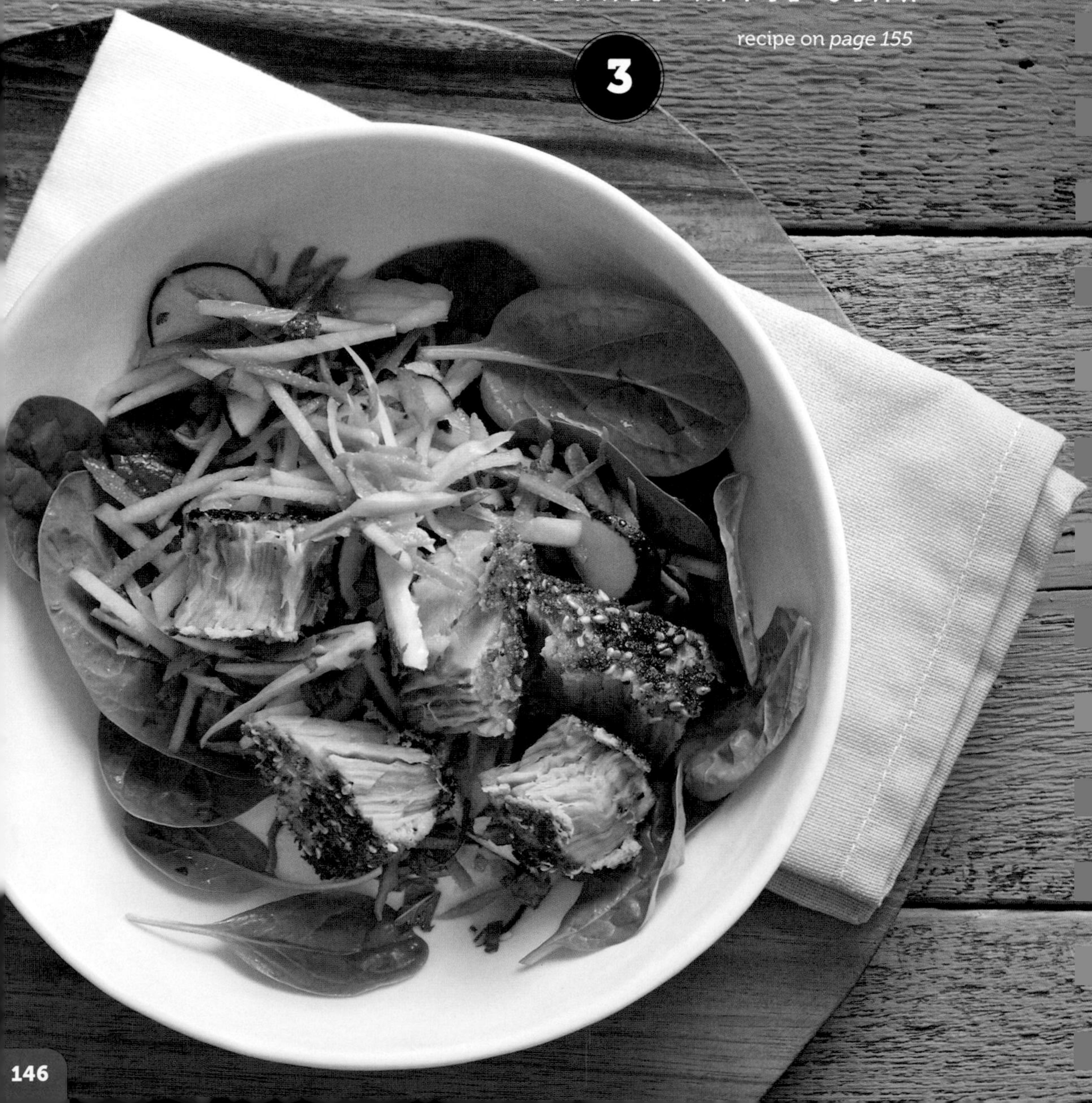

4

STEAK and
CHIMICHURRI SALAD

recipe on *page 155*

147

PRETZEL-PISTACHIO-
CRUSTED TOFU SALAD

recipe on *page 156*

5

6

SALMON
SALAD with
ORANGE
VINAIGRETTE

recipe on *page 156*

BBQ CHICKEN and ROASTED
CORN SALAD

7

recipe on *page 157*

8 SPICY SWEET POTATO
and PORK SALAD

recipe on page 157

BACON-WRAPPED TURKEY MEATBALL and CABBAGE SALAD

recipe on *page 158*

9

CAULIFLOWER-
WATERCRESS
SALAD with
DILL-SHALLOT
DRESSING

10

recipe on *page 158*

11

GRILLED PORTOBELLO-CHICKEN ROW SALAD

recipe on *page 159*

12

POTATO and BRUSSELS SPROUTS SALAD with LEMON-HONEY VINAIGRETTE

recipe on *page 159*

1 Chicken-Broccoli Salad with Buttermilk Dressing

SERVINGS 4 (2 cups each)
CARB. PER SERVING 29 g
PREP 20 minutes   CHILL 2 hours

- 3 cups packaged shredded broccoli slaw
- 2 cups coarsely chopped cooked chicken breast
- 1/2 cup dried cherries
- 1/3 cup thinly sliced celery
- 1/4 cup finely chopped red onion
- 1 recipe Buttermilk Dressing
- 4 cups fresh baby spinach

1. In a large bowl combine shredded broccoli, chicken, dried cherries, celery, and red onion.
2. Pour Buttermilk Dressing over broccoli mixture; toss gently to combine. Cover and chill at least 2 hours or up to 24 hours.
3. Just before serving, add baby spinach and toss gently.

BUTTERMILK DRESSING: In a small bowl whisk together 1/3 cup buttermilk, 1/3 cup light mayonnaise, 1 tablespoon honey, 1 tablespoon cider vinegar, 1 teaspoon dry mustard, 1/2 teaspoon salt, and 1/8 teaspoon black pepper.

PER SERVING: 278 cal., 7 g total fat (2 g sat. fat), 64 mg chol., 585 mg sodium, 29 g carb. (4 g fiber, 19 g sugars), 26 g pro.

2 Shrimp and Edamame Salad with Ginger Dressing

SERVINGS 4 (2 cups each)
CARB. PER SERVING 25 g
START TO FINISH 45 minutes

- 6 ounces fresh or frozen peeled, cooked medium shrimp, halved lengthwise if desired
- 1/2 cup frozen edamame
- 1 cup dried radiatore or rotini pasta
- 3 cups shredded napa cabbage
- 2 cups shredded romaine lettuce
- 1 cup halved fresh strawberries
- 3/4 cup packaged julienned carrots
- 3/4 cup fresh snow pea pods, ends trimmed, strings removed, and halved
- 1 small yellow sweet pepper, cut into thin bite-size strips
- 1/4 cup thinly sliced green onions (2)
- 1 recipe Ginger Dressing

1. Thaw shrimp, if frozen. Cook edamame according to package directions; drain. Cook pasta according to package directions; drain. Rinse with cold water; drain again.
2. In an extra-large bowl combine shrimp, edamame, pasta, cabbage, romaine, strawberries, carrots, pea pods, sweet pepper, and green onions.
3. Drizzle Ginger Dressing over salad. Toss gently to coat.

GINGER DRESSING: In a screw-top jar combine 3 tablespoons cider vinegar; 2 tablespoons reduced-sodium soy sauce; 1 tablespoon canola oil; 4 cloves garlic, minced; 2 teaspoons grated fresh ginger; 1 teaspoon toasted sesame oil; and 1/8 teaspoon crushed red pepper. Cover and shake well.

PER SERVING: 224 cal., 6 g total fat (1 g sat. fat), 80 mg chol., 351 mg sodium, 25 g carb. (5 g fiber, 8 g sugars), 17 g pro.

3 Seared Tuna with Fennel-Apple Slaw

SERVINGS 4 (2$^{1}/_{2}$ ounces tuna, $^{3}/_{4}$ cup slaw, and 1 cup spinach each)
CARB. PER SERVING 16 g
PREP 25 minutes COOK 5 minutes

  2 5- to 6-ounce fresh or frozen tuna steaks, cut about $^{3}/_{4}$ inch thick
  1 recipe Fennel-Apple Slaw
  2 egg whites
  1 tablespoon water
  $^{1}/_{4}$ cup panko bread crumbs
  2 tablespoons sesame seeds
  1 tablespoon canola oil
  4 cups fresh spinach

1. Thaw fish, if frozen. Rinse fish; pat dry with paper towels. Prepare Fennel-Apple Slaw; cover.
2. In a shallow dish whisk together egg whites and water. In a separate shallow dish combine bread crumbs and sesame seeds. Pat tuna steaks dry with paper towels. Sprinkle steaks on both sides with $^{1}/_{4}$ teaspoon each *salt* and *black pepper*. Dip steaks on the tops and bottoms in egg white mixture. Allow excess to drip off. Dip steaks in bread crumb mixture to coat tops and bottoms, pressing crumbs lightly onto steaks.
3. In a large nonstick skillet cook steaks in hot oil over medium-high heat 5 to 7 minutes or until well browned on the outside, turning once; steaks will be pink in the center. Transfer steaks to a cutting board. Cut into $^{1}/_{4}$-inch-thick slices.
4. To serve, divide spinach leaves among four plates. Top with slaw and tuna slices.

FENNEL-APPLE SLAW: In a bowl combine 1 medium green apple, cored and cut into matchstick-size pieces; $^{1}/_{2}$ cup thinly sliced fennel bulb; $^{1}/_{2}$ cup shredded carrot; and 2 radishes, halved and thinly sliced. In a bowl whisk 3 tablespoons rice vinegar, 2 tablespoons snipped fresh mint, 4 teaspoons canola oil, $^{1}/_{4}$ teaspoon toasted sesame oil (if desired), $^{1}/_{4}$ teaspoon salt, and $^{1}/_{8}$ to $^{1}/_{4}$ teaspoon crushed red pepper. Add to fennel mixture; toss to coat.

PER SERVING: 251 cal., 10 g total fat (1 g sat. fat), 28 mg chol., 435 mg sodium, 16 g carb. (5 g fiber, 6 g sugars), 22 g pro.

4 Steak and Chimichurri Salad

SERVINGS 4 (1$^{3}/_{4}$ cups each)
CARB. PER SERVING 22 g
PREP 30 minutes GRILL 13 minutes

  12 ounces beef flank steak
  $^{1}/_{4}$ teaspoon salt
  $^{1}/_{4}$ teaspoon black pepper
  1 recipe Chimichurri Sauce
  4 ounces whole grain baguette-style French bread, cut into $^{1}/_{2}$-inch cubes and toasted
  1$^{1}/_{2}$ cups cherry tomatoes, halved
  $^{1}/_{2}$ cup very thinly sliced, quartered red onion
  4 cups fresh arugula or baby mixed greens

1. Score both sides of steak in a diamond pattern by making shallow diagonal cuts at 1-inch intervals. Sprinkle both sides of steak with salt and pepper. Let stand 5 minutes.
2. Meanwhile, prepare the Chimichurri Sauce.
3. For a charcoal or gas grill, grill steak on the rack of a covered grill directly over medium heat until desired doneness or 13 to 18 minutes for medium doneness (160°F), turning once halfway through grilling. Brush steak with 2 tablespoons Chimichurri Sauce during the last 5 minutes of grilling.
4. In a large bowl combine bread cubes, tomatoes, onion, arugula, and remaining Chimichurri Sauce; toss until well coated.
5. Thinly slice steak across the grain. Divide bread and salad mixture among four plates. Top with steak slices.

CHIMICHURRI SAUCE: In a blender combine $^{3}/_{4}$ cup tightly packed fresh Italian (flat-leaf) parsley, $^{3}/_{4}$ cup tightly packed fresh cilantro, $^{1}/_{4}$ cup lime juice, 2 tablespoons red wine vinegar, 1 tablespoon olive oil, 1 tablespoon water, 3 cloves garlic, $^{1}/_{4}$ teaspoon crushed red pepper, and $^{1}/_{4}$ teaspoon salt. Cover and pulse until nearly smooth.

PER SERVING: 284 cal., 12 g total fat (4 g sat. fat), 49 mg chol., 514 mg sodium, 22 g carb. (2 g fiber, 3 g sugars), 23 g pro.

5 Pretzel-Pistachio-Crusted Tofu Salad

SERVINGS 4 (1¹/₂ cups salad, 2 tofu slices, and 1 tablespoon dressing each)
CARB. PER SERVING 26 g
START TO FINISH 25 minutes

- 8 ounces extra-firm tofu, cut into 8 slices
- 2 egg whites, lightly beaten
- 1 ounce unsalted pretzels, crushed (¹/₄ cup)
- 3 tablespoons chopped pistachios
  Nonstick cooking spray
- 5 teaspoons olive oil
- 2 tablespoons white wine vinegar
- 2 tablespoons horseradish mustard
- 1 teaspoon honey
- ¹/₄ teaspoon salt
- 6 cups fresh baby spinach
- 1 medium apple, cored and thinly sliced
- ¹/₄ cup dried cranberries

1. Place tofu slices on paper towels; pat dry. Set aside.
2. Place egg whites in a shallow dish. In another shallow dish combine pretzels and nuts. Dip tofu slices in egg whites, turning to coat. Dip in pretzel mixture, turning to coat evenly.
3. Coat an extra-large nonstick skillet with cooking spray. Add 1 teaspoon of the oil to the skillet. Heat over medium-high heat. Add tofu slices; cook 4 to 6 minutes or until golden and crisp, turning once halfway through cooking.
4. Meanwhile, for dressing, in a screw-top jar combine the remaining 4 teaspoons oil, the vinegar, mustard, honey, and salt. Cover and shake well.
5. In a large salad bowl combine spinach, apple, and dried cranberries. Arrange tofu slices on top. Serve immediately with the dressing.

PER SERVING: 259 cal., 12 g total fat (2 g sat. fat), 0 mg chol., 353 mg sodium, 26 g carb. (5 g fiber, 12 g sugars), 12 g pro.

6 Salmon Salad with Orange Vinaigrette

SERVINGS 4 (1 salmon fillet, 2 cups salad, and 2 tablespoons vinaigrette each)
CARB. PER SERVING 16 g
PREP 20 minutes   GRILL 8 minutes

- 4 4- to 5-ounce fresh or frozen skinless salmon fillets, about 1 inch thick
- ¹/₄ teaspoon salt
- ¹/₄ teaspoon black pepper
  Nonstick cooking spray
- 8 cups packaged mixed salad greens
- 2 oranges, peeled and thinly sliced
- ¹/₄ cup thinly sliced red onion
- 1 recipe Orange Vinaigrette
- 2 tablespoons sliced almonds

1. Thaw salmon, if frozen. Rinse salmon; pat dry with paper towels. Sprinkle with salt and pepper. Coat both sides of salmon with cooking spray. For a charcoal or gas grill, grill salmon on the rack of a covered grill directly over medium heat 8 to 12 minutes or just until salmon flakes when tested with a fork, turning once halfway through grilling.
2. To serve, divide salad greens among four plates. Top with oranges and red onion. Arrange salmon on top of salads. Drizzle with Orange Vinaigrette and sprinkle with almonds.
ORANGE VINAIGRETTE: In a screw-top jar combine 3 tablespoons balsamic vinegar, ¹/₄ teaspoon finely shredded orange peel, 3 tablespoons orange juice, 2 tablespoons snipped fresh mint, 2 tablespoons olive oil, and ¹/₈ teaspoon salt. Cover and shake well.

PER SERVING: 306 cal., 16 g total fat (2 g sat. fat), 62 mg chol., 286 mg sodium, 16 g carb. (4 g fiber, 10 g sugars), 25 g pro.

7 BBQ Chicken and Roasted Corn Salad

SERVINGS 4 ($1^{3}/_{4}$ cups salad, 4 ounces chicken, and 1 tablespoon dressing each)
CARB. PER SERVING 31 g
PREP 25 minutes   BROIL 6 minutes

- 1 to $1^{1}/_{4}$ pounds skinless, boneless chicken breast halves
- 2 teaspoons chili powder
- 1 teaspoon dried oregano
- 1 teaspoon dried thyme
- 1 tablespoon canola oil
- 1 15-ounce can no-salt-added black beans, rinsed and drained
- 1 cup frozen whole kernel corn, thawed
- 2 tablespoons bottled light ranch dressing
- 2 tablespoons reduced-sodium barbecue sauce
- 1 tablespoon white wine vinegar
- 4 cups chopped romaine lettuce
- 1 cup cherry tomatoes, halved
- 1 ounce queso fresco, crumbled

1. Place each chicken piece between two pieces of plastic wrap. Pound to about $^{1}/_{2}$-inch thickness. Remove plastic wrap.
2. Preheat broiler. Combine chili powder, oregano, thyme, $^{1}/_{4}$ teaspoon each *salt* and *black pepper*. Rub half of the mixture over chicken. Mix oil and remaining spice mixture. Stir half of the oil mixture into beans.
3. Line a 15×10×1-inch baking pan with foil. Place chicken on one side and corn on the other side of pan; drizzle corn with the remaining oil-spice mixture. Broil 4 to 5 inches from the heat 6 to 8 minutes or until chicken is no longer pink (165°F), turning chicken and stirring corn once. In a bowl combine salad dressing, barbecue sauce, and vinegar.
4. To serve, slice chicken. Arrange romaine in a shallow serving bowl. Top with corn mixture, tomatoes, chicken, and bean mixture. Sprinkle with queso fresco. Serve with dressing mixture.

PER SERVING: 347 cal., 11 g total fat (2 g sat. fat), 80 mg chol., 435 mg sodium, 31 g carb. (8 g fiber, 6 g sugars), 33 g pro.

8 Spicy Sweet Potato and Pork Salad

SERVINGS 4 ($1^{1}/_{2}$ cups spinach, $2^{1}/_{2}$ ounces pork, and $^{3}/_{4}$ cup sweet potato mixture each)
CARB. PER SERVING 44 g
PREP 30 minutes   ROAST 30 minutes

- 1 pound pork tenderloin, trimmed of fat
- $^{3}/_{4}$ teaspoon paprika
- 1 pound sweet potatoes, peeled and cut into 1-inch cubes
- 1 tablespoon canola oil
- 1 medium poblano pepper, seeded and chopped (tip, *page 252*)
- 1 small onion, halved and thinly sliced
- 2 cloves garlic, minced
- $^{1}/_{2}$ teaspoon ground cumin
- 1 large fresh tomato, cored and chopped
- $^{3}/_{4}$ cup canned reduced-sodium black beans, rinsed and drained
- $^{1}/_{4}$ cup golden raisins
- 6 cups fresh spinach
- $^{1}/_{4}$ cup light sour cream
- 2 tablespoons roasted pumpkin seeds

1. Preheat oven to 425°F. Line a shallow baking pan with foil; add pork. Sprinkle pork with $^{1}/_{4}$ teaspoon of the paprika and $^{1}/_{4}$ teaspoon *black pepper*. Roast, uncovered, 10 minutes.
2. Meanwhile, in a large bowl toss sweet potatoes with oil. After the pork loin has roasted 10 minutes, add sweet potatoes in a single layer to the baking pan with the pork. Roast an additional 20 minutes or until potatoes are lightly browned and pork is done (145°F).
3. Coat a large nonstick skillet with *nonstick cooking spray*. Add poblano pepper, onion, and garlic; cook 5 minutes, stirring occasionally. Stir in $^{1}/_{2}$ teaspoon *salt*, the remaining paprika, and the cumin. Add tomato, beans, and raisins. Cook, covered, 5 minutes, stirring occasionally. Remove from heat. Stir in sweet potatoes.
4. To serve, thinly slice pork. Divide spinach among four plates. Top with pork, vegetable mixture, sour cream, and pumpkin seeds.

PER SERVING: 401 cal., 11 g total fat (2 g sat. fat), 78 mg chol., 555 mg sodium, 44 g carb. (9 g fiber, 12 g sugars), 34 g pro.

9 Bacon-Wrapped Turkey Meatball and Cabbage Salad

SERVINGS 4 (1 cup salad, 4 meatballs, and 2 tablespoons dressing each)
CARB. PER SERVING 26 g
PREP 25 minutes   BAKE 15 minutes
BROIL 5 minutes

- ¼ cup refrigerated or frozen egg product, thawed, or 1 egg, lightly beaten
- ¼ cup fat-free milk
- ¼ cup dry whole wheat bread crumbs
- ½ teaspoon caraway seeds, crushed
- 12 ounces ground turkey breast
- 8 strips lower-sodium, less fat-bacon, halved
- 2 tablespoons honey
- 2 teaspoons Dijon-style mustard
- ½ teaspoon cornstarch
- ⅓ cup cider vinegar
- 7 cups coarsely chopped green cabbage
- 2 medium carrots, peeled
- ⅓ cup reduced-fat blue cheese dressing
- 2 tablespoons fat-free milk

1. Preheat oven to 375°F. Line a 15×10×1-inch baking pan with foil. In a bowl combine egg, ¼ cup milk, bread crumbs, and caraway seeds. Add turkey; mix. Shape into 16 balls. Wrap balls with bacon. Place balls with bacon, seam sides down, in prepared pan. Bake 15 to 18 minutes or until meatballs are cooked through (165°F).
2. Meanwhile, in a small saucepan combine honey, mustard, and cornstarch. Whisk in vinegar. Cook and stir over medium heat until thickened and bubbly. Remove from heat. Brush on meatballs. Let meatballs cool slightly.
3. Preheat broiler. Spread cabbage in a 15×10×1-inch baking pan. Lightly coat cabbage with *nonstick cooking spray*. Broil 4 to 5 inches from heat 4 to 5 minutes or until lightly browned and charred in places, stirring once.
4. Using a vegetable peeler, peel long thin strips from carrots. Place cabbage in four bowls. Top with carrots and meatballs. If desired, drizzle with additional glaze. Combine dressing and 2 tablespoons milk. Drizzle over salads.

PER SERVING: 285 cal., 6 g total fat (2 g sat. fat), 41 mg chol., 585 mg sodium, 26 g carb. (5 g fiber, 16 g sugars), 31 g pro.

10 Cauliflower-Watercress Salad with Dill-Shallot Dressing

SERVINGS 4 (3½ cups salad and 3 tablespoons dressing each)
CARB. PER SERVING 18 g
PREP 35 minutes   COOK 10 minutes

- 12 ounces fresh asparagus, trimmed and cut into bite-size pieces
- 6 cups small cauliflower florets
- 3 cups fresh baby spinach
- 3 cups fresh watercress, tough stems trimmed and coarsley chopped
- 1 medium orange or yellow sweet pepper, cut into thin bite-size strips
- 1 recipe Dill-Shallot Dressing
- 3 hard-cooked eggs, peeled and sliced
- ¼ cup thinly sliced, pitted Kalamata olives
- 1 ounce Parmesan cheese, shaved

1. Place asparagus in a 2-quart casserole with 2 tablespoons *water*. Microwave, covered, on 100 percent power (high) 2 to 4 minutes or until crisp-tender; drain. Transfer to a plate; let cool.
2. Meanwhile, place cauliflower in a food processor. Cover and pulse with several on/off turns until cauliflower is evenly chopped. Process in batches if necessary. Add cauliflower to the same casserole dish with 2 tablespoons *water*. Cover and microwave on high 6 to 9 minutes or until cauliflower is crisp-tender. Drain; cool about 5 minutes.
3. To assemble salads, toss spinach and watercress with one-fourth of the Dill-Shallot Dressing. Divide greens among four plates. In a large bowl combine asparagus, cauliflower, sweet pepper, and remaining dressing. Spoon cauliflower mixture evenly over greens. Top with eggs, olives, and cheese.

DILL-SHALLOT DRESSING: Combine ⅓ cup each chopped shallot and white wine vinegar. Cover; let stand 15 minutes. Whisk in 2 tablespoons light mayonnaise, 2 teaspoons snipped fresh dill, 1 tablespoon olive oil, 1 teaspoon Dijon-style mustard, and ⅛ teaspoon salt.

PER SERVING: 229 cal., 12 g total fat (3 g sat. fat), 146 mg chol., 485 mg sodium, 18 g carb. (6 g fiber, 7 g sugars), 14 g pro.

11 Grilled Portobello-Chicken Row Salad

SERVINGS 4 (2$\frac{1}{2}$ cups salad and 2 tablespoons dressing each)
CARB. PER SERVING 18 g
PREP 25 minutes **GRILL** 15 minutes

- 1 teaspoon fennel seeds, finely crushed*
- 1 teaspoon Italian seasoning, crushed
- $\frac{1}{8}$ to $\frac{1}{4}$ teaspoon crushed red pepper
- 12 ounces skinless, boneless chicken breast halves
- 4 large fresh portobello mushrooms (14 to 16 ounces total)
- 1 medium red sweet pepper, halved and seeded
- 1 small red onion, cut into 1-inch crosswise slices
- 3 cups torn, trimmed fresh kale
- 3 cups torn fresh romaine lettuce
- $\frac{1}{2}$ cup torn fresh basil
- $\frac{1}{2}$ cup reduced-fat shredded Italian cheese blend
- $\frac{1}{2}$ cup bottled light balsamic vinaigrette dressing
- 2 tablespoons chopped walnuts, toasted

1. In a small bowl combine the fennel, Italian seasoning, and crushed red pepper. Sprinkle evenly over chicken.

2. For a charcoal or gas grill, grill chicken, portobello mushrooms, red sweet pepper, and onion slices on the rack of a covered grill directly over medium heat. Allow 15 to 18 minutes for the chicken, 10 to 12 minutes for the mushrooms, and 8 to 10 minutes for the peppers and onion slices or until vegetables are tender and chicken is done (165°F). Slice chicken, mushrooms, and pepper into strips. Coarsely chop onion.

3. On a platter arrange chicken, vegetables, greens, cheese, and basil. Drizzle with dressing and sprinkle with nuts.

*TEST KITCHEN TIP: Use a spice grinder or clean coffee grinder to finely crush the fennel seeds.

PER SERVING: 266 cal., 9 g total fat (2 g sat. fat), 70 mg chol., 392 mg sodium, 18 g carb. (5 g fiber, 10 g sugars), 29 g pro.

12 Potato and Brussels Sprouts Salad with Lemon-Honey Vinaigrette

SERVINGS 6 (2 cups each)
CARB. PER SERVING 34 g
PREP 25 minutes **COOK** 20 minutes

- 12 ounces medium red potatoes, quartered
- 6 slices lower-sodium, less-fat bacon, chopped
- 2 cups fresh Brussels sprouts, trimmed and quartered
- $\frac{1}{2}$ medium red onion, halved and thinly sliced ($\frac{1}{2}$ cup)
- 3 tablespoons water
- 2 medium tomatoes, chopped (1 cup)
- 1 15-ounce can no-salt-added garbanzo beans (chickpeas), rinsed and drained
- 6 cups torn fresh butterhead lettuce or baby spinach
- 1 recipe Lemon-Honey Vinaigrette
- $\frac{1}{2}$ cup crumbled reduced-fat feta cheese

1. In a medium saucepan cook potatoes, covered, in enough boiling water to cover 12 to 15 minutes or until tender. Drain; set aside.

2. In a large skillet cook bacon over medium heat until crisp. Remove bacon from skillet; drain on paper towels. Wipe out skillet.

3. Add Brussels sprouts, red onion, and the water to skillet. Cook, covered, 4 to 6 minutes or until sprouts are crisp-tender, stirring occasionally. Add tomatoes. Cook, uncovered, 2 to 3 minutes or until tomatoes are softened and sprouts are lightly browned, stirring occasionally. Remove from heat. Add potatoes and garbanzo beans; stir gently to combine.

4. To serve, divide lettuce among six plates. Spoon potato mixture evenly over lettuce. Drizzle with Lemon-Honey Vinaigrette. Sprinkle with feta and reserved bacon.

LEMON-HONEY VINAIGRETTE: In a screw-top jar combine $\frac{1}{3}$ cup lemon juice, 2 tablespoons each olive oil and honey, 2 teaspoons Dijon-style mustard, and $\frac{1}{8}$ teaspoon salt. Cover; shake.

PER SERVING: 246 cal., 8 g total fat (2 g sat. fat), 7 mg chol., 351 mg sodium, 34 g carb. (6 g fiber, 10 g sugars), 11 g pro.

Salads are always a healthful choice, right? Not always. Use these tips to ensure your salad bar choices are working for you.

BUILD a BETTER salad

DRESSING

Your best choice is a light vinaigrette dressing on the side. Dip your fork into the dressing before spearing a bite.

CHEESE

Shredded cheese adds protein and calcium but can be high in fat. Keep your portion to 1 tablespoon.

STARCHY VEGGIES

Starchy veggies and legumes, such as corn and beans, add carbohydrate but are also a good source of fiber. Keep your serving to ¼ cup.

NONSTARCHY VEGGIES

Load salads with nonstarchy veggies, such as carrots, peppers, and cucumbers. One cup contains about 25 calories and 5 g carb.

LEAN PROTEIN

Opt for a source of lean protein, such as 2 ounces of chicken or pork or ½ cup low-fat cottage cheese. Nuts, beans, and cheese provide some protein, too.

HEALTHY HABIT:
EAT LESS MEAT

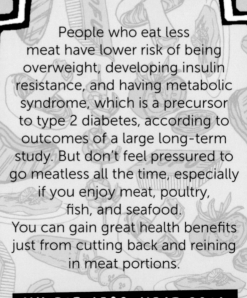

People who eat less meat have lower risk of being overweight, developing insulin resistance, and having metabolic syndrome, which is a precursor to type 2 diabetes, according to outcomes of a large long-term study. But don't feel pressured to go meatless all the time, especially if you enjoy meat, poultry, fish, and seafood.
You can gain great health benefits just from cutting back and reining in meat portions.

MY EAT-LESS-MEAT GOAL

This week I'll prepare a large batch of beans to use in meals.

> "Quitting smoking gave me confidence to lose weight. And it saved my life."

JOE DRAGON | age 37

By the time Joe was 32 years old, he was smoking two packs of cigarettes a day and weighed 400 pounds. Not long after, he found himself in the emergency room with an A1C of 9.5%. He was diagnosed with type 2 diabetes and put on metformin right away.

Kick-start into action: "My father had his first of three heart attacks at the age of 32. I feared following in his footsteps," Joe says. When he was diagnosed, Joe had already been smoke-free for a year. He knew addressing his weight was the next step, so he joined Weight Watchers and gave up regular soda in favor of diet soda, iced tea, or water. "I trimmed the amount of bread, pasta, and large portions of many foods I ate in excess." Joe knows his actions saved his life and have given him new opportunities. He is now taking classes and on the road to becoming a registered dietitian.

Words of wisdom: "Be patient with yourself and trust in yourself. Believe you can be the inspiration for people around you. Be open—the effort can change your life."

3 oz. cooked
chicken breast
26 g protein

BECOME A
protein
pro

It may seem that everywhere you look, Americans are crazy for protein. Is this trend being fed by one of the many low-carbohydrate diets, such as Paleo, or by new research that suggests eating a bit more protein may increase satiety and assist with weight control? The jury is still out.

Yet food manufacturers have jumped on this protein craze and have brought protein-padded products to market. But do you really need more protein, especially in your cereal, bars, and drinks? Hardly! According to the Dietary Guidelines for Americans, we eat more than enough protein, with too much of that protein being animal-based. That's not a wise plan when it comes

to type 2 diabetes. Some major studies have shown an association between eating less red meat and reducing the odds of developing type 2 diabetes.

To become a protein pro and learn about healthier protein choices, it's good to understand that protein and fat are generally paired together in protein foods (such as red meat, poultry, cheese, seafood, nuts, and eggs). There are some exceptions: Protein is also in some fat-free foods, such as beans and nonfat dairy.

Choose a variety of protein foods from all sources. Follow the tips on page 164 for your best protein picks.

2 Tbsp.
almonds
4 g protein

3 oz. cooked
salmon
21 g protein

1½ oz.
cheese
11 g protein

3 oz. cooked
shrimp
20 g protein

¾ cup
cottage
cheese
21 g protein

1 cup milk
9 g protein

PICKING proteins

1 Eat protein in small servings. As a rule of thumb, don't let protein foods fill more than one-fourth of your plate.

2 Choose lean and low-fat protein most often, especially sources also low in saturated fat and cholesterol (beans, nuts, low-fat dairy, tofu, and chicken).

3 Cook protein in ways that don't add a lot of fat, such as grilling, roasting, and sautéing.

4 When planning meals, get away from thinking about proteincentric dishes. Use meat as a side dish or stretch the protein in a main course.

3 oz. cooked
beef steak
21 g protein

3 oz. cooked
pork tenderloin
22 g protein

MAKING THE MOST
of meat

Protein is good for you, but too much protein results in an unwanted increase in calories, saturated fat, and cholesterol. Choose recipes like these that feature healthful 2- to 3-ounce portions of lean proteins.

CHEESY TURKEY
SLOPPY JOES

recipe on *page 166*

Cheesy Turkey Sloppy Joes

photo on *page 165*

SERVINGS 6 (1 sandwich each)
CARB. PER SERVING 21 g
START TO FINISH 45 minutes

　1　cup chopped onion
　2　teaspoons olive oil
　1　pound ground turkey breast
　$^3/_4$　cup chopped red sweet pepper
　3　cloves garlic, minced
　1　cup shredded reduced-fat cheddar
　　　cheese (4 ounces)
　$^1/_2$　cup light mayonnaise
　1　tablespoon Worcestershire sauce
　2　teaspoons Dijon mustard
　6　light whole wheat hamburger buns,
　　　split and toasted.
　　　Leaf lettuce, sliced red onion, and thinly
　　　sliced fresh jalapeño chile peppers
　　　(tip, *page 252*)

1. In a large nonstick skillet cook chopped onion, covered, in hot oil over medium-low heat 10 to 15 minutes or until onion is tender, stirring occasionally. Uncover; cook and stir over medium-high heat 3 to 5 minutes or until golden brown. Remove from skillet; set aside.
2. In the same skillet cook turkey, sweet pepper, and garlic over medium heat until turkey is no longer pink, using a spoon to break up turkey as it cooks. Drain off fat.
3. Add cooked onion, cheddar cheese, mayonnaise, Worcestershire sauce, and mustard to turkey mixture. Cook and stir over medium-low heat just until cheese is melted and mixture is well mixed.
4. Top buns with lettuce and sliced red onion. Spoon turkey mixture onto buns. Top with chile pepper slices.

PER SERVING: 295 cal., 12 g total fat (4 g sat. fat), 53 mg chol., 551 mg sodium, 21 g carb. (7 g fiber, 6 g sugars), 27 g pro.

Mustard Pork, Fennel, and Broccoli Pasta

SERVINGS 2 ($1^1/_2$ cups each)
CARB. PER SERVING 31 g
START TO FINISH 40 minutes

　1　cup reduced-sodium chicken broth
　$^1/_4$　ounce dried porcini mushrooms ($^1/_3$ cup)
　$1^1/_2$　ounces dried multigrain penne pasta
　$1^1/_2$　cups broccoli florets
　8　ounces pork tenderloin, cut into strips
　2　teaspoons olive oil
　1　tablespoon Dijon-style mustard
　1　small bulb fennel, cored and cut into
　　　thin wedges ($^3/_4$ cup)
　1　medium shallot, cut into thin wedges
　$^1/_2$　teaspoon snipped fresh thyme
　$^1/_8$　teaspoon black pepper
　2　teaspoons flour
　1　tablespoon shaved Parmesan cheese
　　　(optional)

1. In a saucepan bring broth to boiling. Stir in mushrooms; let soak 15 to 20 minutes or until tender. Using a slotted spoon, transfer the mushrooms to a fine-mesh sieve. Rinse under cold running water; drain. Coarsely chop mushrooms; place in a medium bowl. Line sieve with a paper towel or coffee filter; strain broth through lined sieve into bowl with mushrooms.
2. Meanwhile, cook pasta according to package directions, adding broccoli the last 3 minutes of cooking. Drain pasta and broccoli.
3. In a large skillet cook pork in hot oil over medium-high heat about 4 minutes or until pork is just cooked through, stirring occasionally. Using a slotted spoon, transfer pork to bowl with mushrooms. Add mustard to pork mixture and stir to combine. Set aside.
4. Add fennel, shallot, thyme, and pepper to skillet. Cook and stir about 3 minutes or until fennel is crisp-tender. Stir in the flour; cook and stir 1 minute. Return pork mixture to skillet. Cook and stir until slightly thickened. Cook and stir 1 minute more. Add pasta mixture to skillet; cook and stir until heated through. If desired, sprinkle each serving with Parmesan cheese.

PER SERVING: 326 cal., 8 g total fat (1 g sat. fat), 74 mg chol., 584 mg sodium, 31 g carb. (7 g fiber, 3 g sugars), 33 g pro.

MUSTARD PORK, FENNEL, and BROCCOLI PASTA

EAT LESS MEAT

Pork Tacos with Summer Peach Salsa

SERVINGS 4 (2 tacos each)
CARB. PER SERVING 25 g
PREP 20 minutes   **GRILL** 25 minutes
STAND 3 minutes

- 1   1-pound pork tenderloin
- 1   teaspoon salt-free fiesta lime seasoning blend, such as Mrs. Dash brand
- ½   teaspoon salt
- 2   peaches, halved and pitted
- ½   cup finely chopped red onion (1 medium)
- ½   of a fresh jalapeño chile pepper, seeded and chopped (tip, *page 252*)
- ¼   cup snipped fresh cilantro
- 1   tablespoon lime juice
- 8   5½- to 6-inch corn tortillas, warmed

1. Trim any visible fat from pork. Sprinkle pork with seasoning blend and ¼ teaspoon of the salt. For a charcoal grill, arrange medium coals on one side of grill. Place a drip pan on the other side of grill. Place pork on greased grill rack over drip pan. Cover; grill 25 to 30 minutes or until an instant-read thermometer inserted in center of pork registers 145°F. Meanwhile, place peach halves, pitted sides down, on the greased grill rack directly over coals. Cover and grill about 6 minutes or until tender and lightly browned, turning once. (For a gas grill, preheat grill. Reduce heat to medium. Adjust for indirect cooking. Place meat on greased grill rack over burner that is off. Place peaches on greased grill rack over burner that is on. Grill as directed.) Remove pork from grill; tent with foil and let stand 3 minutes. Thinly slice pork.

2. Coarsely chop peaches. In a bowl combine peaches, red onion, chile pepper, cilantro, lime juice, and the remaining ¼ teaspoon salt.

3. Serve thinly sliced pork topped with peach mixture in tortillas.

PER SERVING: 238 cal., 3 g total fat (1 g sat. fat), 73 mg chol., 346 mg sodium, 25 g carb. (4 g fiber, 9 g sugars), 27 g pro.

EXPERT TIP

"Holding steady on a weight loss plateau? Alter your walking routine. Add bursts of speed. Walk regular speed a few minutes, then walk faster for a few minutes. As you're able, spend more time walking faster."

– Suzanne Pecoraro, MPH, RDN, CDE, President Diabetes Education Support Services

PORK TACOS with SUMMER PEACH SALSA

STEAK and MUSHROOM PIZZAS

Steak and Mushroom Pizzas

SERVINGS 6 (¹/₂ of a pizza each)
CARB. PER SERVING 18 g
PREP 35 minutes   **BAKE** 10 minutes

 Nonstick cooking spray
3 artisan pizza thin-crust flatbreads, such as Flatout brand
12 ounces boneless beef top sirloin steak, trimmed
¹/₂ cup thinly slivered red onion
4 cloves garlic, minced
1 tablespoon olive oil or canola oil
8 ounces fresh shiitake or oyster mushrooms, stemmed and sliced, and/or button mushrooms, sliced
¹/₈ teaspoon salt
1¹/₃ cups shredded part-skim mozzarella cheese
¹/₄ cup purchased basil pesto

1. Preheat oven to 375°F. Lightly coat an extra-large baking sheet with cooking spray. Place crusts on baking sheet. Bake 5 to 7 minutes or until crisp.

2. Meanwhile, cut meat into very thin bite-size strips. Coat an extra-large nonstick skillet with cooking spray; heat over medium-high heat. Add meat. Cook and stir 2 to 3 minutes or until slightly pink in center. Remove meat; keep warm. Wipe skillet. In same skillet cook onion and garlic in hot oil over medium-high heat 1 minute. Add mushrooms and salt. Cook 5 to 7 minutes or until liquid has evaporated.

3. Top crusts with mushroom mixture, meat, and cheese. Bake 5 minutes more or until cheese is melted. Drizzle with pesto.

PER SERVING: 295 cal., 14 g total fat (5 g sat. fat), 53 mg chol., 481 mg sodium, 18 g carb. (2 g fiber, 3 g sugars), 25 g pro.

Grilled Flank Steak and Romaine Salad with Beets

SERVINGS 2 (2¼ ounces cooked beef, ½ heart of romaine, and about ½ cup beet mixture each)
CARB. PER SERVING 23 g
PREP 20 minutes **MARINATE** 2 hours
GRILL 15 minutes

- 6 ounces beef flank steak
- ¼ cup balsamic vinegar
- 2 tablespoons lemon juice
- 1 tablespoon reduced-sodium soy sauce
- 1 tablespoon Worcestershire sauce
- 2 teaspoons Dijon-style honey mustard
- 1 clove garlic, minced
- Black pepper
- 12 ounces cooked fresh beets,* cut into wedges
- 2 teaspoons olive oil
- 1 8-ounce heart of romaine lettuce
- ½ ounce freshly shredded Parmesan cheese (optional)

1. Score both sides of the flank steak in a diamond pattern by making shallow diagonal cuts at 1-inch intervals. Place steak in a large resealable plastic bag set in a shallow dish. For marinade, in a small bowl whisk together 2 tablespoons of the balsamic vinegar, 1 tablespoon of the lemon juice, the soy sauce, Worcestershire sauce, mustard, garlic, and a pinch of the pepper. Pour marinade over the steak. Seal bag and turn to coat. Marinate in the refrigerator 2 to 4 hours, turning bag occasionally.

2. In a medium bowl combine beets, remaining 2 tablespoons balsamic vinegar, 1 teaspoon of the olive oil, and a pinch pepper; set aside.

3. Cut heart of romaine in half lengthwise (do not remove the core so the leaves remain attached). In a small bowl whisk together remaining 1 tablespoon lemon juice and 1 teaspoon olive oil. Brush mixture on the romaine; set aside.

4. Drain steak, discarding marinade. Heat a grill pan over medium heat. Grill steak 15 minutes for medium rare (145°F), turning once halfway through grilling. Cover and let stand. Grill romaine 5 minutes, turning once.

5. Thinly slice steak diagonally across the grain. Serve with romaine and beets. If desired, top with Parmesan to serve.

***TEST KITCHEN TIP:** To cook fresh beets, wash and trim the beets; pat dry. Wrap beets in foil and bake at 400°F for 1¼ to 1½ hours or until tender. Remove from oven and cool slightly. Unwrap and slip off skins under cool running water. Place beets in a covered container and refrigerate until needed. Or use packaged refrigerated cooked whole baby beets.

PER SERVING: 294 cal., 12 g total fat (4 g sat. fat), 40 mg chol., 535 mg sodium, 23 g carb. (4 g fiber, 16 g sugars), 22 g pro.

 **EXPERT TIP**

"Implementing portion control can lead to thoughts and feelings of deprivation and starvation. Instead, enlarge your portions and figure out how to eat more like this: Fill half your plate with steamed vegetables tossed with fresh herbs or a huge helping of greens drizzled with a rich, thick balsamic vinegar."

– Ann Constance, RD, CDE, Program Director, Upper Peninsula Diabetes Outreach Network, Marquette, Michigan

GRILLED FLANK STEAK and
ROMAINE SALAD with BEETS

QUINOA SALAD with
SEARED TUNA

Quinoa Salad with Seared Tuna

SERVINGS 6 (1 cup each)
CARB. PER SERVING 31 g
PREP 30 minutes   **COOK** 19 minutes

12 ounces fresh or frozen tuna steaks
1½ cups quinoa
3 cups water
¼ teaspoon salt
1 large tomato, coarsely chopped
1 cup coarsely chopped, seeded cucumber
½ cup crumbled reduced-fat feta cheese (2 ounces)
¼ cup chopped red onion
2 tablespoons olive oil
2 tablespoons lemon juice
1 teaspoon honey
½ teaspoon snipped fresh oregano or ¼ teaspoon dried oregano, crushed
¼ teaspoon black pepper
Nonstick cooking spray
⅛ teaspoon salt
⅛ teaspoon black pepper

1. Thaw tuna steaks, if frozen. Rinse fish; pat dry with paper towels. Measure thickness of fish. Set aside.

2. Place quinoa in a fine-mesh sieve; rinse well under cold running water. In a large saucepan bring the 3 cups water and the ¼ teaspoon salt to boiling. Add quinoa; reduce heat. Simmer, covered, about 15 minutes or until most of the water is absorbed and quinoa is tender. Drain if necessary. Spread on a baking sheet to cool slightly.

3. On a platter combine quinoa, tomato, cucumber, feta cheese, and red onion.

4. In a screw-top jar combine olive oil, lemon juice, honey, oregano, and the ¼ teaspoon pepper. Cover and shake well. Add to quinoa mixture; toss to combine.

5. Lightly coat a grill pan or large skillet with cooking spray. Sprinkle tuna steaks with the ⅛ teaspoon salt and the ⅛ teaspoon pepper. Cook on grill pan over medium-high heat 4 to 6 minutes per ½-inch thickness of fish or until browned on both sides, fish begins to flake when tested with a fork, and center is just pink; turn once halfway through cooking. Thinly slice tuna steaks; arrange on top of quinoa mixture. If desired, garnish with *fresh oregano leaves*.

PER SERVING: 316 cal., 11 g total fat (3 g sat. fat), 25 mg chol., 332 mg sodium, 31 g carb. (4 g fiber, 2 g sugars), 22 g pro.

SKEWERED SHIMP and
TOMATO LINGUINE

recipe on *page 174*

Skewered Shrimp and Tomato Linguine

photo on *page 173*
SERVINGS 4 (1¼ cups each)
CARB. PER SERVING 40 g
START TO FINISH 40 minutes

- 12 ounces fresh or frozen large shrimp in shells
- 24 red and/or yellow cherry or grape tomatoes
- 1 tablespoon olive oil
- 1 clove garlic, minced
- ¼ teaspoon black pepper
- ⅛ teaspoon salt
- 6 ounces dried whole grain linguine
- 1 tablespoon butter
- 1 tablespoon lemon juice
- 4 cups torn baby arugula or packaged baby spinach
- ¼ cup finely shredded Parmesan cheese
- 1 tablespoon snipped fresh oregano
  Freshly cracked black pepper
  Lemon wedges

1. Thaw shrimp, if frozen. Peel and devein shrimp. Rinse shrimp; pat dry with paper towels. Thread shrimp and tomatoes onto four 10-inch metal skewers. In a small bowl whisk together the olive oil, garlic, ¼ teaspoon pepper, and salt. Brush over shrimp and tomatoes on skewers.
2. For a charcoal grill, place skewers on the grill rack directly over medium-hot coals. Grill, uncovered, 5 to 8 minutes or until shrimp turn opaque, turning once halfway through grilling. (For a gas grill, preheat grill. Reduce heat to medium-hot. Place skewers on grill rack over heat. Cover and grill as directed.)
3. Meanwhile, prepare linguine according to package directions. Drain, reserving ⅓ cup cooking water. Return pasta to saucepan. Add butter and lemon juice. Toss to combine. Add the reserved cooking water, the grilled shrimp and tomatoes, arugula, Parmesan cheese, and oregano. Toss to combine. Sprinkle with cracked black pepper and serve with lemon wedges.

PER SERVING: 321 cal., 10 g total fat (3 g sat. fat), 118 mg chol., 603 mg sodium, 40 g carb. (7 g fiber, 5 g sugars), 20 g pro.

Dijon Beef Stew

SERVINGS 6 (1¼ cups each)
CARB. PER SERVING 14 g
PREP 25 minutes   SLOW COOK 8 to 10 hours (low) or 4 to 5 hours (high)

- 2 cups frozen small whole onions
- 2 cups packaged peeled fresh baby carrots
- 1 pound beef stew meat, cut into 1-inch cubes and trimmed of fat
- 1 14.5-ounce can no-salt-added diced tomatoes, undrained
- 1 14.5-ounce can 50%-less-sodium beef broth
- 2 tablespoons Dijon-style mustard
- 4 cloves garlic, minced
- 1 teaspoon dried thyme, crushed
- ½ teaspoon dried tarragon, crushed
- ¼ teaspoon black pepper
  Fresh tarragon or parsley sprigs

1. Place onion and carrots in a 3½- or 4-quart slow cooker. Top with stew meat. In a small bowl stir together tomatoes, broth, mustard, garlic, thyme, the dried tarragon, and the pepper. Pour over beef in cooker.
2. Cover and cook on low-heat setting 8 to 10 hours or on high-heat setting for 4 to 5 hours. Ladle into bowls. Garnish individual servings with fresh tarragon sprigs.

SERVING SUGGESTION: If your meal plan allows, serve this stew with thin slices of baguette-style whole grain French bread, toasted.

PER SERVING: 164 cal., 4 g total fat (2 g sat. fat), 48 mg chol., 370 mg sodium, 14 g carb. (4 g fiber, 7 g sugars), 19 g pro.

DIJON BEEF STEW

OPEN-FACE PHILLY-STYLE CHICKEN SANDWICHES

SERVINGS 6 (1 sandwich each)
CARB. PER SERVING 26 g
START TO FINISH 30 minutes

- 1¼ pounds skinless, boneless chicken breast halves, cut into thin strips
- 1 tablespoon olive oil
- 2 cups thinly sliced onions
- 1 cup green, red, and/or yellow sweet pepper strips (3½ ounces)
- 1 to 2 cloves garlic, minced
- 1 teaspoon dried Italian seasoning, crushed
- ½ teaspoon black pepper
- 6 slices reduced-fat Provolone cheese (4 ounces)
- 6 ½-inch-thick slices whole grain bread (9 ounces)

1. Preheat broiler. In a large skillet cook chicken in hot oil over medium-high heat about 5 minutes or until no longer pink, stirrring occasionally. Reduce heat to medium. Add the onions, pepper strips, garlic, Italian seasoning, and black pepper. Cook and stir 5 to 8 minutes or until vegetables are tender. Reduce heat to low. Place the cheese slices in a single layer over the chicken mixture. Cover and cook about 1 minute more or until the cheese is melted.

2. Meanwhile, arrange the bread on a baking sheet. Broil bread 4 to 5 inches from the heat 1 to 2 minutes per side or until toasted. Using a spatula, transfer portions of cheese-topped chicken mixture onto toasted bread slices.

PER SERVING: 321 cal., 10 g total fat (3 g sat. fat), 71 mg chol., 435 mg sodium, 26 g carb. (5 g fiber, 6 g sugars), 31 g pro.

GARLIC CASHEW
CHICKEN CASSEROLE

recipe on *page 178*

Garlic Cashew Chicken Casserole

photo on *page 177*
SERVINGS 6 (1⅓ cups each)
CARB. PER SERVING 40 g
PREP 35 minutes **BAKE** 24 minutes

    Nonstick cooking spray
  1 cup reduced-sodium chicken broth
  ¼ cup hoisin sauce
  2 tablespoons grated fresh ginger
  4 teaspoons cornstarch
  ½ teaspoon crushed red pepper
  ⅛ teaspoon black pepper
  1 pound skinless, boneless chicken breast
     halves, cut into 1-inch strips
  2 medium onions, cut into thin wedges
  2 cups sliced bok choy
  1 cup sliced celery (2 stalks)
  1 cup sliced carrots (2 medium)
  ¾ cup chopped green sweet pepper
  6 cloves garlic, minced
  2 cups cooked brown rice
  1 cup chow mein noodles, coarsely broken
  ½ cup cashews
  ¼ cup thinly sliced green onions (2)

1. Preheat oven to 400°F. Coat a 2-quart baking dish with cooking spray. Set aside.

2. For sauce, in a medium bowl whisk together broth, hoisin sauce, ginger, cornstarch, crushed red pepper, and black pepper; set aside.

3. Coat an extra-large skillet with cooking spray; heat over medium-high heat. Add chicken to skillet; cook until lightly browned. Remove from skillet. Add onion wedges, bok choy, celery, carrots, and sweet pepper to the skillet. Cook 3 to 4 minutes or until vegetables start to soften. Add garlic; cook 30 seconds more. Stir in sauce. Cook and stir about 3 minutes or until sauce is thickened and bubbly. Stir in rice and browned chicken.

4. Spoon chicken mixture into the prepared baking dish. Cover and bake about 20 minutes or until casserole is bubbly. Sprinkle with chow mein noodles and cashews. Bake, uncovered, 4 to 5 minutes or until noodles and cashews are golden brown. Sprinkle with green onions.

PER SERVING: 340 cal., 10 g total fat (2 g sat. fat), 49 mg chol., 480 mg sodium, 40 g carb. (4 g fiber, 8 g sugars), 23 g pro.

Creamy Spinach and Artichoke Chicken

SERVINGS 6 (1⅓ cups chicken mixture and ⅔ cup noodles each)
CARB. PER SERVING 40 g
PREP 25 minutes **SLOW COOK** 4 to 5 hours (low) **STAND** 5 minutes

  1 pound skinless, boneless chicken breast
     halves, cut crosswise into 1-inch strips
  1 9-ounce package frozen artichoke
     hearts, thawed and cut up
  2 large onions, cut into wedges
  1 medium red sweet pepper, cut into thin
     bite-size strips
  1 10.75-ounce can reduced-fat and
     reduced-sodium condensed cream of
     chicken soup
  ⅓ cup water
  1 teaspoon dried Italian seasoning,
     crushed
  ¼ teaspoon salt
  ¼ teaspoon black pepper
  4 ounces reduced-fat cream cheese
     (Neufchâtel), cut into cubes
  3 cloves garlic, minced
  3 cups fresh baby spinach
  6 ounces dried wide whole wheat noodles,
     cooked according to package directions

1. In a 3½- or 4-quart slow cooker combine chicken, artichokes, onions, and sweet pepper. In a medium bowl combine soup, the water, Italian seasoning, salt, and black pepper. Pour over chicken mixture in cooker.

2. Cover and cook on low-heat setting 4 to 5 hours.

3. Add cream cheese and garlic to mixture in cooker. Cover and let stand 5 minutes. Stir until cream cheese is melted and smooth. Stir in spinach. To serve, divide noodles among six serving plates. Top with chicken mixture.

PER SERVING: 323 cal., 8 g total fat (3 g sat. fat), 64 mg chol., 474 mg sodium, 40 g carb. (8 g fiber, 9 g sugars), 25 g pro.

CREAMY SPINACH and
ARTICHOKE CHICKEN

SHOULD YOU GO
vegetarian?

More and more research indicates that a plant-based eating plan may be a good choice for people with prediabetes and type 2 diabetes by helping them lose weight, lower blood glucose and blood pressure, and prevent heart disease. In a 72-week study published by Neal Barnard, M.D., president of the Physicians Committee for Responsible Medicine, people with type 2 diabetes followed either a low-fat vegan diet or a moderate-carbohydrate plan. Both groups lost weight and improved their cholesterol. When people who didn't complete the study or had medication changes were omitted from the study analysis, there was a significantly greater decrease in A1C and LDL (bad) cholesterol in those who had eaten a low-fat vegan diet.

MEATLESS OR JUST
less meat?

Even if you're not interested in eliminating meat completely—or if you want to ease into the habit—here are some practical pointers to help you get the benefits of vegetarian eating.

1 Think of animal protein as a side dish or garnish. Prepare meals that stretch small amounts of animal protein, such as a tomato-and-meat sauce, shrimp-and-vegetable stir-fry, and chili with turkey and beans.

2 Start participating in Meatless Monday, a movement created to help people conserve meat to aid the war effort during World War I. Every week, try a new meatless meal, such as vegetable lasagna, bean tacos or burritos, pizza topped with sautéed veggies, tofu stir-fry, or a bean-based chili. Build up to serving a couple of meatless meals a week.

3 Stock a variety of dried beans. Prepare them in batches and freeze the leftovers so you can thaw small amounts as you need them. Keep edamame in the freezer. A side of beans or grains on your plate can take up the room previously occupied by meat.

4 To hold the line on your carbohydrate counts, round out meals with low-fat cheese, eggs or egg whites, and nuts and nut butters that don't contain added sugars.

5 Go meatless at breakfast. Mix and match fruit, yogurt, cottage cheese, hot or cold high-fiber cereal, whole grain pancakes or waffles, or a veggie omelet or egg scramble.

3 MUST-HAVES IN A meatless meal

2

1

3

FALAFEL and VEGETABLE PITAS

When a vegetarian dish hits all the right spots,
you won't miss the meat. Look for meatless recipes like
these that provide flavor, nutrition, and satisfaction.

Falafel and Vegetable Pitas

SERVINGS 4 ($\frac{1}{2}$ of a pita bread with filling each)
CARB. PER SERVING 43 g
PREP 25 minutes **COOK** 4 minutes

- 1 15-ounce can reduced-sodium garbanzo beans (chickpeas), rinsed and drained
- 2 tablespoons whole wheat flour
- 2 tablespoons snipped fresh Italian (flat-leaf) parsley
- 3 cloves garlic, sliced
- 2 teaspoons finely shredded lemon peel
- 2 tablespoons lemon juice
- $\frac{1}{2}$ teaspoon ground coriander
- $\frac{1}{4}$ teaspoon salt
- $\frac{1}{4}$ teaspoon black pepper
- $\frac{1}{8}$ teaspoon ground cumin
- Olive oil nonstick cooking spray
- $\frac{1}{2}$ cup plain fat-free yogurt
- 2 tablespoons snipped fresh Italian (flat-leaf) parsley
- $\frac{1}{8}$ teaspoon salt
- $\frac{1}{8}$ teaspoon black pepper
- 2 whole grain pita breads
- $\frac{3}{4}$ cup fresh spinach or watercress
- 8 thin roma tomato slices
- $\frac{1}{2}$ cup thinly sliced cucumber

1. For falafel, in a food processor combine garbanzo beans, flour, the 2 tablespoons parsley, the garlic, lemon peel, lemon juice, coriander, the $\frac{1}{4}$ teaspoon salt, the $\frac{1}{4}$ teaspoon pepper, and the cumin. Cover and process until finely chopped and mixture just holds together (should have some visible pieces of garbanzo beans).

2. Using your hands, shape garbanzo bean mixture into four $\frac{1}{2}$-inch-thick oval patties. Coat a large nonstick skillet with cooking spray; heat skillet over medium-high heat. Add patties. Cook 4 to 6 minutes or until browned and heated through, turning once halfway through cooking time.

3. For yogurt sauce, in a small bowl combine yogurt, 2 tablespoons parsley, the $\frac{1}{8}$ teaspoon salt, and the $\frac{1}{8}$ teaspoon pepper.

4. Cut pita breads in half crosswise. Open pita halves to make pockets. Divide spinach, tomato slices, and cucumber slices evenly among pockets. Add a falafel to each. Spoon yogurt sauce over falafels in pockets. Serve warm.

PER SERVING: 217 cal., 3 g total fat (0 g sat. fat), 1 mg chol., 582 mg sodium, 43 g carb. (8 g fiber, 4 g sugars), 11 g pro.

1) FLAVOR

The garlic, lemon juice, herbs, and spices really bump up the flavor in these bean patties. The herbed yogurt sauce adds a tasty acidic contrast.

2) NUTRITION

The beans and yogurt supply protein, and the mix of veggies delivers vitamins C and K. The beans and whole grain pita are good sources of fiber and minerals.

3) SATISFACTION

There's a perception that meatless meals aren't as filling, but this recipe proves that's not true. It's high in fiber, has many textures, and tastes great.

Moroccan Vegetable Quinoa with Golden Raisins and Almonds

SERVINGS 5 (1 cup each)
CARB. PER SERVING 41 g
PREP 20 minutes   COOK 45 minutes

  2 cups no-salt-added vegetable broth
    or water
  2 teaspoons garam masala
  ½ teaspoon ground turmeric
  1 cup halved green beans (4 ounces)
  1½ cups cauliflower florets (8 ounces)
  1 cup chopped red sweet pepper (1 large)
  1 tablespoon olive oil
  ½ cup chopped onion (1 medium)
  2 cloves garlic, minced
  ½ teaspoon salt
  ⅛ to ¼ teaspoon cayenne pepper
  ¾ cup red or white quinoa
  ⅓ cup golden raisins
  1 orange
  ½ cup slivered almonds, toasted
  ¼ cup finely snipped fresh mint

1. In a large saucepan bring stock, garam masala, and turmeric to boiling; reduce heat. Add green beans; simmer 4 minutes. Add cauliflower; simmer 6 minutes more. Add sweet pepper; simmer 2 minutes more. Drain vegetables, reserving the cooking liquid. Measure cooking liquid. Add enough water to equal 1¾ cups; set aside.

2. In the same large saucepan heat oil over medium heat. Add onion, garlic, salt, and cayenne pepper. Cook, stirring occasionally, about 5 minutes or until onion is tender. Add reserved broth and bring to boiling. Add quinoa and raisins; reduce heat. Simmer, covered, 15 to 20 minutes or until quinoa is tender and water is absorbed. Add reserved vegetable mixture. Heat through.

3. Meanwhile, finely shred 1 teaspoon of peel from the orange. Squeeze orange to get 2 tablespoons juice.

4. Before serving, fold in almonds, mint, orange peel, and orange juice.

PER SERVING: 271 cal., 10 g total fat (1 g sat. fat), 0 mg chol., 535 mg sodium, 41 g carb. (8 g fiber, 13 g sugars), 8 g pro.

1 FLAVOR

Garam masala and turmeric add a warm spiciness to this dish. Stirring in orange peel, orange juice, and fresh mint just before serving gives it a bold, fresh finish.

2 NUTRITION

Golden raisins add iron and fiber along with their sweetness. Quinoa and almonds deliver protein. The sweet pepper and orange juice make this dish an excellent source of vitamin C.

3 SATISFACTION

Before you even take a bite, the rich aromas and bold colors of this dish satisfy two of your senses. The variety of textures and flavors take care of your hunger.

1

2

3

MOROCCAN VEGETABLE
QUINOA with
GOLDEN RAISINS
and ALMONDS

EXPERT TIP

"Do you think exercise must be done continuously and intensely to benefit your health. Not true! Accumulate 30 minutes of exercise each day by simply breaking up sitting time. Fit in 5-minute activity breaks once every hour or two during the day to rack up your exercise and achieve better glucose control and improve your overall health."

– Sheri R. Colberg, Ph.D., FACSM, exercise physiologist, professor, author, and founder of DiabetesMotion.com

ARTICHOKE FLATBREADS
with SPINACH, PARMESAN,
and LEMON

1 FLAVOR

Lemon, fresh garlic, and fresh oregano bring bright flavors to the artichokes without overwhelming them.

2 NUTRITION

Artichokes are high in fiber and vitamin C, which is a potent antioxidant. Raw spinach provides plenty of B vitamins and even some vitamin C.

3 SATISFACTION

Flatbread is a filling and flavorful base for hearty toppings. A sprinkling of melty cheese contributes enough protein to satisfy.

Artichoke Flatbreads with Spinach, Parmesan, and Lemon

SERVINGS 4 ($^1/_2$ flatbread each)
CARB. PER SERVING 23 g
PREP 20 minutes **BAKE** 10 minutes

- 2 artisan pizza thin-crust flatbreads, such as Flatout brand
- 2 cloves garlic
- 1 14-ounce can artichoke hearts, drained and quartered
- 1 teaspoon finely shredded lemon peel
- 1 tablespoon lemon juice
- 1 teaspoon dried oregano or basil, crushed
- $^1/_4$ teaspoon salt
- $^1/_4$ teaspoon black pepper
- 2 teaspoons olive oil
- 1 cup shredded part-skim mozzarella cheese
- 2 tablespoons grated Parmesan cheese
- $^1/_2$ cup chopped fresh spinach
- $^1/_4$ cup thinly sliced red onion

1. Preheat oven to 450°F. Place flatbreads on a baking sheet. Bake 5 to 7 minutes or until lightly browned and crisp. Remove from oven; set aside. In a food processor pulse garlic with several on/off turns until minced. Add the artichoke quarters, lemon peel, lemon juice, oregano, salt, and pepper. Pulse until coarsely chopped.

2. Brush the surface of each flatbread with 1 teaspoon olive oil. Top with the artichoke mixture and mozzarella and Parmesan cheeses.

3. Return flatbreads to oven. Bake 5 to 6 minutes or until cheeses melt and crust is browned. Top each with the spinach and red onion.

PER SERVING: 212 cal., 8 g total fat (4 g sat. fat), 20 mg chol., 632 mg sodium, 23 g carb. (5 g fiber, 2 g sugars), 14 g pro.

Sweet Potato and Zucchini Enchiladas with Queso Fresco

SERVINGS 4 (2 enchiladas each)
CARB. PER SERVING 41 g
PREP 25 minutes **COOK** 17 minutes
BAKE 10 minutes

- 1 8-ounce can no-salt-added tomato sauce
- 1 cup low-sodium salsa, such as Newman's Own All Natural Mild Chunky Salsa
- ¼ cup finely snipped fresh cilantro
- 2 tablespoons lime juice
- 1 teaspoon chile powder
- ¼ teaspoon salt
- ¼ teaspoon ground cumin
- 1 tablespoon vegetable oil
- 1 medium onion, chopped (½ cup)
- 1 fresh jalapeño chile pepper, halved, seeded, and finely chopped (tip, *page 252*)
- 1 cup peeled and chopped sweet potato
- ¼ cup low-sodium vegetable broth or water
- 1½ cups chopped zucchini
- ½ cup fresh or frozen corn kernels, thawed
  Dash salt
  Nonstick cooking spray
- 8 6-inch corn tortillas, warmed
- ½ cup queso fresco

1. Preheat oven to 375°F. In a blender or food processor combine tomato sauce, salsa, cilantro, lime juice, chile powder, ¼ teaspoon salt, and cumin. Cover and blend until smooth; set aside.

2. In a large skillet heat oil over medium-high heat. Add onion and chile pepper. Cook and stir onion about 6 minutes or until tender. Add sweet potato and broth. Simmer, covered, about 6 minutes or until sweet potato is tender and liquid is nearly evaporated.

3. Add zucchini and corn to the sweet potato mixture; cook and stir about 5 minutes or until zucchini is crisp-tender. Stir in ½ cup of the reserved salsa mixture and the dash salt. Remove from heat.

4. Coat a 2-quart rectangular baking dish with cooking spray. Fill each tortilla with about ⅓ cup sweet potato filling. Roll to enclose filling and place, seam sides down, in the prepared baking dish. Top with remaining salsa mixture and sprinkle with queso fresco. Bake 10 to 15 minutes or until heated through.

PER SERVING: 303 cal., 12 g total fat (4 g sat. fat), 20 mg chol., 592 mg sodium, 41 g carb. (8 g fiber, 12 g sugars), 10 g pro.

1 FLAVOR

Adding salsa to sauces is a shortcut to flavor. Enhance its flavors with a sprinkling of ingredients classic in Southwestern fare—fresh cilantro, lime, chiles, and cumin.

2 NUTRITION

Sweet potatoes are high in beta-carotene, an antioxidant, and are an excellent source of vitamin A, which is important for eye health and a strong immune system.

3 SATISFACTION

The lower-fat, fresh veggie-packed filling allows you to enjoy two of these robust enchiladas.

SWEET POTATO and
ZUCCHINI ENCHILADAS
with QUESO FRESCO

1

2

3

THAI EGGPLANT
VEGETABLE CURRY
with BROWN RICE

Thai Eggplant Vegetable Curry with Brown Rice

SERVINGS 4 ($^3/_4$ cup curry and $^1/_3$ cup brown rice each)

CARB. PER SERVING 37 g

PREP 30 minutes **COOK** 15 minutes

- 1 tablespoon vegetable oil
- 2 tablespoons minced fresh ginger
- 1 tablespoon minced garlic
- 1 serrano chile pepper, seeded and minced (tip, *page 252*)
- 1 tablespoon prepared Thai green curry paste
- $^1/_2$ of a small eggplant, cut into 1-inch cubes (2 cups)
- 4 ounces green beans, trimmed and halved crosswise
- 1 medium carrot, thinly sliced ($^1/_2$ cup)
- 1 small yellow sweet pepper, coarsely chopped ($^1/_2$ cup)
- 1 14-ounce can unsweetened light coconut milk
- $^1/_2$ cup low-sodium vegetable broth
- 1 tablespoon reduced-sodium soy sauce
- 6 cherry or grape tomatoes, halved
- 1 tablespoon lime juice
- $^1/_2$ cup snipped fresh cilantro
- 1$^1/_3$ cups cooked brown rice
- 4 lime wedges

1. In a large skillet heat oil over medium-high heat. Add ginger, garlic, and chile pepper. Cook and stir about 1 minute or until fragrant. Add the curry paste and mash with a spoon about 30 seconds or until it darkens slightly.

2. Stir in eggplant, beans, carrot, and sweet pepper. Cook and stir 3 to 5 minutes or until vegetables begin to soften.

3. Add the coconut milk, broth, and soy sauce; stir to combine. Simmer, uncovered, 10 minutes or until eggplant is tender, the other vegetables are crisp-tender, and sauce has reduced slightly. Remove from heat.

4. Add tomatoes, lime juice, and $^1/_4$ cup of the cilantro. Serve over brown rice with lime wedges. Sprinkle with remaining cilantro.

PER SERVING: 239 cal., 10 g total fat (6 g sat. fat), 0 mg chol., 382 mg sodium, 37 g carb. (7 g fiber, 8 g sugars), 5 g pro.

1 **FLAVOR**

There is no shortage of flavor in a Thai dish. Fresh ginger, garlic, chiles, and green curry paste provide a delicious punch.

2 **NUTRITION**

The colorful assortment of vegetables used in this curry contributes high levels of vitamins C and A and fiber.

3 **SATISFACTION**

This bowl is full of goodness that is both filling and delicious. Use a spoon to get every last bite.

Penne with Five Herbs and Ricotta Salata

SERVINGS 6 (1½ cups each)
CARB. PER SERVING 33 g
PREP 20 minutes **COOK** 13 minutes

  8 ounces dried penne pasta
  2 tablespoons olive oil
  ⅓ cup snipped fresh basil
  1 teaspoon snipped fresh oregano
  1 teaspoon fresh thyme leaves
  ½ teaspoon cracked black pepper
  4 cups grape tomatoes
  2 cloves garlic, minced
  ½ cup vegetable broth
  ¼ cup snipped fresh Italian
     (flat-leaf) parsley
  2 tablespoons snipped fresh chives
  1½ cups crumbled ricotta salata

1. Cook pasta according to package directions; drain well. Transfer drained pasta to a large bowl. Add 1 tablespoon of the oil, the basil, oregano, thyme, and pepper. Toss to combine; cover to keep warm.

2. In an extra-large skillet heat the remaining 1 tablespoon oil over medium-high heat. Add tomatoes and garlic; cook and stir 5 to 6 minutes or until tomatoes caramelize, skins burst, and flesh begins to break down. Stir in broth; bring to boiling.

3. Add tomato mixture, parsley, and chives to pasta mixture; gently toss to combine. Divide pasta mixture among six plates. Top with ricotta salata.

PER SERVING: 285 cal., 11 g total fat (1 g sat. fat), 25 mg chol., 556 mg sodium, 33 g carb. (3 g fiber, 4 g sugars), 11 g pro.

---

1 FLAVOR

The fresh herbs release their bright flavors when warmed by the hot pasta. Skillet-roasting tomatoes caramelizes their skins and intensifies their flavor.

2 NUTRITION

Tomatoes are a good source of vitamins A and C. The penne pasta contributes protein and good levels of B vitamins.

3 SATISFACTION

Pasta never fails to satisfy. A sprinkling of slightly salty ricotta salata provides a delicious finish to this simple dish.

1

2

3

PENNE with
FIVE HERBS and
RICOTTA SALATA

1

2

3

MEDITERRANEAN LENTIL
SKILLET with PITA CHIPS

Mediterranean Lentil Skillet with Pita Chips

SERVINGS 6 ($^2/_3$ cup each)
CARB. PER SERVING 36 g
PREP 30 minutes   **COOK** 40 minutes

 1 tablespoon olive oil
$^1/_2$ cup finely chopped onion
$^1/_4$ cup finely chopped carrot
$^1/_4$ cup finely chopped celery
 1 teaspoon dried thyme, crushed
 2 cups low-sodium vegetable broth
$^3/_4$ cup dry brown lentils
$^1/_4$ cup dried currants or golden raisins
 1 bay leaf
 3 cups packed torn fresh kale
$^1/_2$ teaspoon salt
$^1/_2$ teaspoon black pepper
 1 cup cherry or grape tomatoes, halved
 1 tablespoon red wine vinegar
 1 tablespoon lemon juice
$^1/_4$ cup chopped walnuts, toasted
 3 tablespoons goat cheese ($1^1/_2$ ounces)
 3 ounces unsalted pita chips

1. In a large skillet with a tight-fitting lid heat oil over medium heat. Add the onion, carrot, celery, and thyme; cook and stir about 5 minutes or until vegetables are crisp-tender. Stir in the broth, lentils, currants, and bay leaf. Bring to boiling; reduce heat. Simmer, covered, 30 minutes or until lentils are tender. Remove and discard bay leaf.

2. Stir in the kale, salt, and pepper. Cook, uncovered, 5 minutes more or until kale is slightly wilted and any remaining liquid is absorbed. Remove from heat.

3. Add tomatoes, vinegar, and lemon juice; stir to combine. Sprinkle with walnuts and goat cheese. Serve warm with pita chips.

PER SERVING: 281 cal., 11 g total fat (2 g sat. fat), 6 mg chol., 434 mg sodium, 36 g carb. (10 g fiber, 8 g sugars), 12 g pro.

1 FLAVOR

Sweet, toasty, and salty flavors come together with a combo of dried currants, toasted nuts, and goat cheese.

2 NUTRITION

Kale and tomatoes boast high levels of vitamins C and A. Tiny lentils pack a punch as a good-for-you source of fiber and protein.

3 SATISFACTION

Using the pita chips as scoops makes this lentil skillet a fun twist on chips 'n' dip, but it's really a filling main dish.

MACARONI PANCAKES
with MUSHROOMS, SPINACH,
and TOMATOES

1

2

3

Macaroni Pancakes with Mushrooms, Spinach, and Tomatoes

SERVINGS 6 (1 wedge each)
CARB. PER SERVING 22 g
PREP 1 hour   **BAKE** 5 minutes
STAND 10 minutes

- 3 ounces dried whole wheat elbow macaroni
- 2 cloves garlic, thinly sliced
- 5 teaspoons olive oil
- 1 14.5-ounce can no-salt-added diced tomatoes, undrained
- ¾ teaspoon kosher salt
- ½ teaspoon black pepper
- ½ teaspoon dried Italian seasoning, crushed
- 10 ounces fresh cremini mushrooms, sliced
- 1 10-ounce package frozen chopped spinach, thawed and well drained
- 6 eggs
- 1½ cups finely shredded carrots (2 to 3 medium)
- 1 cup shredded reduced-fat mozzarella cheese (4 ounces)

1. Cook macaroni according to package directions. Drain; set aside.
2. In a large skillet cook garlic in 1 teaspoon of the hot oil 30 seconds. Add tomatoes, a pinch of the salt, a pinch of the pepper, and ¼ teaspoon of the Italian seasoning. Bring to boiling; reduce heat. Simmer, uncovered, 5 to 8 minutes or until most of the liquid is evaporated. Transfer to a bowl; set aside.
3. In the same skillet cook mushrooms in another 1 teaspoon of the hot oil about

5 minutes or until liquid is evaporated. Stir in thawed spinach, another pinch of the salt, another pinch of the pepper, and the remaining ¼ teaspoon Italian seasoning. Cook and stir until most of the liquid from the spinach is evaporated. Set aside.
4. Preheat oven to 375°F. For each macaroni pancake, in a medium bowl whisk two of the eggs until combined. Stir in one-third of the shredded carrot and one-third of the cooked macaroni. Season with another pinch of the salt and another pinch of the pepper. In a nonstick skillet heat another 1 teaspoon of the oil over medium-low heat. Add macaroni mixture; cook until macaroni mixture is set and lightly browned on one side. Remove from heat. Place a plate over the skillet; holding plate and skillet firmly, invert macaroni pancake onto the plate. Slide pancake back into the skillet. Cook until lightly browned. Slide pancake onto a greased cookie sheet and keep warm. Repeat two more times to make three pancakes total.
5. Place one of the pancakes in a greased 9-inch pie plate. Spread mushroom-spinach mixture to within ½ inch of the edge of the pancake. Sprinkle with ¼ cup of the shredded cheese. Top with a second pancake; spread tomato mixture over pancake to within ½ inch of the edge of the pancake. Sprinkle with ¼ cup of the shredded cheese. Top with the final pancake; sprinkle with the remaining ½ cup shredded cheese.
6. Bake 5 to 8 minutes or until hot in center and cheese is melted. Let stand 10 minutes before serving. To serve, cut into six wedges.

PER SERVING: 259 cal., 12 g total fat (3 g sat. fat), 193 mg chol., 536 mg sodium, 22 g carb. (5 g fiber, 5 g sugars), 17 g pro.

1 FLAVOR

Mushrooms provide a "meaty" umami quality; the garlic-herb tomato layer tastes like a good marinara sauce. Cheese helps mesh the flavorful layers.

2 NUTRITION

The eggs contribute a big helping of protein, and the olive oil is a good source of healthful fats. Tomatoes, carrots, and spinach supply vitamins.

3 SATISFACTION

This tall stack is both fun to serve and fun to eat. The layers are filling, and the cheese gives each bite a nice salty hit. There's a lot to chew and savor.

"Start eating less meat by going meatless on Mondays. Snack on hummus with crackers or raw veggies. For dinner, try whole grain pasta with sautéed veggies and marinara sauce."
– *Mary Lou Perry, M.S., RD, CDE, dietitian at the University of Virginia's Heart and Vascular Center*

Salad Tacos

SERVINGS 4 (2 tacos each)
CARB. PER SERVING 30 g
START TO FINISH 30 minutes

1 tablespoon olive oil
1 tablespoon lime juice
¾ teaspoon honey
⅛ teaspoon ground cumin
⅛ teaspoon ground ancho chile pepper
Pinch salt
1 medium carrot, chopped
½ of a small cucumber, chopped
½ cup chopped radishes
½ cup chopped fresh pineapple
½ cup canned black beans, rinsed and drained
¼ cup thinly sliced green onions (2)
¼ cup cilantro leaves
2 cups shredded romaine lettuce
8 hard taco shells
¼ cup shredded reduced-fat cheddar cheese (1 ounce)

1. In a small bowl whisk together oil, lime juice, honey, cumin, ground chile pepper, and salt. Set aside.

2. In a medium bowl combine carrot, cucumber, radishes, pineapple, beans, green onions, and cilantro; set aside. In another medium bowl combine lettuce and reserved dressing; toss to coat.

3. Divide carrot mixture among taco shells. Top with lettuce and sprinkle with cheese.

PER SERVING: 219 cal., 11 g total fat (2 g sat. fat), 5 mg chol., 387 mg sodium, 30 g carb. (9 g fiber, 5 g sugars), 7 g pro.

1 FLAVOR

Honey, lime juice, and pineapple give these tacos an unexpected sweet-tart tang.

2 NUTRITION

A crunchy collection of raw veggies makes these tacos vitamin A powerhouses. And sodium is kept in check because the fresh ingredients require little enhancement.

3 SATISFACTION

Here's a taco salad you can eat with your hands. What would be more fun? Eating two of them!

SALAD TACOS

1

2

3

VEGETARIAN Q&A

Q: Does eating vegetarian guarantee you'll eat healthier?

A: Considering the variety of vegetarian eating plans, you're likely to eat healthier just by virtue of the foods that are prominent in this diet. However, if you eat lots of cheese, full-fat dairy foods, and sweets, you probably won't see your health improve.

Q: If I become a vegetarian, should I have any nutritional concerns?

A: The more food groups you include and the greater variety of foods you eat, the easier it will be to meet your nutrition needs. The nutrients that may be hardest to get in sufficient supply are vitamins B12 and D, omega-3 fats, iron, and zinc.

Q: How do I stop missing meat?

A: One reason you may miss meat is habit. If your meal planning has a "Where's the beef?" focus, start with planning the nonmeat things you'll prepare. A reason people enjoy cooked meat is umami, considered the fifth taste, but meat is not the only source of umami. You can taste it in roasted vegetables, mushrooms, nuts, avocado, soy sauce, and cheese.

Q: Will I get enough protein?

A: Americans tend to eat more protein than they need, and too much is from animal sources that contain saturated fat and cholesterol. Nonmeat sources of protein are grains, beans, nuts, vegetables, eggs, and dairy foods. These can meet your protein requirements if you eat sufficient calories.

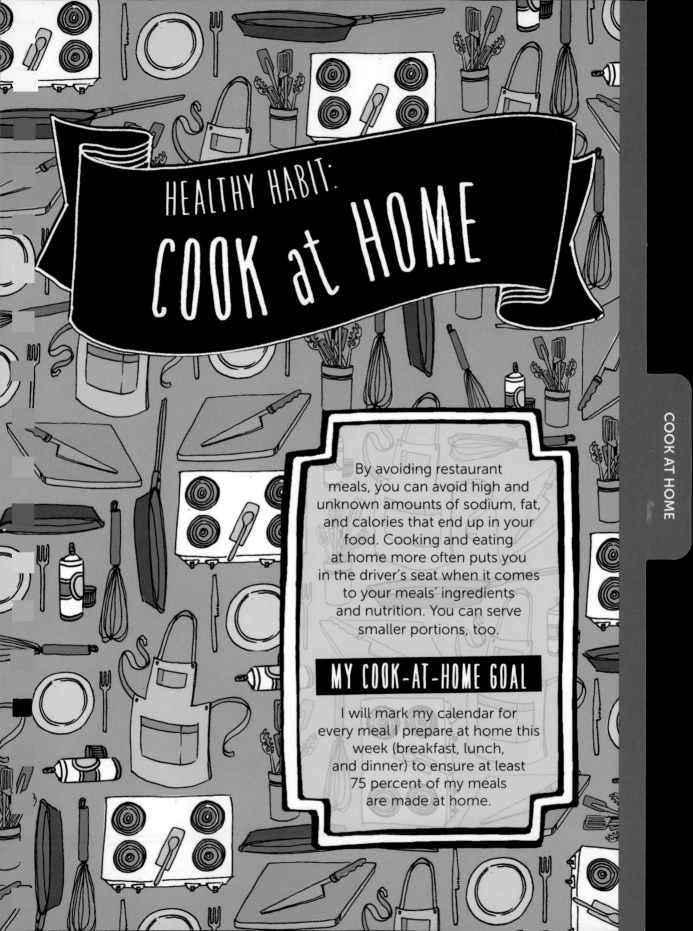

HEALTHY HABIT: COOK at HOME

By avoiding restaurant meals, you can avoid high and unknown amounts of sodium, fat, and calories that end up in your food. Cooking and eating at home more often puts you in the driver's seat when it comes to your meals' ingredients and nutrition. You can serve smaller portions, too.

MY COOK-AT-HOME GOAL

I will mark my calendar for every meal I prepare at home this week (breakfast, lunch, and dinner) to ensure at least 75 percent of my meals are made at home.

" My two lightbulb moments were when the scale neared 200 pounds and I saw a photo of myself looking so unhealthy. "

SHUN PLEDGER | age 47

With a family history of type 2 diabetes and after having gestational diabetes 17 years ago, Shun is currently living with prediabetes. After remarrying, she watched the scale slowly creep up until she had gained almost 50 pounds over seven years. That's when she signed up for the yearlong diabetes prevention program offered at her local hospital.

Kick-start into action: "My keys to success are having healthy foods in the house and keeping sweets out, planning my meals for the week, and learning ways to deal with stress without eating." Shun has lost 20 pounds so far and gets in 150 minutes of exercise each week. She's off her cholesterol medication and her last A1C was 5.7%.

Words of wisdom: "Just get started. It's never too late to change your ways, especially when it's for your health. If you make a mistake, don't beat yourself up. Learn from it, then get right back on track."

healthy cooking IS EASY!

Master these simple techniques and tips as the basis for cooking more healthfully every day. Each fills a role in reducing calories, fat, and carbs while improving overall nutrition in recipes.

LEARN HOW to OVEN-FRY

Think adding fat is essential for crisping foods? Think again. Oven-frying lets you fit crunchy-coated "fried" foods into your healthful meal plan.

Crispy Oven-Fried Chicken

SERVINGS 4 (4 ounces chicken each)
CARB. PER SERVING 13 g
PREP 15 minutes **MARINATE** 2 hours
BAKE 20 minutes

- ⅔ cup buttermilk
- ½ teaspoon paprika
- ¼ teaspoon salt
- ¼ teaspoon black pepper
- ⅛ teaspoon crushed red pepper
- 2 8-ounce skinless, boneless chicken breast halves, halved crosswise
- ¾ cup whole wheat or regular panko bread crumbs
- 1½ teaspoons onion powder
- ¾ teaspoon garlic powder
- ¾ teaspoon paprika
- ⅛ teaspoon salt
- ⅛ teaspoon black pepper
  Nonstick cooking spray

1. In a medium bowl combine buttermilk, the ½ teaspoon paprika, the ¼ teaspoon salt, the ¼ teaspoon black pepper, and the crushed red pepper. Place chicken in a large resealable plastic bag set in a shallow dish. Pour buttermilk mixture over chicken in bag. Seal bag; turn to coat chicken. Marinate in the refrigerator at least 2 hours or up to 8 hours, turning occasionally.
2. Preheat oven to 425°F. Line a baking sheet with foil. Place a rack on top of the foil; set aside. Drain chicken well. Discard buttermilk mixture.
3. In a shallow dish combine panko, onion powder, garlic powder, the ¾ teaspoon paprika, the ⅛ teaspoon salt, and the ⅛ teaspoon black pepper; mix well. Add chicken pieces to panko mixture, one piece at a time. Coat all sides, pressing to adhere panko mixture to chicken.
4. Place chicken pieces on the prepared rack. Coat tops of chicken pieces with cooking spray. Bake, uncovered, about 20 minutes or until a thermometer inserted in center of each chicken piece registers 165°F. (Do not turn chicken while baking.) If desired, sprinkle with *snipped fresh parsley* before serving.

PER SERVING: 194 cal., 4 g total fat (1 g sat. fat), 73 mg chol., 261 mg sodium, 13 g carb. (2 g fiber, 1 g sugars), 27 g pro.

Baking coated foods on an elevated rack placed over a foil-lined baking sheet ensures all sides get crispy.

Instead of cutting a smaller piece of quiche, cut carbs and fat with a cauliflower-based crust rather than a traditional pastry crust.

Cauliflower-Crusted Dinner Quiche

SERVINGS 6 (1 wedge each)
CARB. PER SERVING 11 g
PREP 30 minutes   **COOK** 8 minutes
BAKE 58 minutes   **STAND** 10 minutes

- 1   medium head cauliflower, cored and cut into florets (about 4 cups)
- 2   tablespoons water
- ¼   cup refrigerated or frozen egg product, thawed, or 1 egg, lightly beaten
- 1   cup shredded reduced-fat mozzarella or cheddar cheese (4 ounces)
- 2   tablespoons whole wheat panko bread crumbs
- 2   tablespoons snipped fresh chives
- 1   medium green sweet pepper, cut into thin bite-size strips
- ½   cup chopped onion (1 medium)
- 1   tablespoon olive oil
- 3   fully cooked chicken with spinach and feta cheese sausage links, chopped*
- 1¼ cups refrigerated or frozen egg product, thawed, or 4 eggs, lightly beaten
- ¼   cup fat-free half-and-half
- 1   tablespoon all-purpose flour
- ½   cup chopped, seeded tomato
- ¼   cup torn fresh basil

1. Preheat oven to 375°F. Grease a 9-inch pie plate; set aside. In a food processor finely chop the cauliflower, half at a time. In a large microwave-safe bowl combine cauliflower and water. Cover with vented plastic wrap. Microwave on 100 percent power (high) 3 to 5 minutes or until tender, stirring once. Let cauliflower cool slightly. Cut a 15-inch square of double-thickness cheesecloth. Spoon cauliflower into center of cheesecloth. Bring corners up and around cauliflower; squeeze the water from the cauliflower (should remove about 1 cup of liquid from cauliflower).

2. In a large bowl stir together ¼ cup egg, ½ cup of the cheese, the panko, and chives. Add cauliflower; stir until well combined. Spoon cauliflower mixture into prepared pie plate, pressing mixture onto bottom and up the sides of the plate.

3. Bake cauliflower crust about 25 minutes or until golden. Set on a wire rack. Decrease oven temperature to 325°F.

4. Meanwhile, in a large skillet cook green pepper and onion in hot oil over medium heat 5 minutes, stirring occasionally. Add sausage. Cook 3 minutes more, stirring occasionally. Spoon sausage mixture into cauliflower crust, spreading evenly. In a medium bowl whisk together the 1¼ cups egg, the half-and-half, and flour. Pour over sausage mixture in crust.

5. Bake, uncovered, 30 to 40 minutes or until a knife inserted near center comes out clean (Cover edges of quiche with foil if needed to keep crust from overbrowning.) Sprinkle with remaining ½ cup cheese. Bake 3 minutes more. Let stand on a wire rack 10 minutes before serving. Sprinkle with tomato and basil just before serving. Cut into wedges.

***TEST KITCHEN TIP:** Save the remaining chicken sausage from the package to cut up and add to omelets and scrambled eggs.

PER SERVING: 214 cal., 9 g total fat (3 g sat. fat), 40 mg chol., 552 mg sodium, 11 g carb. (2 g fiber, 4 g sugars), 21 g pro.

This is a loose mixture. Be sure to press it evenly over the bottom and sides of dish for a solid crust.

MASTER YOUR NONSTICK COOKWARE

Using nonstick cookware can help you cut back on the amount of oil used during cooking. Spray the skillet with cooking spray and heat it over medium to ensure foods brown evenly.

Sautéed Pork Chops with Balsamic Grape Sauce

SERVINGS 4 (1 pork chop and $^1/_2$ cup sauce each)
CARB. PER SERVING 18 g
START TO FINISH 25 minutes

Nonstick cooking spray
4   5- to 6-ounce bone-in pork loin chops, cut $^3/_4$ inch thick
$^1/_4$ cup thinly sliced onion
1   clove garlic, minced
$^3/_4$ cup apple juice or apple cider
$^1/_2$ cup reduced-sodium chicken broth
1   tablespoon cornstarch
1   tablespoon balsamic vinegar
1   teaspoon honey
1   cup seedless red grapes, halved

1. Generously coat an extra-large nonstick skillet with cooking spray. Heat skillet over medium heat. Add chops to hot skillet; cook about 5 minutes or until browned on both sides, turning to brown evenly. Remove chops from skillet.
2. Add onion and garlic to hot skillet; cook and stir 2 minutes. Add apple juice and broth to skillet. Bring to boiling; reduce heat. Return chops to skillet. Simmer, covered, about 4 minutes or until a thermometer inserted in centers of chops registers 145°F. Transfer chops to a serving platter; cover with foil and keep warm.
3. In a small bowl whisk together cornstarch, balsamic vinegar, and honey. Whisk vinegar mixture into juice mixture in skillet; cook and whisk 1 to 2 minutes or until thickened and bubbly. Stir in grapes; heat through.
4. To serve, spoon grape mixture over chops.

PER SERVING: 188 cal., 4 g total fat (1 g sat. fat), 47 mg chol., 117 mg sodium, 18 g carb. (1 g fiber, 13 g sugars), 19 g pro.

Off heat, coat nonstick skillet with cooking spray. Heat skillet over medium.

To help foods brown, let skillet heat before adding food and keep the lid off.

STRETCH with GRAINS and VEGGIES

Serve a more satisfying meat loaf by using low-calorie whole grains and chopped vegetables to extend higher-fat ground beef.

Southwest Meat Loaf

SERVINGS 8 (1 slice each)
CARB. PER SERVING 8 g
PREP 25 minutes **BAKE** 55 minutes
STAND 10 minutes

- ¼ cup dried quinoa
- ¾ cup water
- 1 stalk celery, finely chopped
- ½ cup finely chopped onion
- ½ cup finely chopped red or green sweet pepper
- ½ cup refrigerated or frozen egg product, thawed, or 2 eggs, lightly beaten
- ½ cup finely shredded carrot
- 1 tablespoon chili powder
- 3 cloves garlic, minced
- ¼ teaspoon salt
- 1½ pounds 90% or higher lean ground beef
- ⅓ cup reduced-sugar ketchup
- 2 tablespoons taco sauce
- 1 teaspoon chili powder

1. Preheat oven to 350°F. Place quinoa in a fine-mesh sieve; rinse with cold water. Drain well. In a small saucepan combine quinoa and water. Bring to boiling; reduce heat. Simmer, covered, 10 minutes. Stir in celery, onion, and sweet pepper. Return to a simmer. Simmer, covered, 2 to 5 minutes more or until quinoa is tender and most of the liquid is absorbed. Drain if necessary. Cool slightly.

2. In a large bowl combine egg, carrot, 1 tablespoon chili powder, the garlic, salt, and quinoa mixture. Add beef; mix well. Pat mixture into a 9×5×3-inch loaf pan.

3. Bake 45 minutes. Carefully tip the pan over a heatproof bowl; pour off fat. Meanwhile, in a small bowl combine ketchup, taco sauce, and 1 teaspoon chili powder. Spoon over meat loaf, spreading evenly. Bake 10 to 15 minutes more or until internal temperature reaches 160°F.

4. Let meat loaf stand 10 minutes on a wire rack. Carefully tip the pan over a heatproof bowl; pour off fat. Cut into eight slices while still in the pan and serve using a spatula.

PER SERVING: 197 cal., 9 g total fat (4 g sat. fat), 55 mg chol., 326 mg sodium, 8 g carb. (2 g fiber, 2 g sugars), 20 g pro.

Drain off accumulated fat in the loaf pan so the meat loaf doesn't reabsorb what has cooked off.

Test for doneness by inserting the tip of a thermometer into the center of the meat loaf.

GET SKILLED at STIR FRYING

Keeping the ingredients in constant motion while cooking is key to making sure vegetables are cooked but still crisp.

Beef-and-Vegetable Stir-Fry

SERVINGS 4 (1 cup stir-fry and $^1/_3$ cup cooked brown rice each)
CARB. PER SERVING 27 g
START TO FINISH 35 minutes

- 8 ounces boneless beef sirloin steak
- $^1/_3$ cup cold water
- $2^1/_2$ teaspoons cornstarch
- 3 tablespoons reduced-sodium soy sauce
- 1 tablespoon dry sherry or reduced-sodium chicken broth
- $^1/_8$ teaspoon salt
- Nonstick cooking spray
- 4 teaspoons vegetable oil
- 2 cloves garlic, minced
- 2 teaspoons grated fresh ginger
- 1 medium onion, cut into thin bite-size strips
- $^1/_2$ cup thinly sliced carrot (1 medium)
- $^1/_2$ cup thinly sliced celery (1 stalk)
- $^1/_2$ to 1 fresh jalapeño chile pepper, seeded and finely chopped (tip, *page 252*)
- 1 cup thin bite-size strips green and/or red sweet pepper (1 medium)
- 1 cup sliced fresh mushrooms
- 1 small zucchini, halved lengthwise and thinly sliced (1 cup)
- $1^1/_3$ cups hot cooked brown rice
- 2 tablespoons chopped dry-roasted unsalted peanuts or toasted unsalted cashews
- 2 tablespoons snipped fresh basil or parsley (optional)

1. If desired, partially freeze meat for easier slicing. Trim fat from meat. Thinly slice meat across the grain into bite-size strips. For sauce, in a small bowl stir together the cold water and cornstarch; stir in soy sauce, dry sherry, and salt. Set meat and sauce aside.

2. Coat a large nonstick skillet with cooking spray; heat over medium-high heat. Add 2 teaspoons of the oil. Add garlic and ginger; cook and stir 15 seconds. Add onion, carrot, celery, and chile pepper to hot skillet. Stir-fry 3 minutes, using a wide wooden spatula to constantly stir and lift vegetables. Add sweet pepper; stir-fry 1 minute. Add mushrooms and zucchini; stir-fry 3 to 4 minutes more or just until vegetables are crisp-tender. Remove vegetables from skillet.

3. Add the remaining 2 teaspoons oil to hot skillet. Add meat strips; stir-fry 1 to 2 minutes or until browned. Stir sauce; stir into meat in skillet. Cook and stir until thickened and bubbly. Return cooked vegetables to skillet, stirring to coat. Cook and stir 1 minute more. Serve with hot cooked rice. Sprinkle with peanuts. If desired, sprinkle with basil.

PER SERVING: 275 cal., 10 g total fat (2 g sat. fat), 34 mg chol., 548 mg sodium, 27 g carb. (4 g fiber, 6 g sugars), 18 g pro.

It's easier to cut thin slices of meat if you freeze the meat for a few minutes before slicing.

Have all your ingredients cut and measured before you start cooking. Once the stir-fry starts, it cooks fast.

UNDERSTAND COOKING with LOW-FAT CHEESE

Low-fat cheese melts differently than full-fat cheese. Stirring it into a hot roux made of milk and flour helps it melt into a creamy sauce.

Veggie Mac and Cheese

SERVINGS 8 (1 cup each)
CARB. PER SERVING 34 g
START TO FINISH 45 minutes

- ½ cup panko bread crumbs
- ¼ teaspoon paprika
- 8 ounces dried whole grain elbow macaroni (about 2 cups)
- 1 cup sliced carrots (2 medium)
- 1 cup green beans cut into 1-inch pieces
- ⅔ cup finely chopped onion (2 small)
- 2 cups small broccoli florets
- 1¾ cups fat-free milk
- 3 tablespoons all-purpose flour
- ½ teaspoon salt
- ⅛ teaspoon black pepper
- 3 ounces reduced-fat cream cheese (Neufchâtel)
- 1½ teaspoons Dijon-style mustard
- 2 cups shredded reduced-fat Mexican-style four-cheese blend (8 ounces)
  Nonstick cooking spray

To avoid overcooking the cheese, remove the sauce from the heat, then gradually stir in the shredded cheese.

EXPERT TIP

"If no one in your home will eat veggies, sneak them in by sautéing and pureeing tomatoes, carrots, onions, zucchini, garlic, and peppers—then add them to chili, spaghetti sauce, or meat loaf to add flavor, vitamins, minerals, and fiber."

– Tonya Olsen, RN, diabetes educator at Northeastern Tribal Health System, Oklahoma

1. Preheat broiler. In a small bowl stir together panko and paprika; set aside.

2. In a large saucepan cook macaroni, carrots, green beans, and onion according to package directions for macaroni, except omit salt; add broccoli the last 3 minutes of the cooking time. Drain. Return cooked macaroni and vegetables to hot saucepan; keep warm.

3. Meanwhile, in a medium saucepan whisk together milk, flour, salt, and pepper. Cook and stir over medium heat until slightly thickened and bubbly. Add cream cheese and mustard, stirring until smooth. Remove from heat. Add shredded cheese, stirring constantly until melted.

4. Immediately pour cheese mixture over cooked macaroni mixture; toss gently to coat. Spoon into a 2½- or 3-quart broilerproof oval baking dish.

5. Sprinkle panko mixture over macaroni mixture in baking dish. Lightly coat panko mixture with cooking spray. Broil 4 to 6 inches from the heat 1 to 2 minutes or until golden brown.

PER SERVING: 269 cal., 8 g total fat (5 g sat. fat), 24 mg chol., 495 mg sodium, 34 g carb. (4 g fiber, 6 g sugars), 16 g pro.

LEARN to BOOST FLAVORS

Flavor doesn't have to come with fat. Pair high- and low-sodium ingredients to balance those flavors. A splash of an acid, like lemon juice, makes other flavors pop.

Crispy Smoked Fish Roll-Ups

SERVINGS 4 (1 roll-up each)
CARB. PER SERVING 16 g
PREP 20 minutes **BAKE** 18 minutes

4 4-ounce fresh or frozen tilapia, flounder, or sole fillets
Nonstick cooking spray
3 ounces thinly sliced smoked salmon (lox-style)
¼ cup snipped fresh chives
2 tablespoons finely chopped red onion
1 teaspoon finely shredded lemon peel
½ cup refrigerated or frozen egg product, thawed, or 2 eggs, lightly beaten
1 cup whole wheat or plain panko bread crumbs
4 lemon wedges

1. Thaw fish, if frozen. Preheat oven to 425°F. Coat a 2-quart square baking dish with cooking spray; set aside. Rinse fish and pat dry with paper towels. Lay fish on a large cutting board.
2. Cut the smoked salmon into thin strips and place evenly in a single layer on top of tilapia. Sprinkle salmon with chives, red onion, and lemon peel. Roll fish up around filling. If necessary, secure with wooden toothpicks.
3. Pour egg into a shallow dish. Place panko in another shallow dish. Dip fish rolls in egg, turning to coat all sides. Allow excess to drip off; dip fish in panko, turning to coat all sides. Arrange fish in prepared baking dish; lightly coat tops of fish rolls with cooking spray.
4. Bake fish, uncovered, 18 to 20 minutes or until fish is browned and flakes easily when tested with a fork. To serve, divide fish rolls among four plates. Garnish with lemon wedges to squeeze over fish rolls.

PER SERVING: 224 cal., 3 g total fat (1 g sat. fat), 66 mg chol., 350 mg sodium, 16 g carb. (2 g fiber, 1 g sugars), 33 g pro.

Carefully lift and wrap fish fillets around filling and secure with toothpicks as needed.

Coating the panko mixture with cooking spray helps it brown and crisp during baking.

Grilling your dinner is an easy way to add great flavor but not add fat. The meat cooks slowly over indirect heat, and vegetables are added later to cook over direct heat.

Apricot-Chipotle Grilled Pork Tenderloin and Zucchini

SERVINGS 4 (3 ounces pork and $\frac{1}{2}$ of a zucchini each)
CARB. PER SERVING 12 g
PREP 25 minutes   GRILL 20 minutes
STAND 3 minutes

- 1 1-pound pork tenderloin
- 3 green onions
- 2 tablespoons apricot preserves or jam
- 2 tablespoons reduced-sodium soy sauce
- 2 teaspoons finely chopped canned chipotle pepper in adobo sauce (tip, *page 252*)
- 2 medium zucchini (about 8 ounces each)
- 1 tablespoon olive oil
- $\frac{1}{4}$ teaspoon salt
- $\frac{1}{4}$ teaspoon black pepper
- 2 tablespoons snipped fresh cilantro

1. Trim fat from pork. Thinly slice green onions, keeping white parts separate from green tops. Reserve green tops. In a small microwave-safe bowl combine white parts of onions, the apricot preserves, soy sauce, and chipotle pepper. Microwave on 100 percent power (high) 30 to 60 seconds or until heated. Set aside.
2. Trim ends off zucchini. Cut zucchini in half lengthwise. Brush zucchini with olive oil; sprinkle with salt and black pepper.
3. For a charcoal grill, arrange medium-hot coals around a drip pan. Test for medium heat above pan. Place pork on a greased grill rack over pan. Cover; grill 20 to 25 minutes or until slightly pink in the center (145°F), brushing with 2 tablespoons of the apricot sauce the last 5 minutes of grilling. Add zucchini to the grill with pork, placing them over the coals; grill 8 to

10 minutes or until tender, turning once. (For a gas grill, preheat grill. Reduce heat to medium. Adjust for indirect cooking. Place pork on greased rack over burner that is off. Grill as directed. Add zucchini to the grill with pork, placing it over the heat; grill as directed.) Remove pork and zucchini from grill; tent pork with foil and let stand 3 minutes before slicing.
4. Slice pork and divide among four plates. Cut zucchini halves into large pieces; divide among plates. Top with remaining apricot sauce. Sprinkle with reserved green onion tops and the cilantro.

PER SERVING: 210 cal., 6 g total fat (1 g sat. fat), 74 mg chol., 507 mg sodium, 12 g carb. (2 g fiber, 8 g sugars), 26 g pro.

Using a sharp knife, carefully trim fat and silverskin from the pork tenderloin.

Tenting pork with foil keeps the sauce on the pork from sticking while juices redistribute in the meat.

BEEF and BROCCOLI NOODLES

RESTAURANT FAVORITES
at home

Save some money, avoid the crowds, and feel good about the healthful and delicious bites you're about to indulge in. These restaurant-style recipes really deliver.

Beef and Broccoli Noodles

SERVINGS 4 (1$\frac{1}{2}$ cups beef-broccoli mixture and $\frac{1}{2}$ cup noodles each)
CARB. PER SERVING 39 g
START TO FINISH 45 minutes

- 3 teaspoons cornstarch
- 1 tablespoon reduced-sodium soy sauce
- 3 cloves garlic, minced
- $\frac{1}{4}$ teaspoon crushed red pepper
- 12 ounces boneless beef top sirloin steak, bias-cut into $\frac{1}{8}$-inch-thick slices
- 4 ounces dried Chinese egg noodles* or whole wheat vermicelli
- 1 pound broccoli
- 3 tablespoons hoisin sauce*
- 2 tablespoons water
- 2 teaspoons toasted sesame oil**
- 1 tablespoon canola oil
- $\frac{3}{4}$ cup reduced-sodium beef broth
- 1 cup quartered and/or halved cherry tomatoes

1. In a medium bowl stir together 2 teaspoons of the cornstarch, the soy sauce, garlic, and crushed red pepper; add beef and stir to coat. Marinate at room temperature 20 minutes.

2. Meanwhile, cook Chinese noodles or vermicelli according to package directions, except omit salt; drain and set aside.

3. Cut broccoli into 2-inch florets. If desired, peel broccoli stem and cut into $\frac{1}{2}$-inch-thick slices; set aside. For sauce, stir together hoisin sauce, the water, sesame oil, and the remaining 1 teaspoon cornstarch; set aside.

4. In an extra-large skillet or wok heat canola oil over medium-high heat. Add beef mixture; stir-fry 1 to 2 minutes or just until slightly pink in center. Remove beef mixture from skillet; set aside.

5. Stir broth into skillet, scraping up any browned bits from bottom of skillet. Add broccoli; bring to boiling. Reduce heat to medium. Cover and cook 3 to 4 minutes or until broccoli is crisp-tender.

6. Add sauce to broccoli; cook and stir until thickened. Add beef and tomatoes; heat through. Serve over cooked Chinese noodles or vermicelli.

*CHEF'S SECRET: Look for Chinese egg noodles and hoisin sauce in the Asian section of a large supermarket or at an Asian food store.

**CHEF'S SECRET: Toasted sesame oil, which is nutty brown in color and robust in flavor, is used in small amounts to add a pleasant nuttiness to Asian dishes. You don't want to skip it.

PER SERVING: 379 cal., 14 g total fat (4 g sat. fat), 48 mg chol., 532 mg sodium, 39 g carb. (8 g fiber, 7 g sugars), 26 g pro.

VIETNAMESE-STYLE BEEF and NOODLE BOWLS

recipe on *page 222*

Vietnamese-Style Beef and Noodle Bowls

photo on *page 221*

SERVINGS 4 (1¹/₂ cups each)
CARB. PER SERVING 31 g
PREP 20 minutes   **COOK** 5 minutes

  4 ounces banh pho* (Vietnamese wide rice noodles)
  2 teaspoons chili oil
 12 ounces beef flank steak or beef top round steak, sliced into bite-size strips
  2 stalks bok choy, stalk and leaf separated and each thinly sliced
 ¹/₂ cup chopped red sweet pepper
  2 teaspoons grated fresh ginger
  2 cloves garlic, minced
 ¹/₄ teaspoon crushed red pepper
  1 cup lower-sodium beef broth
  1 tablespoon reduced-sodium soy sauce
 ¹/₂ cup canned bean sprouts, drained
  2 tablespoons snipped fresh basil
     Fresh basil
     Lime wedges

1. Prepare noodles according to package directions. Set aside.
2. Heat oil in a wok or large skillet over medium-high heat. Add beef; stir-fry 1 minute. Add the stalk portions of the bok choy, the sweet pepper, ginger, garlic, and crushed red pepper; stir-fry 1 to 2 minutes more or until beef is browned on all sides. Push beef from the center of the wok. Add beef broth and soy sauce. Bring to boiling; reduce heat. Stir meat into broth mixture. Cook and stir 1 to 2 minutes more or until beef is done.
3. Add noodles, bok choy leaf portions, bean sprouts, and snipped basil to mixture in wok; toss to combine. Ladle mixture into soup bowls. Garnish with fresh basil. Serve with lime wedges.
*CHEF'S SECRET: Look for banh pho in the Asian section of a large supermarket or at an Asian food store.

PER SERVING: 274 cal., 7 g total fat (2 g sat. fat), 51 mg chol., 397 mg sodium, 31 g carb. (2 g fiber, 2 g sugars), 21 g pro.

Chicken Honey-Nut Stir-Fry

SERVINGS 4 (1 cup stir-fry and ¹/₃ cup rice each)
CARB. PER SERVING 28 g
START TO FINISH 25 minutes

  4 teaspoons vegetable oil
 ¹/₂ cup diagonally sliced carrot
 ¹/₂ cup sliced celery
  1 pound skinless, boneless chicken breast halves, cut into 1-inch pieces
 ¹/₂ cup orange juice
  2 teaspoons cornstarch
  2 tablespoons reduced-sodium soy sauce
  2 teaspoons honey
 ¹/₂ teaspoon grated fresh ginger
 ¹/₄ cup cashews
 ¹/₄ cup sliced green onions (2)
 1¹/₃ cups hot cooked brown rice

1. In a wok or large skillet heat 2 teaspoons of the oil over high heat. Add carrot and celery; stir-fry vegetables 2 minutes. Add 1 teaspoon of the remaining oil. Add half of the chicken; stir-fry 3 to 5 minutes more or until chicken is no longer pink. Transfer chicken mixture to a bowl. Repeat with remaining 1 teaspoon oil and the remaining chicken. Return all to wok.
2. In a small bowl whisk together orange juice and cornstarch. Add soy sauce, honey, and ginger, whisking until well mixed. Add soy sauce mixture to chicken mixture in wok. Cook and stir over medium heat until thickened; cook and stir 1 minute more. Top with cashews and green onions. Serve stir-fry with hot cooked rice.

PER SERVING: 336 cal., 12 g total fat (2 g sat. fat), 73 mg chol., 353 mg sodium, 28 g carb. (2 g fiber, 8 g sugars), 28 g pro.

CHICKEN HONEY-NUT
STIR-FRY

LIGHT 'n' CRISP EGG ROLLS

Light 'n' Crisp Egg Rolls

SERVINGS 8 (1 egg roll each)
CARB. PER SERVING 23 g
PREP 30 minutes **BAKE** 15 minutes

  8 ounces lean pork loin, cut into
       ½-inch pieces, or ground pork
  ½ cup chopped red sweet pepper
  1 teaspoon grated fresh ginger or
       ¼ teaspoon ground ginger
  1 clove garlic, minced
  2 teaspoons toasted sesame oil or
       canola oil
  ¾ cup finely chopped bok choy or
       napa cabbage
  ½ cup chopped canned water chestnuts
  ½ cup coarsely shredded carrot (1 medium)
  ¼ cup sliced green onions (2)
  ¼ cup bottled light Asian sesame
       ginger vinaigrette
  8 egg roll wrappers

1. Preheat oven to 425°F. Lightly coat a large baking sheet with *nonstick cooking spray;* set aside. For filling, in a medium nonstick skillet cook pork, sweet pepper, ginger, and garlic in hot oil over medium-high heat 3 to 4 minutes or until pork is no longer pink, stirring occasionally. If using ground pork, drain off fat. Add bok choy, water chestnuts, carrot, and green onions to skillet. Cook and stir 1 minute more or until liquid evaporates. Stir in vinaigrette. Cool slightly.
2. For each egg roll, place an egg roll wrapper on a flat surface with a corner pointing toward you. Spoon about ⅓ cup of the filling across and just below the center of each egg roll wrapper. Fold bottom corner over filling, tucking it under on the other side. Fold side corners over filling, forming an envelope shape. Roll egg roll toward remaining corner. Moisten top corner with water; press firmly to seal.
3. Place egg rolls, seam sides down, on the prepared baking sheet. Coat tops and sides of the egg rolls with cooking spray. Bake 15 to 18 minutes or until egg rolls are golden brown and crisp. Cool slightly before serving.

PER SERVING: 167 cal., 4 g total fat (1 g sat. fat), 22 mg chol., 282 mg sodium, 23 g carb. (1 g fiber, 2 g sugars), 10 g pro.

Pizza Margherita

SERVINGS 6 (1 piece each)
CARB. PER SERVING 27 g
PREP 15 minutes **BAKE** 15 minutes

    Nonstick cooking spray
  1 11-ounce package refrigerated thin-crust
       pizza dough
  1 tablespoon olive oil
  2 cups grape tomatoes, halved
  8 ounces small fresh mozzarella cheese
       balls, sliced
  2 cloves garlic, minced
  ½ cup fresh basil
    Coarse ground black pepper (optional)

1. Preheat oven to 400°F. Coat a 15x10x1-inch baking pan with cooking spray. Unroll pizza dough in the prepared pan. Press onto the bottom and slightly up the sides of the pan. Brush with oil. Bake 7 minutes.
2. Top with tomato, cheese, and garlic. Bake 8 to 10 minutes more or until crust is golden brown. Tear or snip large basil leaves. Sprinkle pizza with basil and, if desired, pepper. Cut into six pieces.

PER SERVING: 291 cal., 15 g total fat (7 g sat. fat), 27 mg chol., 418 mg sodium, 27 g carb. (2 g fiber, 4 g sugars), 12 g pro.

Beef Burgundy

SERVINGS 8 (³⁄₄ cup beef mixture and about ¹⁄₂ cup potatoes each)
CARB. PER SERVING 28 g
PREP 25 minutes
SLOW COOK 8 to 10 hours (low) or 4 to 5 hours (high)
COOK 20 minutes (potatoes)

- 2 pounds boneless beef chuck roast, cut into 1-inch pieces
- 4 teaspoons olive oil
- 1¹⁄₂ cups chopped onions
- 4 medium carrots, cut into ³⁄₄-inch pieces
- 2 cups frozen small whole onions
- 2 cloves garlic, minced
- 2 tablespoons quick-cooking tapioca*
- 1 cup red wine or 50%-less-sodium beef broth
- ¹⁄₂ cup 50%-less-sodium beef broth
- ¹⁄₄ cup brandy or 50%-less-sodium beef broth
- 1 tablespoon tomato paste
- 1 teaspoon dried thyme, crushed
- ¹⁄₂ teaspoon dried rosemary, crushed
- ¹⁄₂ teaspoon black pepper
- 2 bay leaves
- 1 cup quartered fresh cremini mushrooms**
- 1 recipe Skins-On Garlic Mashed Potatoes
  Snipped fresh thyme (optional)

1. In a large nonstick skillet brown half of the beef in 1 teaspoon of the oil over medium-high heat; remove from skillet. Repeat with remaining beef and another 1 teaspoon of the oil.

2. In a 3¹⁄₂- or 4-quart slow cooker combine chopped onions, carrots, whole onions, and garlic. Sprinkle with tapioca. Place beef on top of the vegetables. In a medium bowl whisk together wine, broth, brandy, tomato paste, thyme, rosemary, and pepper. Pour over all in cooker. Add bay leaves, tucking them down into the liquid.

3. Cover and cook on low-heat setting 8 to 10 hours or on high-heat setting 4 to 5 hours. Discard bay leaves.

4. Near the end of cooking time, in a large skillet cook mushrooms in the remaining

EXPERT TIP

2 teaspoons hot oil over medium-high heat until browned. Stir mushrooms into beef mixture. Serve beef mixture with Skins-On Garlic Mashed Potatoes. If desired, sprinkle with thyme.

SKINS-ON GARLIC MASHED POTATOES: Cut 1¹⁄₂ pounds red-skin, Yukon gold, or russet potatoes into quarters. Peel and halve 4 cloves garlic. In a covered large saucepan cook potatoes and garlic in enough boiling lightly salted water to cover 20 to 25 minutes or until tender; drain. Mash with potato masher or beat with an electric mixer on low speed. Add 1 tablespoon butter, ¹⁄₈ teaspoon salt, and ¹⁄₈ teaspoon black pepper. Slowly beat in 3 to 5 tablespoons fat-free milk to make potato mixture light and fluffy.

***CHEF'S SECRET:** The tapioca thickens the sauce without curdling or breaking down during the long cooking period.

****CHEF'S SECRET:** Dark brown cremini mushrooms are firmer in texture than button mushrooms. If you prefer, use fresh portobello mushrooms cut into 1-inch pieces.

PER SERVING: 344 cal., 9 g total fat (3 g sat. fat), 78 mg chol., 255 mg sodium, 28 g carb. (4 g fiber, 6 g sugars), 29 g pro.

BEEF BURGUNDY

ALFREDO-SAUCED CHICKEN

2. Coat a large nonstick skillet with cooking spray.* Heat over medium heat. Add 2 teaspoons of the butter. Add chicken; cook and stir about 8 minutes or until cooked through. Remove chicken. Add the remaining 1 teaspoon butter to skillet. Add mushrooms, onion, and garlic; cook 3 minutes. Stir in wine and chicken.

3. Whisk together half-and-half and flour. Whisk in sour cream, salt, and pepper; stir into chicken mixture. Cook and stir just until bubbly; cook and stir 2 minutes more. Add tomatoes and the $^1/_2$ cup cheese, stirring until cheese is melted. Serve over pasta. Sprinkle with green onion and the 2 tablespoons cheese.

***CHEF'S SECRET:** Coat unheated skillet with cooking spray. Then heat the skillet before adding food for cooking.

PER SERVING: 340 cal., 10 g total fat (5 g sat. fat), 68 mg chol., 516 mg sodium, 34 g carb. (4 g fiber, 6 g sugars), 26 g pro.

Alfredo-Sauced Chicken
SERVINGS 6 ($^3/_4$ cup chicken mixture and $^1/_3$ cup pasta each)
CARB. PER SERVING 34 g
START TO FINISH 40 minutes

 6 ounces dried whole grain fettuccine
Nonstick cooking spray
 3 teaspoons butter
 1 pound skinless, boneless chicken breast halves, cut up
 1 cup sliced fresh mushrooms
 $^1/_4$ cup finely chopped onion
 1 clove garlic, minced
 $^1/_2$ cup dry white wine or reduced-sodium chicken broth
 $1^1/_2$ cups fat-free half-and-half
 3 tablespoons all-purpose flour
 $^1/_2$ cup light sour cream
 $^1/_2$ teaspoon salt
 $^1/_8$ teaspoon black pepper
 1 cup halved cherry tomatoes
 $^1/_2$ cup shredded Parmesan cheese
 2 tablespoons sliced green onion (1)
 2 tablespoons shredded Parmesan cheese

1. In a Dutch oven cook pasta according to package directions, except omit the salt. Drain well. Return to hot pan; cover and keep warm.

Baked Cavatelli
SERVINGS 8 ($^3/_4$ cup each)
CARB. PER SERVING 30 g
PREP 30 minutes **COOK** 15 minutes
BAKE 40 minutes

 8 ounces dried cavatelli or dried multigrain penne pasta
 12 ounces uncooked ground Italian turkey sausage*
 1 cup chopped eggplant or zucchini
 1 cup chopped fresh cremini or button mushrooms
 $^3/_4$ cup chopped red sweet pepper
 $^1/_2$ cup chopped onion
 2 cloves garlic, minced
 1 14.5-ounce can no-salt-added diced tomatoes, undrained
 1 8-ounce can no-salt-added tomato sauce
 $^1/_4$ cup snipped fresh basil or 1 tablespoon dried basil, crushed
 1 tablespoon snipped fresh oregano or 1 teaspoon dried oregano, crushed
 $^1/_4$ teaspoon salt
 $^1/_4$ teaspoon black pepper
 1 cup shredded reduced-fat Italian cheese blend (4 ounces)

1. Preheat oven to 350°F. Cook pasta according to package directions, omitting any salt or oil. Drain; set aside.

2. Meanwhile, in an extra-large skillet cook sausage, eggplant, mushrooms, sweet pepper, onion, and garlic over medium heat until sausage is browned and vegetables are just tender, stirring to break up sausage as it cooks. Drain off fat. Add tomatoes, tomato sauce, dried basil and dried oregano (if using), salt, and black pepper. Bring to boiling; reduce heat. Simmer, covered, 10 minutes, stirring occasionally. Stir in fresh basil and fresh oregano (if using).

3. In a very large bowl stir together the pasta and sausage mixture. Spoon mixture into a 3-quart baking dish.

4. Bake, covered, 35 to 40 minutes or until heated through. Uncover; sprinkle with cheese. Bake about 5 minutes more or until cheese is melted.

*CHEF'S SECRET: For a less spicy pasta dish, use half regular ground turkey and half Italian turkey sausage.

PER SERVING: 254 cal., 7 g total fat (3 g sat. fat), 34 mg chol., 492 mg sodium, 30 g carb. (3 g fiber, 6 g sugars), 17 g pro.

BAKED CAVATELLI

Spinach Alfredo Lasagna

SERVINGS 8 (1 piece each)
CARB. PER SERVING 24 g
PREP 25 minutes **BAKE** 1 hour 15 minutes
STAND 20 minutes

Nonstick cooking spray
1 egg, lightly beaten
1 15-ounce carton part-skim ricotta cheese
1 10-ounce package frozen chopped spinach, thawed and well drained
4 cloves garlic, minced
1/4 teaspoon freshly ground black pepper
1 15-ounce jar light Alfredo sauce
1/2 cup fat-free milk
6 whole grain lasagna noodles
2 cups shredded carrots (4 medium)
2 cups sliced fresh mushrooms
1/2 cup shredded part-skim mozzarella cheese (2 ounces)
1/4 cup finely shredded Parmesan cheese (1 ounce)

1. Preheat oven to 350°F. Lightly coat a 2-quart rectangular baking dish with cooking spray.
2. In a medium bowl stir together egg, ricotta cheese, spinach, garlic, and pepper. In a separate bowl combine Alfredo sauce and milk.
3. Spread about 1/2 cup of the Alfredo sauce mixture into the bottom of the prepared baking dish. Arrange three of the uncooked noodles in a layer over the sauce. Spread half of the spinach mixture over the noodles; top with half of the carrots and half of the mushrooms. Arrange the remaining three uncooked noodles over the vegetables. Top noodles with the remaining spinach mixture. Top with the remaining carrots and the remaining mushrooms. Cover with the remaining Alfredo mixture. Sprinkle with the mozzarella cheese and Parmesan cheese.
4. Lightly coat a sheet of foil with cooking spray. Cover dish with foil, coated side down.
5. Bake 60 to 70 minutes. Uncover and bake 15 to 20 minutes more or until top is lightly browned. Let stand 20 minutes before serving. Cut into eight pieces.

PER SERVING: 262 cal., 12 g total fat (7 g sat. fat), 69 mg chol., 527 mg sodium, 24 g carb. (4 g fiber, 4 g sugars), 16 g pro.

Crab Cakes with Spring Greens Salad

SERVINGS 6 (1 crab cake and 1 1/2 cups salad each)
CARB. PER SERVING 7 g
PREP 40 minutes **CHILL** 30 minutes
COOK 8 minutes

1 egg white
3 tablespoons light mayonnaise
1 tablespoon Dijon-style mustard
Bottled hot pepper sauce
3 tablespoons finely chopped red or green sweet pepper
2 tablespoons snipped fresh parsley
1 tablespoon sliced green onion
2 teaspoons snipped fresh dill weed or cilantro or 1/2 teaspoon dried dill weed
1 pound cooked fresh lump crabmeat or three 6- to 6.5-ounce cans lump crabmeat, drained, flaked, and cartilage removed

SPINACH ALFREDO
LASAGNA

CRAB CAKES with
SPRING GREENS SALAD

1¼ cups soft whole wheat bread crumbs
5 ounces mixed baby salad greens (8 cups)
1 head Belgian endive, sliced crosswise
1 medium tomato, seeded and chopped
Nonstick cooking spray
1 recipe Lime Dressing

1. In a large bowl whisk together egg white, mayonnaise, mustard, and hot pepper sauce. Stir in sweet pepper, parsley, green onion, and dill. Add crab and ½ cup of the bread crumbs; stir until well mixed. Using wet hands, firmly shape mixture into six ½-inch-thick patties. Place in a 15×10×1-inch baking pan. Cover and chill 30 minutes.

2. In an-extra large bowl combine greens, Belgian endive, and tomato. Cover and chill until ready to serve.

3. Preheat oven to 300°F. Place the remaining ¾ cup bread crumbs in a shallow dish. Dip crab cakes into bread crumbs, turning to coat both sides. Coat a large nonstick skillet generously with cooking spray; heat over medium heat. Add three of the crab cakes. Cook 8 to 10 minutes or until golden brown and heated through (160°F), very carefully turning once halfway through cooking time. Transfer to a baking sheet; keep warm in the oven. Repeat with the remaining three crab cakes.

4. To serve, toss greens mixture with Lime Dressing; divide among six plates. Top with warm crab cakes.

LIME DRESSING: In a bowl whisk together 2 tablespoons olive oil; 2 tablespoons lime juice; 1 clove garlic, minced; ⅛ teaspoon salt; and ⅛ teaspoon black pepper.

PER SERVING: 167 cal., 8 g total fat (1.25 g sat. fat), 76 mg chol., 512 mg sodium, 7 g carb. (1.38 g fiber, 1.9 g sugars), 16 g pro.

Pork Tenderloin Sandwiches

SERVINGS 4 (1 sandwich and $1/2$ cup slaw each)
CARB. PER SERVING 31 g
PREP 25 minutes **CHILL** 2 hours
COOK 8 minutes

- 12 ounces pork tenderloin
- 2 tablespoons flour
- $1/4$ teaspoon salt
- $1/4$ teaspoon onion powder or garlic powder
- $1/4$ teaspoon cayenne pepper
- $1/4$ teaspoon black pepper
- 2 tablespoons vegetable oil
- 4 whole wheat hamburger buns, split and toasted
- Ketchup, yellow mustard, and/or pickles (optional)
- 1 recipe Broccoli Slaw

1. Cut pork crosswise into four pieces. Place one pork piece between two sheets of plastic wrap. Pound lightly with the flat side of a meat mallet, working from center to edges until $1/4$ inch thick. Repeat with remaining pork.
2. In a shallow dish combine flour, salt, onion powder, cayenne pepper, and black pepper. Dip meat into the flour mixture, turning to coat. In an extra-large skillet heat oil over medium heat. Add pork; cook 8 to 10 minutes or until no pink remains and juices run clear, turning once. (If all the pork slices won't fit in the skillet, cook in two batches, adding additional oil if necessary.)

3. To serve, place pork pieces on buns. If desired, serve with a small drizzle of ketchup, mustard, and/or pickles. Serve Broccoli Slaw on the side or on top of pork pieces.

BROCCOLI SLAW: For dresssing, whisk together 2 tablespoons vinegar, 1 tablespoon honey. $1/4$ teaspoon salt, and $1/8$ teaspoon black pepper. Combine 2 cups broccoli slaw mix, 2 tablespoons thinly sliced green onion, and 1 tablespoon snipped fresh parsley. Add dressing; toss. Cover and chill 2 to 24 hours.

PER SERVING: 310 cal., 10 g total fat (1 g sat. fat), 55 mg chol., 560 mg sodium, 31 g carb. (3 g fiber, 10 g sugars), 23 g pro.

Curried Chicken Salad

SERVINGS 4 (1 cup each)
CARB. PER SERVING 24 g
PREP 25 minutes **CHILL** 1 hour

- 2 skinless, boneless chicken breast halves (about 8 ounces total)
- Dash onion powder
- Dash garlic powder
- 1 Gala or Fuji apple, cored and chopped
- $1/2$ cup sliced green onions (4)
- $1/2$ cup chopped celery
- $1/3$ cup golden raisins
- $1/4$ cup sliced almonds, toasted
- 1 recipe Curried Salad Dressing
- 4 Boston or Bibb lettuce leaves

1. Heat a medium nonstick skillet over medium heat. Coat chicken with *nonstick cooking spray* and sprinkle with onion and garlic powders. Cook in hot skillet 8 to 10 minutes or until no longer pink (165°F). Cool; cut into bite-size pieces.
2. In a bowl combine chicken, apple, green onions, celery, raisins, and almonds. Add Curried Salad Dressing; toss. Cover; chill 1 to 4 hours.
3. To serve, spoon 1 cup of the salad into each lettuce leaf.

CURRIED SALAD DRESSING: In a bowl stir together $1/2$ cup light sour cream, 1 to 2 teaspoons curry powder, 1 teaspoon honey, $1/2$ teaspoon ground ginger, and a dash cayenne pepper.

PER SERVING: 217 cal., 7 g total fat (2 g sat. fat), 50 mg chol., 61 mg sodium, 24 g carb. (3 g fiber, 15 g sugars), 16 g pro.

PORK TENDERLOIN
SANDWICHES

CURRIED
CHICKEN SALAD

OPEN-FACE REUBENS

Open-Face Reubens

SERVINGS 4 (1 sandwich each)
CARB. PER SERVING 22 g
START TO FINISH 20 minutes

- 4 slices pumpernickel or dark rye bread
- 6 ounces thinly sliced lower-sodium deli roast beef
- 4 slices reduced-fat Swiss cheese (3 to 4 ounces)
- 5 cups packaged shredded cabbage with carrot (coleslaw mix)
- 1 tablespoon water
- ½ teaspoon caraway seeds, crushed
- 2 tablespoons light mayonnaise
- 1 tablespoon cider vinegar

1. Preheat broiler. Place bread slices on a large baking sheet. Broil 5 to 6 inches from the heat 2 to 4 minutes or until toasted, turning once.
2. To assemble, arrange beef on bread slices. Top with cheese. Broil about 2 minutes more or until cheese is melted.
3. Meanwhile, heat a large skillet over medium heat. Add coleslaw mix, the water, and caraway seeds to hot skillet. Cover and cook 2 to 3 minutes or until cabbage is wilted, stirring often. Remove from heat. Stir in mayonnaise and vinegar.
4. To serve, spoon cabbage mixture over sandwiches and serve open-face.

PER SERVING: 239 cal., 9 g total fat (3 g sat. fat), 39 mg chol., 586 mg sodium, 22 g carb. (4 g fiber, 4 g sugars), 19 g pro.

Peppery, Crispy Oven Fries

SERVINGS 4 (¾ cup each)
CARB. PER SERVING 18 g
PREP 25 minutes **BAKE** 30 minutes

- ½ teaspoon garlic powder
- ½ teaspoon smoked paprika
- ¼ to ½ teaspoon black pepper
- ¼ teaspoon salt
- 1 pound russet potatoes
- 2 tablespoons olive oil
  Nonstick cooking spray

1. Arrange two oven racks in the top and bottom thirds of the oven. Preheat oven to

PEPPERY, CRISPY OVEN FRIES

350°F. In a small bowl combine garlic powder, smoked paprika, pepper, and salt; set aside.
2. Cut potatoes into ¼-inch-wide strips.* Place potato strips in a large bowl; add enough cold water to cover; stir. Drain in a colander. Repeat rinsing and draining two or three times until water runs clear. Drain again, gently tossing potatoes in colander to drain off as much water as you can. Layer several paper towels on a clean work surface. Transfer potato strips to paper towels. Use additional paper towels to pat potatoes as dry as possible.
3. Place potatoes in another dry large bowl. Drizzle with oil; sprinkle with pepper mixture. Toss to coat.
4. Generously coat two large baking sheets with cooking spray. Arrange coated potato strips in a single layer on the prepared baking sheets. Place one baking sheet on each oven rack. Bake 15 minutes. Remove baking sheets from oven. Increase oven temperature to 450°F. Return baking sheets to oven. Bake 15 to 18 minutes more or until browned and crisp, turning potatoes once halfway through.
***CHEF'S SECRET:** Take your time and be sure to cut even-size ¼-inch-wide strips. This is important for evenly cooked potatoes.

PER SERVING: 146 cal., 7 g total fat (1 g sat. fat), 0 mg chol., 164 mg sodium, 18 g carb. (3 g fiber, 1 g sugars), 2 g pro.

PUMPKIN-CHICKEN ENCHILADAS

SERVINGS 4 (2 enchiladas each)
CARB. PER SERVING 44 g
PREP 35 minutes   **BAKE** 25 minutes

- 2 teaspoons olive oil
- 1/2 cup chopped onion (1 medium)
- 1 fresh jalapeño chile pepper, seeded and finely chopped (tip, *page 252*)
- 1 15-ounce can pumpkin
- 1 teaspoon chili powder
- 1/2 teaspoon ground cumin
- 1 cup no-salt-added red kidney beans, rinsed and drained*
- 1 1/2 cups shredded cooked chicken breast
- 1/2 cup shredded part-skim mozzarella cheese (2 ounces)
- 8 6-inch white corn tortillas, softened

1. Preheat oven to 400°F. Lightly coat a 2-quart rectangular baking dish with *nonstick cooking spray;* set aside. In a medium saucepan heat oil over medium-high heat. Add onion and chile pepper; cook and stir 5 minutes. Stir in pumpkin, 1 1/2 cups *water,* chili powder, 1/2 teaspoon *salt,* and the cumin. Heat through. If necessary, stir in 1/4 cup *water* to make desired consistency.

2. In a large bowl slightly mash beans. Stir in half of the pumpkin mixture, the chicken, and 1/4 cup of the cheese.

3. Spoon 1/3 cup of the bean mixture onto each tortilla. Roll up tortillas; place, seam sides down, in the prepared baking dish. Pour the remaining pumpkin mixture over tortilla roll-ups.

4. Bake, covered, 15 minutes. Sprinkle with the remaining 1/4 cup cheese. Bake, uncovered, about 10 minutes more or until heated through. If desired, serve with *pico de gallo.*

*CHEF'S SECRET: Some supermarkets stock no-salt-added beans in the organic area of the store. Also, store brands labeled as unseasoned typically do not contain added salt.

PER SERVING: 357 cal., 8 g total fat (3 g sat. fat), 54 mg chol., 465 mg sodium, 44 g carb. (12 g fiber, 5 g sugars), 28 g pro.

Loaded Nachos

SERVINGS 4 (16 tortilla wedges with toppings each)
CARB. PER SERVING 23 g
PREP 30 minutes **BAKE** 10 minutes

LOADED NACHOS

- 8 6-inch corn tortillas
- Nonstick cooking spray
- 2 teaspoons unsalted butter
- 1 tablespoon all-purpose flour
- ¾ cup fat-free milk
- ½ cup shredded part-skim mozzarella cheese (2 ounces)
- ½ cup shredded reduced-fat cheddar cheese (2 ounces)
- 1 ounce fat-free cream cheese, softened
- ¼ teaspoon paprika
- ¼ teaspoon ground turmeric
- 8 ounces extra-lean ground beef (95% lean)
- ¼ cup water
- 1 recipe Homemade Taco Seasoning
- 1 cup chopped tomato (1 large)
- ½ cup chopped green or red sweet pepper (1 small)
- ¼ cup sliced green onions (2)
- 1 fresh jalapeño chile pepper, stemmed, seeded, and thinly sliced (tip, *page 252*) (optional)
- ½ cup chunky mild salsa*
- 2 tablespoons snipped fresh cilantro

1. Preheat oven to 375°F. Cut each tortilla into eight wedges. Place tortilla wedges in a single layer on a large baking sheet. Coat wedges with cooking spray. Bake 10 to 13 minutes or until wedges are crisp and golden brown on edges. Set aside.

2. Meanwhile, for cheese sauce, in a small saucepan melt butter over medium heat. Stir in flour until combined. Whisk in milk until smooth. Cook and stir until thickened and bubbly. Cook 2 minutes more. Stir in mozzarella cheese, cheddar cheese, cream cheese, paprika, and turmeric. Cook and stir over medium heat until cheese is melted and mixture is smooth. Reduce heat to low. Hold cheese sauce over low heat until needed, stirring occasionally.

3. Coat a large skillet with cooking spray; heat skillet over medium heat. Add meat; cook until browned, using a spoon to break up meat as it cooks. Drain off fat. Stir the water and Homemade Taco Seasoning into meat in skillet. Cook and stir 3 to 5 minutes more or until most of the water has evaporated.

4. To serve, arrange tortilla wedges on a serving plate. Top with meat mixture, cheese sauce, tomato, sweet pepper, green onions, and, if desired, chile pepper. Serve with salsa and cilantro.

HOMEMADE TACO SEASONING: In a bowl stir together 2 teaspoons paprika, 1 teaspoon ground cumin, ½ to 1 teaspoon black pepper, ½ teaspoon ground coriander, ⅛ to ¼ teaspoon ground chipotle chile pepper, and ⅛ teaspoon cayenne pepper.

*CHEF'S SECRET: Read the nutritional facts on the labels of the salsas available at your grocery store. Choose the salsa that's lowest in sodium. Newman's Own Mild Salsa is a good choice.

PER SERVING: 291 cal., 11 g total fat (6 g sat. fat), 61 mg chol., 356 mg sodium, 23 g carb. (3 g fiber, 6 g sugars), 24 g pro.

Shrimp Tacos with Avocado Topper

SERVINGS 4 (2 tacos each)
CARB. PER SERVING 31 g
START TO FINISH 25 minutes

        1   avocado, seeded, peeled, and chopped
      ¼   cup fresh cilantro leaves
        4   teaspoons finely chopped jalapeño chile
            pepper (tip, *page 252*)
      ½   teaspoon finely shredded lime peel
        4   teaspoons lime juice
        1   teaspoon chili powder
        1   pound fresh or frozen medium shrimp
            in shells
        2   teaspoons olive oil
        2   cloves garlic, minced
        1   teaspoon grated fresh ginger*
      ¼   teaspoon black pepper
        8   6-inch white corn tortillas, warmed
            according to package directions
    1½   cups packaged shredded cabbage with
            carrot (coleslaw mix)
      ⅔   cup chopped red sweet pepper
        4   lime wedges

1. In a medium bowl combine avocado, cilantro, chile pepper, lime peel, lime juice, and chili powder. Lightly mash with a fork; cover and set aside.

2. Thaw shrimp, if frozen. Peel, devein, and halve shrimp lengthwise. Rinse shrimp; pat dry with paper towels. In a large skillet heat olive oil over medium heat. Add garlic and ginger; cook and stir 30 seconds. Add shrimp; sprinkle with black pepper. Cook 3 to 4 minutes or until shrimp are opaque.

3. Place two tortillas on each of two plates. Divide coleslaw mix and sweet pepper among tortillas, leaving half of each tortilla uncovered. Add warm shrimp; top with avocado mixture. Fold over each tortilla to form a taco. Serve with lime wedges.

*CHEF'S SECRET: Keep ginger wrapped in plastic wrap and sealed in a resealable plastic bag in the freezer. It will last longer and grates easier than fresh ginger.

PER SERVING: 285 cal., 10 g total fat (1 g sat. fat), 143 mg chol., 589 mg sodium, 31 g carb. (7 g fiber, 3 g sugars), 20 g pro.

Skinny Guacamole

SERVINGS 24 (2 tablespoons each)
CARB. PER SERVING 3 g
PREP 25 minutes   **ROAST** 20 minutes
STAND 15 minutes

- 2 medium green sweet peppers
- 2 medium fresh poblano chile peppers
- 1 bulb garlic
- ½ teaspoon olive oil
- 2 medium avocados, halved, seeded, peeled, and cut up
- 1 teaspoon finely shredded lemon peel
- 2 tablespoons lemon juice
- ½ teaspoon salt
- ¼ teaspoon crushed red pepper
- 2 roma tomatoes, seeded and chopped

1. Preheat oven to 425°F. Line a 15×10×1-inch baking pan with foil; set aside. Quarter, stem, and seed chile peppers (tip, *page 252*). Place pepper quarters, cut sides down, in the prepared pan. Cut off the top ½ inch of the garlic bulb to expose ends of individual cloves. Leaving garlic bulb whole, remove any loose, papery outer layers. Place bulb, cut end up, on a double thickness of foil. Drizzle with the oil. Bring foil up around bulb and fold edges together to loosely enclose. Place foil packet on the pan with the peppers.

2. Roast peppers and garlic 20 to 30 minutes or until pepper skins are charred and garlic cloves feel soft. Bring foil up around pepper quarters and fold edges to enclose. Let stand about 15 minutes or until cool enough to handle. Using a sharp knife, gently pull skins off pepper pieces and discard. When garlic head is cool enough to handle, squeeze garlic paste out of the individual cloves.

3. In a food processor combine roasted pepper quarters and the garlic paste. Cover and process until nearly smooth. Add avocados, lemon peel, lemon juice, salt, and crushed red pepper. Cover and pulse with several on-off turns until mixture is slightly chunky, scraping sides of bowl as needed. Transfer to a serving bowl; stir in tomatoes. Serve immediately or cover the surface with plastic wrap and chill up to 1 hour.

PER SERVING: 29 cal., 2 g total fat (0 g sat. fat), 0 mg chol., 51 mg sodium, 3 g carb. (1 g fiber, 1 g sugars), 1 g pro.

SKINNY GUACAMOLE

Chili-Lime Chicken Tostada with Pico de Gallo and Chipotle Crema

SERVINGS 4 (1 tortilla and about 2 cups toppings each)
CARB. PER SERVING 41 g
PREP 50 minutes **MARINATE** 30 minutes
BAKE 45 minutes

- 2 teaspoons finely shredded lime peel
- ¼ cup lime juice
- 2 tablespoons agave nectar
- 6 cloves garlic, minced
- 2 teaspoons chili powder
- 1¼ pounds bone-in chicken breast halves, skinned
- ¼ teaspoon black pepper
- ⅛ teaspoon salt
- ¼ cup plain fat-free yogurt
- ¼ cup light mayonnaise or salad dressing
- 2 canned chipotle chile peppers in adobo sauce, minced (about 1 tablespoon) (tip, *page 252*)
- 1 tablespoon lime juice
- 1 teaspoon agave nectar
- 4 corn tortillas
  Nonstick cooking spray
- 1 cup no-salt-added canned black beans, rinsed and drained
- ¼ cup reduced-sodium chicken broth
- 4 cups shredded romaine lettuce
- 1 recipe Pico de Gallo
- ¼ cup shredded reduced-fat Mexican-style four-cheese blend (1 ounce)

1. For marinade, in a small bowl combine lime peel, the ¼ cup lime juice, the 2 tablespoons agave nectar, the garlic, and chili powder. Place chicken in a resealable plastic bag set in a shallow dish. Pour marinade over chicken in bag; turn once to coat chicken. Marinate in the refrigerator 30 minutes, turning bag occasionally.

2. Preheat oven to 375°F. Drain chicken, discarding marinade. Arrange chicken in a 15×10×1-inch baking pan. Sprinkle chicken with black pepper and salt. Bake about 45 minutes or until chicken is tender and no longer pink (170°F). When cool enough to handle, remove meat from bone and shred or cut into bite-size pieces.

3. Meanwhile, for the chipotle crema, in a small food processor combine yogurt, mayonnaise, chile peppers, the 1 tablespoon lime juice, and the 1 teaspoon agave nectar. Cover and process until combined.

4. Preheat broiler. Place tortillas on a baking sheet. Coat both sides of each tortilla with cooking spray. Broil 4 inches from the heat 2 to 3 minutes or until crisp and golden brown, turning once halfway through.

5. Meanwhile, in a medium nonstick skillet combine chicken, black beans, and broth. Cook, covered, over medium-high heat until heated through (165°F), stirring occasionally.

6. Place tortillas on four plates. Top each tortilla with 1 cup of the shredded romaine, one-fourth of the chicken-black bean mixture, about ¼ cup of the Pico de Gallo, 2 tablespoons of the chipotle crema, and 1 tablespoon of the cheese.

PICO DE GALLO: In a bowl stir together 1 cup chopped tomatoes; 2 tablespoons chopped red onion; 2 tablespoons snipped fresh cilantro; 1 tablespoon minced fresh jalapeño chile pepper (tip, *page 252*); 1 tablespoon lime juice; 2 cloves garlic, minced; and ⅛ teaspoon salt.

CHEF'S SECRET: The chicken, chipotle crema, and Pico de Gallo can each be prepared, placed in airtight containers, and stored in the refrigerator up to 3 days.

PER SERVING: 402 cal., 11 g total fat (3 g sat. fat), 82 mg chol., 492 mg sodium, 41 g carb. (8 g fiber, 13 g sugars), 36 g pro.

CHILI-LIME CHICKEN
TOSTADA with PICO de GALLO and
CHIPOTLE CREMA

TIPS FOR dining out

Most Americans eat out at least three times a week—that's more than 150 meals a year. This can have a big impact on your health, so eat right when you eat out.

CHEF'S SECRETS
to staying on track

Chef Art Smith gives insights on how to eat out while following a healthful eating plan.

1 START OFF RIGHT. "If you begin your day with a healthy breakfast, I believe you're less likely to cheat later on," Smith says. Some smart protein- and fiber-rich breakfast options at his restaurants are steel-cut oats with fresh berries, an egg white omelet with garden vegetables, and Greek yogurt with fresh blueberries.

2 GUIDE THE RESTAURANT CHOICE. When you're going out with a group, suggest an eating place with healthful choices. For example, Mexican restaurants can be a land mine of carbs and fat thanks to foods such as refried beans and tortilla chips. A restaurant that serves locally grown foods would be a better bet. You can find other good options at *healthydiningfinder.com*.

3 RESEARCH BEFORE YOU GO. Many restaurants provide nutrition information online, but if they don't post the nutrition details, check similar menu items on sites such as *calorieking .com*. "Look into the things you think you can have so you're not blindsided when you get to the restaurant," Smith says.

4 OPT FOR WHOLE, BASIC FOODS. Choose lean grilled meat, such as a skinless, boneless chicken breast or salmon, instead of a pasta entrée smothered in cream sauce. Similarly, pick steamed broccoli over broccoli casserole and choose a baked potato topped with salsa instead of french fries.

5 BEWARE OF HEALTH HALOS. "When people see something is low-fat, they tend to lose sight of how much they're eating and end up consuming too many calories," Smith says. So even if you order a sirloin steak, which is a leaner option, don't pick the 12-ounce cut—opt for the 6-ounce steak, which ends up closer to a sensible 4 ounces after cooking.

6 EAT PLANTS. "Eat vegetarian when you're in doubt about what's healthy on the menu," Smith says. For example, choose a leafy green salad (just watch the toppings) or a vegetarian burger. Swapping a beef burger with a veggie burger could cut calories in half, if not more.

3 questions to ask your waiter

"Waiters are not your doctor, so don't expect them to know everything about eating with diabetes," Chef Art Smith says. "What they can help you with is communicating with the chef about your special dietary needs." Here are some questions to put at the top of your list:

1 Could you use less salt and fat? A study that evaluated menus from 245 restaurants across the country found that an average dinner entrée packs 1,512 milligrams of sodium. That's a full day's allowance for a person with diabetes. Extra fat is also often added for flavor. Smith suggests asking for olive oil instead of butter and for minimal oil in your dish.

2 Would you put condiments on the side? Many restaurants that post nutrition information online list condiments such as sauces and dressings separately rather than in the nutrition count for the main item. These extras typically add 100–200 calories to the dish due to the fat and carbohydrate they contain.

3 Can I substitute? In many cases, there's no charge for a simple swap. And even if a substitution costs a bit more, it's worth it. For example, if your meal comes with french fries, ask if you can sub steamed broccoli. Swapping grilled asparagus might be an upcharge, but it's a treat.

ETIQUETTE CHECK: testing at the table

Check your blood sugar any time and any place you need to—even if you're seated at a restaurant booth. Do what you need to do to keep yourself healthy and safe.

READ BETWEEN THE LINES

Understand the menu. "Fried" and "gravy" are key watch-out words, but other descriptions signal better choices.

Red flags	Lighter lingo
• Bottomless	• Au jus
• Cheese or au gratin	• Blackened
• Cream/creamy	• Broiled
• Crispy/crusted	• Fresh
• Double or triple	• Grilled
• Hand-breaded/battered	• Half-size
• Loaded	• Lighter
• Prime	• Mini
• Smothered	• Seasonal
• Stuffed	• Steamed

CARB alert

A few strategic choices can make all the difference
in whether you control your carbohydrate intake
or completely overshoot your limit.

APPETIZERS Don't order an appetizer instead of an entrée. Many are fried, and most are sized to serve more than one. They can have as many or more carbs and calories as a main dish.

SOUP If you order soup, estimate 15–20 grams of carbohydrate per cup if it contains starchy vegetables, rice, barley, noodles, or beans, or if it's creamy, which often means milk, flour, or cornstarch has been added.

BREAD and BAKED GOODS Halve the carbs in your sandwich by eating it open-face. Watch out for muffins, which can have more calories and carbs than a cupcake.

BREADED MEAT Grilled meats are virtually carb-free. Breaded items, like chicken-fried steak, are loaded with carbohydrate and fat.

SAUCES and GLAZES Gravies and sweet or savory sauces contain carbohydrate grams from the ingredients used to make them, like sugar, flour, and milk. Use sauces sparingly.

STARCHY SIDES Restaurant portions of rice, beans, and french fries are often out of line, so eat half or less of what's served.

BEVERAGES "Don't drink your calories," Chef Art Smith says. "Besides obvious sources such as soda, a lot of cocktails are full of sugar." Additionally, a fancy coffee drink or tall glass of orange juice, lemonade, or sweet tea could chew through your carbohydrate allowance for the meal.

DESSERT A whole serving of dessert is usually out of the question. However, a bite or two of a shared dessert is often doable.

cook it SLOW

Save time and effort by letting your slow cooker do the work to create these humble yet hearty meals. You'll find a collection of classic family pleasers, a few unexpected twists, and several tasty side dishes.

CROCK·POT
◆ THE ORIGINAL SLOW COOKER ◆

Low   High

Off   Warm

BEER-BRAISED POT ROAST
with PARSNIPS and CARROTS

recipe on *page 248*

Beer-Braised Pot Roast with Parsnips and Carrots

photo on *page 247*

SERVINGS 8 (3 to 4 ounces cooked beef and $^1/_2$ cup vegetables with $^1/_4$ cup sauce each)

CARB. PER SERVING 19 g

PREP 30 minutes SLOW COOK 11 to 12 hours (low) or $5^1/_2$ to 6 hours (high)

- 4 parsnips, peeled and cut into 2-inch pieces
- 4 carrots, peeled and cut into 2-inch pieces
- 1 large onion, cut into thin wedges
- 2 bay leaves
- 4 cloves garlic, minced
- 2 tablespoons quick-cooking tapioca
- 1 3- to $3^1/_2$-pound boneless beef chuck or arm roast, trimmed of excess fat
- 2 tablespoons Dijon-style mustard
- $^1/_2$ teaspoon black pepper
- 1 12-ounce bottle dark beer (such as Guinness)
- 1 8-ounce can no-salt-added tomato sauce
- 2 tablespoons Worcestershire sauce
  Snipped fresh parsley

1. Place parsnips, carrots, onion wedges, bay leaves, and garlic in a 6-quart slow cooker. Sprinkle with tapioca. Spread both sides of roast with the mustard and sprinkle with pepper. Place roast on vegetables. In a medium bowl stir together the beer, tomato sauce, and Worcestershire sauce. Pour over meat. Cover and cook on low-heat setting 11 to 12 hours or on high-heat setting $5^1/_2$ to 6 hours.

2. Carefully remove roast and vegetables from cooker and place on a platter. Remove and discard bay leaves. Skim fat from sauce. Drizzle with some of the sauce and sprinkle with parsley. Pass remaining sauce.

PER SERVING: 325 cal., 10 g total fat (5 g sat. fat), 117 mg chol., 308 mg sodium, 19 g carb. (4 g fiber, 6 g sugars), 37 g pro.

Beef Rigatoni Stew

SERVINGS 6 ($1^1/_3$ cups each)

CARB. PER SERVING 32 g

PREP 30 minutes SLOW COOK 10 to 12 hours (low) or 4 to 5 hours (high) + 30 minutes (high)

- 1 2-pound boneless beef chuck arm pot roast, trimmed of fat and cut into 2-inch chunks
- $^1/_2$ teaspoon salt
- $^1/_4$ teaspoon black pepper
- 1 tablespoon olive oil
- 2 cups 50%-less-sodium beef broth
- 1 14.5-ounce can no-salt-added stewed tomatoes, undrained
- $^1/_2$ cup chopped onion
- $^1/_2$ cup chopped celery
- $^1/_2$ cup chopped carrot
- $^1/_2$ cup chopped bottled roasted red peppers
- $^1/_2$ cup dry red wine or cranberry juice
- $^1/_4$ cup fat-free half-and-half
- 1 tablespoon all-purpose flour
- 6 ounces dried rigatoni pasta
- 2 tablespoons Parmesan cheese shavings

1. Season beef with $^1/_4$ teaspoon of the salt and the black pepper. In a large skillet heat oil over medium-high heat; cook meat in hot oil until browned on all sides. Drain off fat.

2. In a $3^1/_2$- or 4-quart slow cooker combine the beef, beef broth, tomatoes, onion, celery, carrot, roasted red peppers, red wine, and remaining $^1/_4$ teaspoon salt. Cover and cook on low-heat setting 10 to 12 hours or on high-heat setting 4 to 5 hours.

3. Using a slotted spoon, transfer meat to a cutting board. Skim fat from cooking liquid. Using two forks, pull meat into shreds; return to cooker.

4. If using low-heat setting, turn to high-heat setting. In a small bowl combine the half-and-half and flour. Stir half-and-half mixture and rigatoni into beef mixture in the cooker. Cover and cook 30 minutes more. Top each serving with Parmesan cheese.

PER SERVING: 401 cal., 10 g total fat (3 g sat. fat), 100 mg chol., 509 mg sodium, 32 g carb. (3 g fiber, 6 g sugars), 40 g pro.

BEEF
RIGATONI STEW

Honey-Orange Chicken with Butternut Squash

SERVINGS 6 (1 chicken thigh, $^2/_3$ cup squash mixture, and $^1/_3$ cup quinoa each)
CARB. PER SERVING 33 g
PREP 25 minutes   **SLOW COOK** 7 to 8 hours (low) or $3^1/_2$ to 4 hours (high)

- 6 skinless, boneless chicken thighs (about $1^1/_2$ pounds total)
- 3 cups $^1/_2$-inch pieces fresh butternut squash
- 1 medium onion, cut into $^1/_2$-inch wedges
- $^1/_4$ cup orange juice
- 2 tablespoons cornstarch
- 2 tablespoons reduced-sodium soy sauce
- 2 tablespoons honey
- 2 teaspoons grated fresh ginger
- 2 cloves garlic, minced
- $^1/_4$ teaspoon salt
- $^1/_4$ teaspoon crushed red pepper
- 2 cups hot cooked quinoa
- 2 tablespoons sliced almonds, toasted

1. Place chicken in a 4- to 5-quart slow cooker. Top with butternut squash and onion. In a small bowl whisk together orange juice, cornstarch, soy sauce, honey, ginger, garlic, salt, and crushed red pepper. Pour over chicken and vegetables. Cover and cook on low-heat setting 7 to 8 hours or on high-heat setting $3^1/_2$ to 4 hours.

2. Serve chicken mixture over hot cooked quinoa. Sprinkle with almonds.

PER SERVING: 297 cal., 7 g total fat (1 g sat. fat), 107 mg chol., 370 mg sodium, 33 g carb. (4 g fiber, 10 g sugars), 26 g pro.

Classic Beef Stroganoff

SERVINGS 6 (about ³⁄₄ cup each)
CARB. PER SERVING 14 g
PREP 30 minutes **SLOW COOK** 8 to 10 hours (low) or 4 to 5 hours (high) + 30 minutes (high)

1¼	pounds beef stew meat
2	teaspoons vegetable oil
2½	cups sliced fresh mushrooms
½	cup sliced green onions (4) or chopped onion (1 medium)
1	bay leaf
2	cloves garlic, minced
½	teaspoon dried oregano, crushed
¼	teaspoon salt
¼	teaspoon dried thyme, crushed
¼	teaspoon black pepper
1½	cups 50%-less-sodium beef broth
¼	cup dry sherry
1	8-ounce carton light sour cream
⅓	cup all-purpose flour
¼	cup water
	Sautéed zucchini "noodles" or hot cooked whole wheat pasta
	Snipped fresh basil or parsley (optional)

1. Cut up any large pieces of meat. In a large nonstick skillet cook half of the meat in hot oil over medium-high heat until browned. Using a slotted spoon, remove meat from skillet. Repeat with the remaining meat. Drain off fat. Set meat aside.

2. In a 3½- or 4-quart slow cooker combine mushrooms, green onions, bay leaf, garlic, oregano, salt, thyme, and pepper. Add meat. Pour broth and sherry over mixture in cooker. Cover and cook on low-heat setting 8 to 10 hours or on high-heat setting 4 to 5 hours. Remove and discard bay leaf.

3. If using low-heat setting, turn to high-heat setting. In a medium bowl stir together sour cream, flour, and the water until smooth. Gradually stir about 1 cup of the hot broth into sour cream mixture. Return sour cream mixture

to cooker; stir to combine. Cover and cook about 30 minutes more or until thickened and bubbly. Serve over sautéed zucchini and, if desired, sprinkle with parsley.

PER SERVING: 257 cal., 10 g total fat (5 g sat. fat), 74 mg chol., 312 mg sodium, 14 g carb. (2 g fiber, 4 g sugars), 26 g pro.

CLASSIC BEEF STROGANOFF

KOREAN-STYLE BEEF TACOS

SERVINGS 10 (1 taco each)
CARB. PER SERVING 25 g or 24 g
PREP 30 minutes   **SLOW COOK** 10 to 12 hours (low) or 5 to 6 hours (high)

- 1 cup 50%-less-sodium beef broth
- 1 cooking apple or pear, peeled, cored, and chopped (1 cup)
- 1 medium onion, cut into wedges (½ cup)
- 3 tablespoons reduced-sodium soy sauce
- 3 tablespoons finely chopped fresh ginger
- 1 fresh serrano chile pepper, halved, seeded, and finely chopped
- 1 tablespoon packed brown sugar*
- 5 cloves garlic, minced
- ½ teaspoon black pepper
- ¼ teaspoon Chinese five-spice powder
- 1 2-pound boneless beef eye round roast, trimmed of fat and cut into 2-inch pieces
- 4 cups packaged shredded cabbage with carrot (coleslaw mix)
- ¼ cup rice vinegar
- ¼ cup thinly sliced green onions
- ¼ cup snipped fresh cilantro
- 10 8-inch low-carb, high-fiber whole wheat tortillas, warmed

1. In a 4- to 5-quart slow cooker combine broth, apple, onion, soy sauce, ginger, chile pepper, brown sugar, garlic, black pepper, and five-spice powder. Stir in beef. Cover and cook on low-heat setting 10 to 12 hours or high-heat setting 5 to 6 hours.

2. Meanwhile, in a large bowl toss together the coleslaw mix, rice vinegar, green onions, and cilantro. Cover and chill slaw until ready to serve.

3. Using a slotted spoon, transfer meat mixture to a large bowl. Using two forks, pull meat into shreds. Moisten meat mixture with cooking liquid. Serve beef mixture topped with slaw in warmed tortillas. Pass additional liquid.

*SUGAR SUBSTITUTE: Use Splenda Brown Sugar Blend. Follow package directions to use product amount equivalent to 1 tablespoon brown sugar.

PER SERVING: 225 cal., 5 g total fat (1 g sat. fat), 43 mg chol., 568 mg sodium, 25 g carb. (13 g fiber, 6 g sugars), 30 g pro.
PER SERVING WITH SUBSTITUE: same as above, except 223 cal., 24 g carb. (5 g sugars).

HANDLING CHILE PEPPERS

Because hot chile peppers contain volatile oils that can burn your skin and eyes, avoid direct contact with chiles as much as possible. When working with chile peppers, wear plastic or rubber gloves. If your bare hands do touch the chile peppers, wash your hands well with soap and water.

PIZZA SPAGHETTI

SERVINGS 8 (1¼ cups each)
CARB. PER SERVING 33 g
PREP 30 minutes **SLOW COOK** 6 to 8 hours (low)
or 3 to 4 hours (high)

- 12 ounces uncooked bulk Italian-style turkey sausage
- 1 8-ounce package fresh sliced button mushrooms
- 1 tablespoon olive oil
- Nonstick cooking spray
- 1 28-ounce can no-salt-added whole peeled tomatoes, drained and snipped

1 14.5-ounce can no-salt-added-fire roasted diced tomatoes, drained
1 cup chopped onion
1 medium green sweet pepper, chopped
2 ounces thinly sliced cooked turkey pepperoni, chopped (¾ cup)
½ cup no-salt-added tomato sauce
1 teaspoon dried oregano, crushed
¼ teaspoon fennel seeds, crushed
¼ teaspoon salt
¼ teaspoon garlic powder
8 ounces dried spaghetti
8 teaspoons finely shredded Parmesan cheese (optional)

1. In a large skillet cook sausage and mushrooms in hot oil over medium heat until meat is browned, stirring to break up meat as it cooks. Drain off fat.

2. Coat the inside of a 3½- or 4-quart slow cooker with cooking spray. Add the cooked sausage mixture, drained tomatoes, onion, sweet pepper, pepperoni, tomato sauce, oregano, fennel, salt, and garlic powder. Cover and cook on low-heat setting 6 to 8 hours or on high-heat setting 3 to 4 hours.

3. Cook pasta according to package directions. Drain. Add cooked pasta to slow cooker. Stir to combine. If desired, top with Parmesan cheese.

PER SERVING: 255 cal., 7 g total fat (2 g sat. fat), 36 mg chol., 587 mg sodium, 33 g carb. (4 g fiber, 7 g sugars), 15 g pro.

Porter and Roasted Red Pepper Sloppy Joes

SERVINGS 12 (1 sandwich each)
CARB. PER SERVING 30 g
PREP 25 minutes   SLOW COOK 7 to 8 hours (low) or 3½ to 4 hours (high)

1½ pounds extra-lean ground beef
1 cup chopped onion (1 large)
1½ cups bottled roasted red sweet pepper strips
1 8-ounce can no-salt-added tomato sauce
½ cup chili sauce
1 tablespoon molasses
1 tablespoon Dijon-style mustard

PORTER and ROASTED RED PEPPER SLOPPY JOES

1 tablespoon reduced-sodium Worcestershire sauce
2 cloves garlic, minced
1 teaspoon dried oregano, crushed
½ teaspoon salt
½ teaspoon dried thyme, crushed
½ teaspoon black pepper
½ cup porter beer or other dark beer
12 whole wheat buns, split and toasted

1. In a large skillet cook ground beef and onion over medium heat until meat is browned, using a spoon to break up meat as it cooks. Drain off fat.

2. In a 3½- or 4-quart slow cooker combine meat mixture, roasted pepper strips, tomato sauce, chili sauce, molasses, Dijon mustard, Worcestershire sauce, garlic, oregano, salt, thyme, and black pepper. Stir in beer. Cover and cook on low-heat setting 7 to 8 hours or on high-heat setting 3½ to 4 hours.

3. Using a slotted spoon, fill buns with meat mixture.

PER SERVING: 225 cal., 4 g total fat (1 g sat. fat), 35 mg chol., 519 mg sodium, 30 g carb. (4 g fiber, 9 g sugars), 17 g pro.

Chicken and Zucchini Stew with Olive Gremolata

SERVINGS 8 (1½ cups each)
CARB. PER SERVING 15 g
PREP 30 minutes **SLOW COOK** 5 to 6 hours (low) or 2½ to 3 hours (high) + 15 minutes (high)

- ¾ cup chopped red sweet pepper
- ½ cup chopped onion
- ½ cup chopped carrot
- ½ ounce dried porcini or shiitake mushrooms
- 6 chicken thighs (2¼ pounds total), skin removed
- 2 14.5-ounce cans no-salt-added diced tomatoes, undrained
- 2 cups reduced-sodium chicken broth
- 3 medium zucchini, halved lengthwise and sliced
- 2 tablespoons balsamic vinegar
- ⅓ cup pimiento-stuffed green olives, chopped
- 2 tablespoons coarsely snipped fresh basil
- 1 tablespoon finely shredded orange or lemon peel
- 1 tablespoon snipped fresh rosemary or 1 teaspoon dried rosemary, crushed

1. In a 4- to 5-quart slow cooker combine sweet pepper, onion, carrot, mushrooms, ¼ teaspoon *salt*, and ¼ teaspoon *black pepper*. Place chicken on top of vegetables, overlapping as needed. Add diced tomatoes and broth. Cover and cook on low-heat setting 5 to 6 hours or on high-heat setting 2½ to 3 hours.
2. Using a slotted spoon, transfer chicken to a large bowl. When chicken is cool enough to handle, remove meat from bones; discard bones. Using two forks, pull meat into shreds. Return chicken to slow cooker; add zucchini pieces and vinegar. If using low-heat setting, turn to high-heat setting. Cover and cook 15 minutes more or until zucchini is just tender.
3. In a small bowl combine olives, basil, lemon peel, and rosemary. Serve stew topped with olive mixture.

PER SERVING: 206 cal., 6 g total fat (1 g sat. fat), 97 mg chol., 555 mg sodium, 15 g carb. (5 g fiber, 10 g sugars), 24 g pro.

Maple-Mustard-Sauced Turkey Thighs

SERVINGS 4 (1 turkey thigh and ¾ cup potatoes each)
CARB. PER SERVING 32 g
PREP 20 minutes **SLOW COOK** 6 to 7 hours (low) or 3 to 3½ hours (high)

- 1 pound tiny new potatoes, quartered
- 4 turkey thighs (2 to 2½ pounds total), skin removed
- ⅓ cup coarse-ground brown mustard
- 3 tablespoons pure maple syrup
- 1 tablespoon quick-cooking tapioca

1. Place potatoes in a 3½- or 4-quart slow cooker. Place turkey thighs on top of potatoes. In a small bowl stir together mustard, maple syrup, and tapioca. Pour mixture over turkey.
2. Cover and cook on low-heat setting 6 to 7 hours or on high-heat setting 3 to 3½ hours. Serve turkey thighs topped with maple sauce.

PER SERVING: 317 cal., 6 g total fat (2 g sat. fat), 128 mg chol., 363 mg sodium, 32 g carb. (2 g fiber, 11 g sugars), 32 g pro.

CHICKEN and ZUCCHINI STEW with OLIVE GREMOLATA

MAPLE-MUSTARD-SAUCED
TURKEY THIGHS

TURKEY BREAST with CURRY and LEMON

SERVINGS 6 (3 ounces turkey,
½ cup couscous, and ⅓ cup sauce each)
CARB. PER SERVING 40 g
PREP 25 minutes **SLOW COOK** 4 to 5 hours
(low) or 2 to 2½ hours (high)
STAND 30 minutes

  1 teaspoon curry powder
  ¾ teaspoon salt
  ½ teaspoon garlic powder
  ¼ teaspoon black pepper
  ¼ teaspoon crushed red pepper
  1 2½- to 3-pound turkey breast half
      with rib cage, skin removed
  1 cup chopped onion
  ½ cup water
  ¼ cup lemon juice
  ¼ cup dry white wine
  1 cup whole wheat couscous
  1 cup frozen peas, thawed
  2 tablespoons water
  2 tablespoons cornstarch
  Snipped fresh mint (optional)

1. In a small bowl combine curry powder,
½ teaspoon of the salt, the garlic powder, black
pepper, and crushed red pepper. Rub both sides
of turkey breast with spice mixture. Let turkey
stand 15 minutes.
2. In a 4- to 5-quart slow cooker place the
onion, ½ cup water, lemon juice, and wine.
Top with the turkey breast. Cover and cook on
low-heat setting 4 to 5 hours or on high-heat
setting 2 to 2½ hours.
3. Remove turkey from cooker. Cover loosely
with foil and let stand 15 minutes before slicing.
4. Meanwhile, prepare couscous according to
package directions. Stir peas into hot couscous;
cover and set aside.
5. Transfer cooking liquid to a small saucepan;
bring to boiling. In a small bowl combine the
remaining 2 tablespoons water, the cornstarch,
and remaining ¼ teaspoon salt; whisk into
boiling liquid. Cook and stir until sauce is
thickened and bubbly. Serve sauce with turkey.
If desired, top with snipped fresh mint.

PER SERVING: 335 cal., 2 g total fat (1 g sat. fat),
74 mg chol., 339 mg sodium, 40 g carb. (6 g fiber,
3 g sugars), 37 g pro.

CHILI VERDE
with WHITE BEANS

Chili Verde with White Beans

SERVINGS 6 (1$^1/_3$ cups each)

CARB. PER SERVING 20 g

PREP 20 minutes **SLOW COOK** 5 to 6 hours
(low) or 2$^1/_2$ to 3 hours (high) + 15 minutes

- 1 pound tomatillos, husked and quartered (about 6 medium)
- 1 cup reduced-sodium chicken broth
- 2 6-inch corn tortillas, torn
- 1 fresh jalapeño chile pepper, halved, seeded (if desired), and chopped (tip, *page 252*)
- 5 cloves garlic
- 1 cup chopped onion (1 large)
- 2 pounds boneless pork shoulder roast, trimmed, cut into 1-inch pieces
- $^1/_2$ teaspoon ground cumin
- $^1/_2$ teaspoon ground coriander
- 1 15-ounce can no-salt-added cannellini beans (white kidney beans), rinsed and drained
- 1 cup snipped fresh cilantro
- $^1/_2$ cup sliced green onions (4)
- 2 tablespoons lime juice

1. In a blender combine the tomatillos, broth, tortillas, chile pepper, and garlic. Cover and blend until smooth.

2. Place chopped onion in a 3$^1/_2$- or 4-quart slow cooker. Top with pork and sprinkle with cumin and coriander. Pour tomatillo mixture over meat. Cover; cook on low-heat setting 5 to 6 hours or high-heat setting 2$^1/_2$ to 3 hours

3. Stir in beans. Cook 15 minutes more. Stir in cilantro, green onions, and lime juice just before serving.

PER SERVING: 307 cal., 10 g total fat (3 g sat. fat), 90 mg chol., 217 mg sodium, 20 g carb. (5 g fiber, 5 g sugars), 34 g pro.

CIDER-MAPLE BRUSSELS SPROUTS

Cider-Maple Brussels Sprouts

SERVINGS 12 ($^1/_2$ cup each)

CARB. PER SERVING 13 g

PREP 25 minutes **SLOW COOK** 3 to 3$^1/_2$ hours
(low) or 1$^1/_2$ to 2 hours (high)

- 2 pounds Brussels sprouts, trimmed and halved
- 1 cup slivered red onion
- $^1/_2$ teaspoon salt
- $^1/_4$ teaspoon black pepper
- $^1/_4$ cup apple cider or juice
- $^1/_4$ cup butter, melted
- $^1/_4$ cup pure maple syrup
- 1 tablespoon snipped fresh thyme

1. In a 4- to 5-quart slow cooker combine Brussels sprouts and onion. Sprinkle with salt and pepper. Pour cider over sprouts mixture. Cover and cook on low-heat setting 3 to 3$^1/_2$ hours or on high-heat setting 1$^1/_2$ to 2 hours.

2. In a small bowl combine melted butter, maple syrup, and thyme. Pour over sprouts in cooker, stirring to combine. If desired, garnish with *fresh thyme leaves.*

PER SERVING: 90 cal., 4 g total fat (2 g sat. fat), 10 mg chol., 151 mg sodium, 13 g carb. (3 g fiber, 7 g sugars), 3 g pro.

Creamed Corn with Red Peppers and Spinach

SERVINGS 10 (½ cup each)
CARB. PER SERVING 16 g
PREP 20 minutes   SLOW COOK 3 hours (low)
or 1½ hours (high)

- 4 cups fresh or frozen corn kernels, thawed if frozen
- 1½ cups chopped red sweet peppers
- 1 cup chopped onion
- ¼ cup unsalted chicken stock
- 2 tablespoons unsalted butter, melted
- ¼ teaspoon salt
- ⅛ teaspoon crushed red pepper
- 6 ounces fat-free cream cheese, cut into small chunks
- 4 cups fresh spinach, chopped
- Cracked black pepper (optional)

1. In a 3½- or 4-quart slow cooker combine the corn, red peppers, onion, stock, butter, salt, and crushed red pepper. Place cream cheese on top of the corn mixture. Cover and cook on low-heat setting 3 hours or on high-heat setting 1½ hours.

2. Stir until mixture is well combined. Gently stir in spinach. Serve immediately. If desired, sprinkle with black pepper.

PER SERVING: 108 cal., 3 g total fat (2 g sat. fat), 8 mg chol., 202 mg sodium, 16 g carb. (2 g fiber, 7 g sugars), 6 g pro.

Slow-Cooked Refried Beans

SERVINGS 16 (⅓ cup each)
CARB. PER SERVING 19 g
PREP 20 minutes   COOK 15 minutes
SLOW COOK 8 to 10 hours (low) or 4 to 5 hours (high)

- 1 pound dried pinto beans
- 7 cups water
- 1 cup reduced sodium chicken or vegetable broth
- 1 large yellow or white onion, cut into chunks (1 cup)
- 2 tablespoons chopped pickled jalapeño peppers
- 5 cloves garlic, peeled
- 2 tablespoons pickling juice from a jar of pickled jalapeño peppers
- ¾ teaspoon salt
- Chopped pickled jalapeño peppers, chopped tomato, and/or sliced green onion (optional)

1. Rinse beans; drain. In a large saucepan combine beans and enough water to cover beans by 2 inches. Bring to boiling; reduce heat. Simmer, covered, 15 minutes. Drain and rinse beans.

2. In a 4- to 5-quart slow cooker combine the beans, 7 cups water, broth, onion, 2 tablespoons chopped pickled jalapeño, and garlic. Cover and cook on low-heat setting 8 to 10 hours or on high-heat setting 4 to 5 hours.

3. Drain beans and vegetables, reserving 1 cup of the cooking liquid. Return beans to the slow cooker and add ¼ cup of the reserved cooking liquid, pickled jalapeño liquid, and salt.

4. Using a potato masher or handheld immersion blender, mash or blend the beans into a chunky mixture or until desired consistency is reached, adding more cooking liquid if necessary. If desired, top with chopped pickled jalapeños, chopped tomato, and/or sliced green onion.

PER SERVING: 106 cal., 0 g total fat, 0 mg chol., 175 mg sodium, 19 g carb. (5 g fiber, 1 g sugars), 6 g pro.

CREAMED CORN with
RED PEPPERS AND SPINACH

EXPERT TIP

"To up your fiber count, set a goal to eat at least one serving of fruits, vegetables, whole grains, and/or legumes at each meal. Do this how? Add banana slices or berries to a high-fiber cereal. Top salads with chopped apples, cooked beans, or chopped nuts."

– Rachel Head, RD, CDE, Diabetes Program Manager, Phoenix Children's Hospital, Arizona

SLOW-COOKED
REFRIED BEANS

Crock-Roasted New Potatoes

SERVINGS 12 ($^2/_3$ cup each)
CARB. PER SERVING 19 g
PREP 20 minutes SLOW COOK 3 to 4 hours
(high)

  3 pounds tiny new potatoes, halved
  8 cloves garlic, peeled
  2 tablespoons olive oil
  1 tablespoon snipped fresh rosemary or
    1 teaspoon dried rosemary, crushed
  1 teaspoon kosher salt or $^1/_2$ teaspoon salt
  $^1/_2$ teaspoon cracked black pepper

1. In a large bowl combine potatoes and garlic.
Drizzle with oil and sprinkle with remaining
ingredients; toss to coat. Transfer potato mixture
to a $3^1/_2$- or 4-quart slow cooker. Cover; cook
on high-heat setting 3 to 4 hours or until tender.

PER SERVING: 103 cal., 2 g total fat (0 g sat. fat),
0 mg chol., 185 mg sodium, 19 g carb. (2 g fiber,
1 g sugars), 2 g pro.

BUTTERNUT SQUASH and
FENNEL with LEMON and HONEY

Butternut Squash and Fennel with Lemon and Honey

SERVINGS 8 ($^3/_4$ cup each)
CARB. PER SERVING 25 g
PREP 25 minutes SLOW COOK $3^1/_2$ to 4 hours
(low) or $1^1/_2$ to 2 hours (high)
COOK 10 minutes

  2 pounds butternut squash, peeled,
    seeded, and cut into $1^1/_2$-inch cubes
  2 medium fennel bulbs, cored, quartered,
    and thinly sliced
  1 cup reduced-sodium chicken broth
  $^1/_4$ cup lemon juice
  3 tablespoons honey
  $^1/_4$ teaspoon black pepper
  $^1/_8$ teaspoon salt
  3 tablespoons light butter with canola oil
  1 ounce Parmesan cheese, shaved
    Snipped fresh tarragon or parsley (optional)

1. Place squash and fennel in a $3^1/_2$- or 4-quart
slow cooker. Whisk together the broth, lemon
juice, honey, pepper, and salt; pour over
vegetables. Cover and cook on low-heat setting
$3^1/_2$ to 4 hours or high-heat setting $1^1/_2$ to
2 hours until vegetables are tender.
2. Transfer vegetables to a dish. In a saucepan
boil cooking liquid 10 minutes or until reduced
to $^1/_2$ cup; swirl in butter. Pour over vegetables.
Top with cheese and, if desired, tarragon.

PER SERVING: 131 cal., 3 g total fat (1 g sat. fat),
4 mg chol., 235 mg sodium, 25 g carb. (4 g fiber,
9 g sugars), 4 g pro.

CROCK-ROASTED
NEW POTATOES

HEALTHY HABIT: FIND FLAVOR the SMART WAY

True, not all fat is bad for you. But fat is the most concentrated source of calories, and most Americans eat a lot more total fat than they realize. Most people take in more sodium than they realize, too. Fat and sodium add great flavor to foods, but it's wise to be mindful of your intake of both. Start by eating fewer restaurant meals and processed foods.

MY SMART-FLAVOR GOAL

To limit my intake of fat grams, this week I will use mustard instead of mayonnaise and olive oil instead of butter.

" I work exercise into my life by walking to and from work. "

MARK YAMAMOTO | age 58

With both parents who had type 2 diabetes, Mark knew he was at high risk. And, as a hospital floor nurse, Mark sees the long-term results of poorly managed diabetes every day. So when a postcard showed up in Mark's mailbox inviting him to join the Diabetes Prevention Program (DPP), a major multicenter clinical research study on people with prediabetes, he jumped at the chance to learn more. That was 15 years ago. Through the study, which includes more than 3,000 participants with prediabetes, Mark feels blessed to have gotten world-class diabetes care and education. "The researchers continue to follow me and do my blood work annually."

Kick-start into action: Mark has held a consistent weight at about 180 pounds for the last 15 years and manages his weight by eating healthfully most of the time. "I eat plenty of produce, I go lighter on rice and pasta, and I eat sweets in moderation."

Words of wisdom: "Don't give up. You aren't in this alone. Lots of people have diabetes, and managing it is possible."

ALL ABOUT fats

You have choices. The types of fats you eat and cook with play a bigger role in your health than the amount you eat.

SHOULD YOU BE USING coconut oil?

Just like all oils, coconut oil contains a mix of fatty acids—some healthier, such as lauric acid, and others less so, such as palmitic acid, which promotes the formation of fatty plaque buildup in arteries. Recently, coconut oil has been crowned with a halo of health by some, but it's still on the fats-to-avoid list for many experts because it increases LDL, the bad cholesterol. A heart-smart move is to use extra virgin olive oil in place of many of the fats and oils you use. It's minimally processed and contains a good supply of antioxidants.

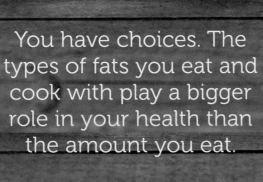

The total amount of fat along with the types of fat you eat can play a big role in the healthiness of your lipid levels and heart. Excess total fat intake (no matter what kind of fat it is) can possibly contribute to weight gain. And when it comes to heart health and glucose control, the American Diabetes Association concludes the types of fats you eat is far more important than the quantity.

You need to eat fats to stay healthy. More specifically, you need to eat two essential fatty acids: linoleic acid and alpha-linolenic acid. They're essential for you because your body can't make them. Fats help maintain healthy skin, are part of some hormones, and help the body absorb fat-soluble vitamins A, D, E, and K.

Fatty acids fall into categories based on whether they're unsaturated (healthier) or saturated (less healthy). The different fats you eat have an impact on your blood lipids, such as your LDL, HDL, and total cholesterol levels, which are important to know.

HEALTHIER FATS

POLYUNSATURATED FATS

Two main types of polyunsaturated fats are omega-3 fats and omega-6 fats. Both are good for your heart and blood lipids. Liquid vegetable oils, such as corn, sunflower, and soybean oils, contain mainly omega-6 polyunsaturated fats. Omega-3 fats are found in fatty fish (salmon, tuna, and sardines) and canola and soybean oils, flax oil and seeds, and walnut oil and walnuts. Research doesn't support recommending omega-3 fat supplements at this time. Unsaturated fats are most beneficial when they replace less-healthy fats in the diet instead of just adding to them.

MONOUNSATURATED FATS

The best sources of monounsaturated fats are nuts, especially almonds, pecans, cashews, pistachios, hazelnuts, and macadamia nuts. Canola, olive, and peanut oils as well as olives and avocados are also good sources. Research increasingly shows that a diet rich in monounsaturated fats has positive effects for heart health and glucose control in people with type 2 diabetes. All unsaturated fats (both monounsaturated and polyunsaturated) lower total cholesterol and LDL cholesterol. Monounsaturated fats also raise HDL cholesterol, which is desired.

LESS-HEALTHY FATS

SATURATED FATS

These fats raise total cholesterol and LDL and also contribute to insulin resistance. Saturated fat is mainly found in foods from animal sources, such as cheese and red meat. Tropical oils, such as coconut and palm, contain saturated fat. Eat no more than 10 percent of your calories from saturated fat. According to the American Heart Association, reducing your intake of saturated fat lowers LDL cholesterol regardless of whether the calories are replaced by healthy carbohydrate, monounsaturated fat, or polyunsaturated fat. To gain this blood lipid benefit, it's important to eat less saturated fat.

TRANS FATS

Much of the trans fats we eat is from processed foods containing partially hydrogenated oils. A small amount of the trans fats we eat is from foods of animal origin, such as meats and dairy foods; for this reason, eating less saturated fat will help you eat less trans fats. Trans fats are unhealthy for your heart and blood vessels because they raise total and LDL cholesterols. Nutrition experts agree you should cut out trans fats as much as possible. Since 2006, the FDA has required the amount of trans fats be listed on the Nutrition Facts label. Due to this raised awareness, most manufacturers now use much less trans fats.

fast FLAVOR

Dinner on the quick can be an indulgent affair. These recipes are refreshingly simple yet full of flavor, and each of them can be ready in about half an hour.

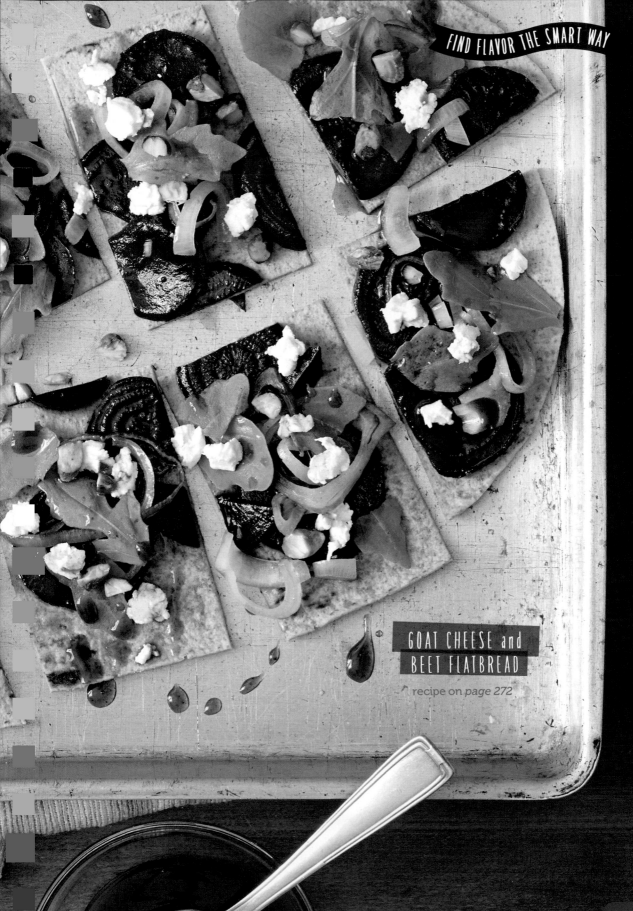

GOAT CHEESE and
BEET FLATBREAD

recipe on page 272

HUMMUS and AVOCADO
SALAD SANDWICHES

2. Lightly coat a large nonstick skillet with cooking spray. Heat skillet over medium heat. Place sandwiches in skillet. Cook about 4 minutes or until toasted, turning once halfway through cooking time.

*TEST KITCHEN TIP: To keep sodium in check, read nutritional labels and choose a hummus that has no more than 120 mg sodium per serving.

PER SERVING: 235 cal., 12 g total fat (3 g sat. fat), 16 mg chol., 354 mg sodium, 26 g carb. (8 g fiber, 3 g sugars), 11 g pro.

Goat Cheese and Beet Flatbread
photo on *pages 270–271*
SERVINGS 4 ($^1/_2$ flatbread [4 pieces] each)
CARB. PER SERVING 18 g
START TO FINISH 25 minutes

> 2 light original-flavor oval flatbreads, such as Flatout Light Original Flatbreads brand
> Nonstick cooking spray
> 1 cup very thinly sliced packaged refrigerated cooked whole baby beets
> 2 medium shallots, very thinly sliced ($^1/_4$ cup)
> 1 cup coarsely chopped fresh arugula or spinach
> 2 ounces semisoft goat cheese, crumbled
> $^1/_4$ cup pistachio nuts, coarsely chopped
> 2 teaspoons balsamic vinegar
> 1 teaspoon reduced-calorie maple-flavored syrup or honey

1. Preheat oven to 400°F. Lightly coat the top of each flatbread with nonstick spray. Arrange flatbreads on a large baking sheet.
2. Bake flatbreads 4 to 6 minutes or until flatbreads are crispy and edges are lightly browned. Top flatbreads evenly with beets and shallots. Bake 2 minutes more or until toppings are heated through.
3. Top flatbreads evenly with arugula, goat cheese, and pistachio nuts. In a small bowl whisk together vinegar and syrup. Drizzle evenly over flatbreads. Cut each flatbread into 8 pieces to serve.

PER SERVING: 173 cal., 9 g total fat (3 g sat. fat), 11 mg chol., 254 mg sodium, 18 g carb. (7 g fiber, 7 g sugars), 10 g pro.

Hummus and Avocado Salad Sandwiches
SERVINGS 4 (1 sandwich each)
CARB. PER SERVING 26 g
START TO FINISH 25 minutes

> $^1/_3$ cup Mediterranean-flavor hummus, such as Sabra Tuscan Herb brand*
> 4 whole wheat sandwich thins or bagel bread squares, split
> $^1/_4$ teaspoon black pepper
> $^1/_2$ of an avocado, peeled and sliced
> 1 cup arugula
> 2 ounces Gruyère cheese, shredded ($^1/_2$ cup)
> Nonstick cooking spray

1. Spread the hummus on cut sides of sandwich thins. Sprinkle with pepper. Divide avocado slices among sandwich thin bottoms. For each sandwich, top avocado slices with $^1/_4$ cup of the arugula and 2 tablespoons of the shredded cheese. Place sandwich thin tops on the cheese, spread sides down. Press down lightly.

CHICKEN-POTATO SKILLET with TOMATOES

SERVINGS 4 (1⅓ cups each)
CARB. PER SERVING 16 g
START TO FINISH 25 minutes

- ½ of a 20-ounce package refrigerated red-skin potato wedges
- 1 medium onion, cut into thin wedges
- 2 cloves garlic, minced
- 2 teaspoons olive oil
- 1 pound skinless, boneless chicken breast halves, cut into bite-size pieces
- ⅓ cup light sour cream
- 2 tablespoons light cream cheese spread, softened
- 2 tablespoons fat-free milk
- ¼ teaspoon salt
- 1 cup grape tomatoes, halved
- 1 tablespoon snipped fresh thyme
- 1 teaspoon finely shredded lemon peel
- Lemon wedges

1. In a large nonstick skillet cook the potatoes, onion, and garlic in hot oil over medium heat about 10 minutes or until onions and potatoes are tender and golden brown. Remove from skillet. Cook chicken, half at a time, in the skillet over medium-high heat 3 to 5 minutes or until no longer pink, stirring occasionally. Return all chicken to the skillet; add cooked potato mixture. In a small bowl stir together sour cream, cream cheese, milk, and salt. Add to chicken mixture. Cook and stir over medium heat 1 to 2 minutes or until heated through. Remove from heat and stir in the tomatoes until well combined.

2. To serve, divide chicken mixture among four plates. Sprinkle each serving with thyme and lemon peel. Serve with lemon wedges.

PER SERVING: 257 cal., 8 g total fat (3 g sat. fat), 83 mg chol., 549 mg sodium, 16 g carb. (3 g fiber, 5 g sugars), 28 g pro.

FISH AMANDINE

SERVINGS 4 (4 ounces each)
CARB. PER SERVING 8 g
START TO FINISH 20 minutes

- 4 4-ounce fresh or frozen skinless tilapia, trout, or halibut fillets, $\frac{1}{2}$ to 1 inch thick
- $\frac{1}{4}$ cup buttermilk
- $\frac{1}{2}$ cup panko bread crumbs or fine dry bread crumbs
- 2 tablespoons snipped fresh parsley or 2 teaspoons dried parsley flakes
- $\frac{1}{2}$ teaspoon dry mustard
- $\frac{1}{4}$ teaspoon salt
- 2 tablespoons grated Parmesan cheese
- $\frac{1}{4}$ cup sliced almonds, coarsely chopped
- 1 tablespoon butter, melted
- $\frac{1}{8}$ teaspoon crushed red pepper

1. Thaw fish, if frozen. Preheat oven to 450°F. Grease a shallow baking pan; set aside. Rinse fish; pat dry with paper towels. Measure thickness of fish.

2. Pour buttermilk into a shallow dish. In another shallow dish combine panko, parsley, dry mustard, and salt. Dip fish into buttermilk, then into panko mixture, turning to coat. Place coated fish in the prepared baking pan.

3. Sprinkle fish with Parmesan cheese and almonds; drizzle with melted butter. Sprinkle with crushed red pepper. Bake 4 to 6 minutes per $\frac{1}{2}$-inch thickness of fish or until fish flakes easily when tested with a fork.

PER SERVING: 200 cal., 8 g total fat (2 g sat. fat), 56 mg chol., 266 mg sodium, 8 g carb. (1 g fiber, 0 g sugars), 24 g pro.

Cashew-Cilantro Pesto with Veggie Noodles

SERVINGS 5 (1 cup each)
CARB. PER SERVING 29 g
START TO FINISH 30 minutes

- 1 daikon radish, peeled (12 ounces)
- 3 carrots, peeled (9 ounces)
- 1 English cucumber, peeled (7 ounces)
- 2 cups thinly sliced savoy cabbage
- ½ teaspoon kosher salt
- 1 cup raw cashews
- ¾ cup snipped fresh cilantro
- ½ cup lime juice
- 3 green onions, chopped
- 2 tablespoons honey
- 1 fresh jalapeño chile pepper, seeded and finely chopped (tip, *page 252*)
- 1 tablespoon tamari sauce
- 2 teaspoons grated fresh ginger
- 2 teaspoons toasted sesame oil
- 3 cloves garlic

1. Using a vegetable peeler, cut the daikon radish, carrots, and English cucumber lengthwise into long julienne "noodles" or "ribbons." (You should have about 2 cups of each.) In a an extra-large bowl toss together the vegetable noodles, cabbage, and salt. Set aside while preparing the pesto.

2. For pesto, in a food processor or blender combine cashews, ½ cup of the cilantro, the lime juice, green onions, honey, chile pepper, tamari sauce, ginger, sesame oil, and garlic. Cover and process or blend until smooth. Drain vegetables well, reserving any liquid that was released from the vegetables as they stood. If necessary, add some of the liquid from the salted vegetables or a little water to thin pesto mixture to a sauce consistency.

3. Toss the vegetable noodles with the pesto. Sprinkle with the remaining ¼ cup cilantro.

PER SERVING: 254 cal., 15 g total fat (3 g sat. fat), 0 mg chol., 454 mg sodium, 29 g carb. (5 g fiber, 14 g sugars), 7 g pro.

CASHEW-CILANTRO PESTO
with VEGGIE NOODLES

EGG-TOPPED SALAD with
TARRAGON-DIJON VINAIGRETTE

Egg-Topped Salad with Tarragon-Dijon Vinaigrette

SERVINGS 4 (1½ cups salad and 1 egg each)
CARB. PER SERVING 8 g
START TO FINISH 30 minutes

- ¼ cup cider vinegar
- 3 tablespoons walnut oil
- 2 teaspoons snipped fresh tarragon or ½ teaspoon dried tarragon, crushed
- 1 teaspoon Dijon-style mustard
- ⅛ teaspoon salt
- ⅛ teaspoon freshly ground black pepper
- 1 teaspoon white vinegar
- 4 eggs
- 6 cups torn mixed salad greens
- 1 small red onion, cut into slivers
- 1 small red sweet pepper, seeded and cut into thin bite-size strips
- ½ cup sliced fresh mushrooms
- ¼ cup crumbed feta cheese (1 ounce)

1. For dressing, in a screw-top jar combine the cider vinegar, walnut oil, tarragon, mustard, salt, and black pepper. Cover; shake well. Set aside.

2. For poached eggs, line a plate with paper towels; set aside. Fill a large skillet with 2 inches of water; add the white vinegar. Bring vinegar mixture to boiling; reduce heat to simmering (bubbles should begin to break the surface of the water). Break one of the four eggs into a cup and slip egg into the simmering water. Repeat with the remaining eggs, allowing each egg an equal amount of space in the skillet. Simmer eggs, uncovered, 3 to 5 minutes or until whites are completely set and yolks begin to thicken but are not hard. Using a slotted spoon, carefully transfer eggs to the prepared plate to dry.

3. Meanwhile, in a large bowl combine salad greens, onion, sweet pepper, and mushrooms. Drizzle with dressing; toss gently to coat.

4. To serve, divide greens mixture among four plates; top greens on each plate with a poached egg. Sprinkle with feta cheese. If desired, sprinkle with additional black pepper.

PER SERVING: 226 cal., 17 g total fat (4 g sat. fat), 194 mg chol., 292 mg sodium, 8 g carb. (2 g fiber, 4 g sugars), 10 g pro. .

SCALLOP TARTINES

SERVINGS 4 (4 tartines each)
CARB. PER SERVING 30 g
START TO FINISH 25 minutes

- 16 fresh or frozen sea scallops
- 6 ounces whole grain baguette
- ¼ teaspoon black pepper
- Nonstick cooking spray
- 3 ounces reduced-fat cream cheese spread with chive and onion
- 1 cup watercress or fresh baby spinach, tough stems trimmed
- 1 medium pink grapefruit, peeled, seeded, sectioned, and chopped
- ⅓ cup thinly sliced green onions or 2 tablespoons snipped fresh chives
- 1 ounce Parmesan cheese, coarsely shredded
- 3 tablespoons chopped macadamia nuts

1. Thaw scallops, if frozen. Rinse scallops; pat dry with paper towels. Set aside. Preheat the broiler. Cut the baguette on a sharp diagonal into 16 thin slices, about ½ inch thick. Arrange baguette slices on a baking sheet. Broil 4 to 5 inches from the heat 2 to 3 minutes or until bread is toasted, turning once. Transfer slices to a wire rack; set aside.

2. Sprinkle both sides of scallops evenly with pepper. Coat a large nonstick skillet with nonstick spray; heat skillet over medium heat. Add scallops; cook 3 to 5 minutes or until browned and opaque, turning once halfway through cooking.

3. Spread baguette slices with cream cheese spread. Divide watercress evenly among the bread slices. Slice scallops in half horizontally. Top bread with scallop slices, grapefruit, green onions, cheese, and macadamia nuts. Serve immediately.

PER SERVING: 313 cal., 13 g total fat (4 g sat. fat), 42 mg chol., 536 mg sodium, 30 g carb. (3 g fiber, 7 g sugars), 20 g pro.

PORK CHOPS with TOMATO-OLIVE PAN SAUCE

SERVINGS 4 (1 pork chop with ⅓ cup sauce each)
CARB. PER SERVING 6 g
START TO FINISH 25 minutes

- 4 boneless pork loin chops, cut ½ inch thick (about 1 pound total)
- ½ teaspoon salt
- ¼ teaspoon black pepper
- 2 teaspoons olive oil
- 4 green onions
- 2 large tomatoes, cored and coarsely chopped (about 2 cups)
- 3 cloves garlic, minced
- 2 tablespoons pitted ripe olives or Kalamata olives, quartered
- 1 tablespoon snipped fresh rosemary or oregano
- 2 tablespoons chopped walnuts, toasted

1. Sprinkle pork chops with ¼ teaspoon of the salt and the pepper. In a large nonstick skillet cook pork chops in hot oil over medium heat 5 to 6 minutes or until pork is just slightly pink in the centers, turning once halfway through cooking. Remove pork chops from skillet; cover to keep warm.

2. Meanwhile, trim ends off green onions and discard. Cut off the white parts of onions; cut white parts in half lengthwise. Slice green tops; set aside. Add white parts to skillet after removing the pork. Cook and stir over medium-high heat 2 minutes.

3. Add tomatoes, garlic, and remaining ¼ teaspoon salt to skillet. Cook, uncovered, 3 to 5 minutes or until tomatoes are softened, stirring occasionally. Add olives and rosemary. Cook and stir 2 minutes more. Lay pork chops on top of tomato mixture; top with green onion tops. Cover and cook 1 minute.

4. Transfer pork chops to four plates. Top with tomato mixture. Sprinkle with walnuts.

PER SERVING: 246 cal., 13 g total fat (3 g sat. fat), 62 mg chol., 386 mg sodium, 6 g carb. (2 g fiber, 3 g sugars), 27 g pro.

Spicy Beef Cabbage Rolls

SERVINGS 6 (2 rolls each)
CARB. PER SERVING 19 g
START TO FINISH 35 minutes

- ⅓ cup hot water
- 2 tablespoons crunchy or creamy peanut butter
- 3 tablespoons reduced-sodium soy sauce
- 1 tablespoon honey
- 2 teaspoons grated fresh ginger
- 1 to 2 teaspoons sriracha sauce
- ½ teaspoon salt
- 12 ounces 93% or higher lean ground beef
- 1½ cups frozen sweet soybeans (edamame)
- 1 cup thin bite-size strips red sweet pepper
- ⅔ cup chopped onion
- 1¼ cups packaged fresh julienned carrots
- 12 green cabbage leaves
- ¼ cup chopped unsalted peanuts

1. In a small bowl whisk together water and peanut butter until combined. Whisk in soy sauce, honey, ginger, sriracha sauce, and salt. Set aside.

2. In an extra-large large skillet cook beef, edamame, red sweet pepper, and onion over medium heat until beef is browned and vegetables are tender, about 7 minutes, stirring to break up beef as it cooks. Drain off any fat. Stir in carrots and reserved sauce mixture. Bring to boiling, stirring to coat the beef mixture with the sauce mixture.

3. Meanwhile, in a Dutch oven cook cabbage leaves, two or three at a time, in boiling water. Cook 1 to 2 minutes or until leaves are just softened and pliable. Carefully remove the leaves from the water so they don't tear. Drain on paper towels. Repeat with remaining leaves.

4. To serve, divide beef mixture among cabbage leaves. Sprinkle with peanuts and roll up. If desired, drizzle with additional sriracha sauce.

PER SERVING: 256 cal., 12 g total fat (3 g sat. fat), 31 mg chol., 576 mg sodium, 19 g carb. (6 g fiber, 10 g sugars), 20 g pro.

SPICY BEEF CABBAGE ROLLS

PEPPER-CRUSTED SALMON
with YOGURT-LIME SAUCE

Pepper-Crusted Salmon with Yogurt-Lime Sauce

SERVINGS 4 (1 salmon fillet and $^1/_4$ cup sauce each)

CARB. PER SERVING 8 g

PREP 15 minutes   **COOK** 6 minutes

- 4   4- to 5-ounce fresh or frozen skinless salmon fillets
- $^1/_2$ teaspoon multicolor peppercorns, coarsely crushed
- $^1/_4$ teaspoon salt
- 2   teaspoons olive oil
- $^3/_4$ cup plain fat-free yogurt
- 1   tablespoon honey
- 1   tablespoon snipped fresh parsley
- $^1/_4$ teaspoon finely shredded lime peel
- 2   teaspoons lime juice
- $^1/_2$ teaspoon minced fresh ginger
  Shredded lime peel (optional)

1. Thaw salmon, if frozen. Rinse salmon; pat dry with paper towels. Sprinkle salmon with crushed peppercorns and salt; use your fingers to gently press peppercorns into the salmon. In a large nonstick skillet heat oil over medium-high heat. Add salmon; cook 6 minutes or until fish flakes easily when tested with a fork, turning once halfway through cooking time.

2. Meanwhile, for yogurt-lime sauce, in a medium bowl combine yogurt, honey, snipped parsley, the $^1/_4$ teaspoon lime peel, the lime juice, and ginger.

3. Serve salmon with yogurt-lime sauce. If desired, garnish with additional lime peel.

PER SERVING: 224 cal., 10 g total fat (1 g sat. fat), 63 mg chol., 232 mg sodium, 8 g carb. (0 g fiber, 8 g sugars), 25 g pro.

CREAMY TUNA-STUFFED SHELLS

SERVINGS 4 (1 cup salad and 3 stuffed shells each)
CARB. PER SERVING 21 g
START TO FINISH 35 minutes

Nonstick cooking spray
12 dried jumbo pasta shells, cooked according to package directions
4 green onions
1 cup finely chopped celery
2 teaspoons olive oil
1 12-ounce can solid white tuna (water pack), drained and flaked
1/3 cup light cream cheese spread
1/4 cup fat-free milk
2 tablespoons light mayonnaise
1/4 cup chopped bottled roasted red sweet peppers
1/4 cup finely shredded Parmesan cheese
4 cups fresh baby spinach
1/4 cup chopped pepperoncini salad peppers
1 tablespoon bottled reduced-fat Italian salad dressing

1. Preheat oven to 375°F. Coat a 2-quart rectangular baking dish with cooking spray; set aside. Set shells, open sides down, on a sheet of foil that has been coated with cooking spray. Lightly coat the shells with cooking spray. Set aside.

2. Meanwhile, thinly slice the green onions, keeping the white parts separate from the green tops; set green tops aside. In a large skillet cook white parts of green onions and the celery in hot oil over medium heat about 5 minutes or until tender, stirring occasionally.

3. Add tuna, cream cheese, milk, mayonnaise, and roasted red sweet peppers to celery mixture. Cook and stir over medium-low heat until mixture is heated through and well combined. Remove from the heat. Stir in half of the green onion tops.

4. Spoon filling evenly into pasta shells. Arrange filled shells in the prepared dish. Sprinkle with cheese. Pour 2 tablespoons *water* into bottom of dish around the shells. Cover dish with vented plastic wrap. Microwave on 100 percent power (high) about 2 minutes or until heated through and cheese is melted.

5. Meanwhile, in a medium bowl toss together the spinach, salad peppers, and Italian dressing. Divide salad among four plates. Top each salad with three stuffed shells.

PER SERVING: 267 cal., 11 g total fat (4 g sat. fat), 41 mg chol., 605 mg sodium, 21 g carb. (3 g fiber, 4 g sugars), 20 g pro.

SODIUM, HEART DISEASE & diabetes

It's no secret that Americans are consuming too much sodium. Cutting back on sodium can lower your blood pressure and decrease your risk of heart disease.

There is a strong connection between sodium, heart disease, and diabetes. Two out of three adults with type 2 diabetes also have hypertension (high blood pressure). And for people with high blood pressure, sodium can have a significant impact on health. Half of the U.S. population, including all people with type 2 diabetes, is advised to limit sodium intake to 2,300 milligrams per day, which is equivalent to a rounded ½ teaspoon salt.

Before you stash your saltshaker, however, you should know that salt added at the dinner table is not to blame (it accounts for only 6 percent of your intake). Almost 80 percent of the sodium you eat comes from restaurant and processed foods, such as packaged snacks, frozen pizzas, hot dogs, fresh meats, canned soups, and condiments.

Because it's hard to control the sodium in these foods, it's best to limit them in your diet and to buy low-sodium versions whenever possible.

Unfortunately, some manufacturers add flavor to lower-carb or lower-fat foods by adding sodium. The best way to know how much sodium is in a food is to check the Nutrition Facts panel.

A high-sodium side dish, snack, or dessert is one that contains more than 400 milligrams of sodium per serving. A high-sodium entrée contains more than 800 milligrams of sodium. The goal for people with diabetes (with or without high blood pressure) is to limit daily sodium intake to 2,300 milligrams or less. Keep in mind that eating enough high-potassium foods (low-fat dairy, fruits, and vegetables) can also help blunt high blood pressure.

6 SODIUM
surprises

Sodium is high in most frozen pizzas, canned soups, and hot dogs. But watch out for sodium in these items, too.

1 FRESH PORK AND POULTRY
Fresh meats, such as pork tenderloins, chicken breasts, and turkey, often are injected with salt to boost flavor. Check packages for salty ingredients, such as broth.

2 SALAD DRESSING
Opt for dressings with less than 240 mg sodium and less than 100 calories per serving.

3 BREAKFAST CEREAL
Many cereals supply more than 240 mg sodium per serving, yet they don't taste salty.

4 INSTANT FOODS
Quick-fix foods, such as instant pudding and instant oatmeal, are often higher in sodium than their regular counterparts. Opt for the regular version when there's a significant sodium savings.

5 SPAGHETTI SAUCE
Seek out no-salt-added versions, which are more prevalent in natural and organic brands.

6 MEDICATIONS
Many drugs have a sodium base to help them dissolve in your digestive tract. Read labels (especially for antacids and pain relievers) and ask your pharmacist about your prescription drugs.

Products labeled as "low sodium" contain 140 mg sodium or less per serving. The wording "no salt added" means salt wasn't added during processing, yet the food will still contain some sodium and won't necessarily be low in sodium.

CHICKEN-NOODLE
CASSEROLE

LOW-SALT
suppers

These recipes (all with less than 400 mg sodium per serving) prove you don't need to coat everything in salt to make it taste good. The fresh flavors reign supreme!

Chicken-Noodle Casserole

SERVINGS 8 (1¼ cups each)
CARB. PER SERVING 33 g
PREP 15 minutes   **COOK** 35 minutes
BAKE 30 minutes

    4   stalks celery, chopped (2 cups)
    1   medium onion, chopped (½ cup)
    2   teaspoons canola oil
    2   pounds chicken legs and/or thighs,
        skinned
    ½   teaspoon black pepper
    1   teaspoon dried thyme, crushed
    ¾   teaspoon salt
    6   cups water
    1   slice bread
   10   ounces jumbo or extra-large
        egg noodles
    1   8-ounce carton light sour cream
    2   tablespoons flour
    ½   teaspoon garlic powder
        Nonstick cooking spray
        Fresh thyme sprigs

1. Preheat oven to 375°F. In a Dutch oven cook two-thirds of the celery and onion in hot oil over medium heat 3 minutes. Add chicken, pepper, thyme, and salt to Dutch oven; cook 2 minutes. Add the water. Bring to boiling;

reduce heat. Simmer, covered, 20 to 25 minutes until chicken is no longer pink.

2. Meanwhile, for topping, tear bread into small pieces. Finely chop remaining celery and onion. In a small bowl toss together the bread, celery, and onion; set aside.

3. Using a slotted spoon, transfer chicken to a cutting board; cool slightly. Add noodles to simmering broth in Dutch oven; simmer 7 to 8 minutes, just until tender, stirring occasionally. Using a slotted spoon, transfer noodles, celery, and onion to a 3-quart baking dish.

4. For sauce, in a bowl whisk together sour cream, flour, and garlic powder. Gradually whisk in 1 cup of the hot broth until smooth. Add sour cream mixture to broth in Dutch oven; cook and stir until boiling.

5. Meanwhile, remove chicken from bones; discard bones. Chop chicken and add to noodles in baking dish. Gently stir in sauce. Sprinkle with bread topping, then lightly coat with cooking spray.

6. Bake, uncovered, 30 to 35 minutes or until casserole is heated through and topping begins to brown. Top with thyme just before serving.

PER SERVING: 288 cal., 9 g total fat (3 g sat. fat), 98 mg chol., 340 mg sodium, 33 g carb. (2 g fiber, 2 g sugars), 19 g pro.

Jerk Chicken and Pineapple Slaw

SERVINGS 4 (1 chicken breast half and about 1½ cups slaw each)
CARB. PER SERVING 19 g
START TO FINISH 25 minutes

- 3 heads baby bok choy, trimmed and thinly sliced
- 2 cups shredded red cabbage
- ½ of a fresh pineapple, peeled, cored, and chopped
- 2 tablespoons cider vinegar
- 4 teaspoons packed brown sugar
- 2 teaspoons all-purpose flour
- 2 teaspoons Jamaican jerk seasoning
- 4 skinless, boneless chicken breast halves (1 to 1¼ pounds total)

1. For pineapple slaw, in an extra-large bowl combine bok choy, cabbage, and pineapple. In a small bowl stir together vinegar and 2 teaspoons of the brown sugar. Drizzle over bok choy mixture; toss to coat. Set aside.

2. In a plastic or paper bag combine the remaining 2 teaspoons brown sugar, the flour, and jerk seasoning. Add chicken to bag. Close bag; shake to coat.

3. Grease a grill pan. Place chicken in pan. Grill over medium heat 8 to 12 minutes or until no longer pink (165°F), turning once halfway through cooking. Transfer chicken to a cutting board; slice chicken. Serve chicken with pineapple slaw.

PER SERVING: 238 cal., 7 g total fat (1 g sat. fat), 72 mg chol., 350 mg sodium, 19 g carb. (3 g fiber, 13 g sugars), 27 g pro.

JERK CHICKEN and PINEAPPLE SLAW

Vegetarian Fried Rice

SERVINGS 6 (1⅓ cups each)
CARB. PER SERVING 30 g
PREP 40 minutes
MARINATE 30 minutes to 4 hours

VEGETARIAN FRIED RICE

8 ounces extra-firm tofu
1 tablespoon sriracha sauce
6 teaspoons olive oil
½ teaspoon grated fresh ginger
1½ cups frozen edamame
1 cup sliced carrots
1 pound fresh asparagus spears, trimmed and cut into 2-inch-long pieces (2 cups)
1 cup fresh or frozen snow pea pods
1 cup refrigerated or frozen egg product, thawed
2 teaspoons toasted sesame oil
2 cups cooked jasmine rice*
1 8-ounce can sliced water chestnuts, drained, rinsed, and cut up
2 tablespoons reduced-sodium soy sauce
1 tablespoon sesame seeds, toasted

1. Drain tofu well. Cut tofu into ½- to ¾-inch cubes. In a small bowl combine tofu and sriracha; gently stir to coat. Marinate tofu at room temperature 30 minutes or in refrigerator up to 4 hours.

2. Meanwhile, in an extra-large nonstick skillet or wok heat 2 teaspoons of the olive oil over medium-high heat. Add ginger; cook 30 seconds. Add edamame and carrots; stir-fry 3 minutes. Add asparagus and pea pods; stir-fry about 5 minutes more or until crisp-tender but still bright green. Quickly transfer vegetables to a large bowl; cover to keep warm.

3. Add 2 teaspoons of the remaining olive oil to the hot skillet. Add marinated tofu to hot oil; fry 5 to 7 minutes or until crisp on all sides, turning to crisp evenly. Transfer tofu to the bowl of vegetables.

4. Add the remaining 2 teaspoons olive oil to the skillet. When oil is heated, pour in egg. Cook over medium heat, without stirring, until egg begins to set on the bottom and around the edges. Using a metal spatula, lift edges of the cooked egg, allowing the uncooked portion to flow underneath. Continue to cook 2 to 3 minutes or until egg is cooked through but still glossy and moist. Remove from heat. Using the spatula, chop the cooked egg into bite-size chunks; transfer to the large bowl.

5. Add the toasted sesame oil to the skillet; heat over medium-high heat. Add the cooked rice. Using a spatula or spoon, break up any chunks; cook rice until grains are coated with oil. Add cooked vegetables, tofu, and egg chunks. Add water chestnuts and soy sauce; stir gently to combine. Heat through. Serve immediately. Sprinkle with sesame seeds.

*TEST KITCHEN TIP: To cut preparation time, use precooked jasmine rice, such as Uncle Ben's Ready Rice brand.

PER SERVING: 283 cal., 12 g total fat (2 g sat. fat), 19 mg chol., 318 mg sodium, 30 g carb. (4 g fiber, 5 g sugars), 15 g pro.

PARMESAN-STUFFED CHICKEN and MELTED STRAWBERRIES

Parmesan-Stuffed Chicken and Melted Strawberries

SERVINGS 6 (1 chicken breast half and ¹/₂ cup strawberry mixture each)
CARB. PER SERVING 11 g
PREP 30 minutes   BAKE 15 minutes

- 3 cups fresh strawberries*
- 2 tablespoons white balsamic vinegar or white wine vinegar
- ¹/₄ cup low-sugar strawberry preserves
- ¹/₂ teaspoon sea salt or salt
- ¹/₄ teaspoon black pepper
- 6 4- to 5-ounce small skinless, boneless chicken breast halves (1¹/₂ to 2 pounds total)
- 2 ounces Parmesan or white cheddar cheese
- 6 large fresh basil leaves
- 2 cloves garlic, minced
- 1 tablespoon olive oil

1. Preheat oven to 400°F. In a 3-quart baking dish combine strawberries, vinegar, and preserves. Sprinkle with ¹/₄ teaspoon of the salt and ¹/₈ teaspoon of the pepper; set aside.
2. Cut a horizontal pocket in each chicken breast half by cutting from one side almost to, but not through, opposite side. Cut cheese into six 3x¹/₂-inch pieces. Wrap a basil leaf around each piece of cheese; stuff into chicken breast pockets. Secure pockets closed with wooden toothpicks or skewers. Sprinkle with remaining ¹/₄ teaspoon salt and ¹/₈ teaspoon pepper.
3. In an extra-large oven-going skillet cook garlic in hot oil over medium heat 30 seconds. Add chicken and cook about 5 minutes or until golden brown, turning once. Transfer skillet with chicken to oven. Bake, uncovered, 5 minutes. Add baking dish with the strawberry mixture to oven. Bake 10 to 13 minutes or until a thermometer inserted in chicken registers 165°F and the berries are softened and jam mixture has thickened. Serve chicken with melted strawberries.

*TEST KITCHEN TIP: Halve or quarter any large strawberries before measuring.

PER SERVING: 229 cal., 6 g total fat (2 g sat. fat), 72 mg chol., 355 mg sodium, 11 g carb. (2 g fiber, 8 g sugars), 30 g pro.

Pork Tenderloin with Cucumber-Mango Salad

photo on *page 290*
SERVINGS 4 (3 slices cooked pork and ¹/₂ cup salad each)
CARB. PER SERVING 18 g or 12 g
PREP 10 minutes   ROAST 25 minutes
STAND 3 minutes

- 2 tablespoons packed brown sugar*
- 2 teaspoons Chinese five-spice powder
- ¹/₂ teaspoon salt
- 2 12-ounce pork tenderloins
- 4 green onions
- 1 mango, peeled, seeded, and chopped
- 1 small English cucumber, thinly sliced
- 1 fresh jalapeño chile pepper, stemmed, seeded, and sliced (see tip, *page 252*) (optional)

1. Preheat oven to 425°F. Line a shallow roasting pan with foil; set aside. In a small bowl combine brown sugar, five-spice powder, and salt; set 1 teaspoon of the brown sugar mixture aside. Sprinkle the remaining brown sugar mixture evenly over pork tenderloins; rub in with your fingers. Place tenderloins in prepared roasting pan.
2. Roast about 25 minutes or until a thermometer inserted in centers of pork tenderloins registers 145°F. Cover with foil; let stand 3 minutes before slicing.
3. Meanwhile, for mango salad, slice the green portions of the green onions into thin strips; chop the white portions. In a medium bowl combine all of the green onions, the mango, cucumber, chile pepper (if desired), and the reserved brown sugar mixture. Slice pork and serve with mango salad.

*SUGAR SUBSTITUTE: Use Splenda Brown Sugar Blend. Follow package directions to use product amount equivalent to 2 tablespoons brown sugar.

PER SERVING: 266 cal., 6 g total fat (2 g sat. fat), 105 mg chol., 365 mg sodium, 18 g carb. (2 g fiber, 15 g sugars), 35 g pro.
PER SERVING WITH SUBSTITUTE: Same as above, except 239 cal., 363 mg sodium , 12 g carb. (8 g sugars).

EXPERT TIP

PORK TEMDERLOIN with
CUCUMBER-MANGO SALAD

recipe on *page 289*

Barbecue-Sauced Pork Sandwiches

SERVINGS 12 (3 ounces meat mixture, about $^1/_3$ cup cabbage mixture, and 2 slices bread each)
CARB. PER SERVING 30 g
PREP 30 minutes   ROAST $1^1/_4$ hours
STAND 10 minutes   COOK 15 minutes

- 2 teaspoons dry mustard
- $1^1/_2$ teaspoons dried marjoram, crushed
- $1^1/_2$ teaspoons paprika
- 1 3-pound boneless pork top loin roast (single loin), trimmed of fat
- 2 8-ounce cans no-salt-added tomato sauce
- $1^1/_2$ cups apple juice or apple cider
- 1 cup chopped onion
- 2 tablespoons white vinegar
- 1 teaspoon bottled hot pepper sauce
- 24 slices 100% whole wheat sandwich bread, toasted
- 4 cups finely shredded cabbage

BARBECUE-SAUCED PORK SANDWICHES

1. Preheat oven to 350°F. In a small bowl stir together 1 teaspoon of the dry mustard, $^1/_2$ teaspoon of the marjoram, $^1/_2$ teaspoon of the paprika, and $^1/_4$ teaspoon *black pepper*. Sprinkle mustard mixture evenly over roast; rub in with your fingers. Place roast on a rack in a shallow roasting pan. Insert an oven-going meat thermometer into center of roast. Roast, uncovered, about $1^1/_4$ hours or until meat thermometer registers 145°F.

2. Remove from oven. Cover with foil; let stand 10 minutes. Thinly slice roast.

3. Meanwhile, in a large saucepan stir together tomato sauce, apple juice, onion, vinegar, the remaining 1 teaspoon dry mustard, the remaining 1 teaspoon marjoram, the remaining 1 teaspoon paprika, the hot pepper sauce, and $^1/_2$ teaspoon *salt*. Bring to boiling; reduce heat. Simmer, uncovered, 15 minutes or until mixture is reduced to $2^3/_4$ cups.

4. Add sliced pork; using tongs, gently turn to coat pork. Heat through. Divide pork among 12 slices of the toasted bread. Add cabbage to the remaining sauce in saucepan. Toss to coat; heat through. Divide cabbage mixture among sandwiches. Top with the remaining slices of toasted bread.

MAKE-AHEAD DIRECTIONS: Prepare as directed through Step 3. Place sliced pork in a resealable plastic freezer bag. Seal, label, and freeze up to 1 month. Place tomato sauce mixture in an airtight freezer container. Seal, label, and freeze up to 1 month. Thaw pork and sauce overnight in the refrigerator. In a large saucepan reheat sauce until boiling. Add sliced pork; using tongs, gently turn to coat. Heat through. Serve as directed in Step 4.

PER SERVING: 313 cal., 6 g total fat (2 g sat. fat), 71 mg chol., 364 mg sodium, 30 g carb. (6 g fiber, 9 g sugars), 33 g pro.

Hungarian Pork Goulash

SERVINGS 6 (1¼ cups each)
CARB. PER SERVING 24 g
PREP 30 minutes
SLOW COOK 5 to 6 hours (low) or
2½ to 3 hours (high) + 30 minutes (high)

- 1 1½- to 2-pound pork sirloin roast
- 1 tablespoon Hungarian paprika or Spanish paprika
- 1 teaspoon caraway seeds, crushed
- ½ teaspoon garlic powder
- 1 tablespoon canola oil
- 1 cup sliced celery
- 1 cup sliced carrots
- 1 cup sliced parsnips
- 1 cup chopped onion
- 1 14.5-ounce can no-salt-added diced tomatoes, undrained
- ½ cup water
- 4 ounces dried wide whole grain noodles (about 2 cups)
- 6 tablespoons light sour cream

1. Trim fat from roast. Cut roast into 2-inch cubes. In a large bowl combine paprika, caraway seeds, garlic powder, ½ teaspoon *black pepper,* and ¼ teaspoon *salt.* Add pork cubes; toss to coat. In a large skillet heat oil over medium heat. Add pork, half at a time; cook until browned, turning occasionally. Transfer pork to a 3½- or 4-quart slow cooker. Add celery, carrots, parsnips, and onion. Pour tomatoes and the water over all ingredients in cooker.

2. Cover and cook on low-heat setting 5 to 6 hours or on high-heat setting 2½ to 3 hours.

3. If using low-heat setting, turn cooker to high-heat setting. Stir noodles into pork mixture in cooker. Cover and cook about 30 minutes more or until noodles are tender, stirring once halfway through cooking. Serve with sour cream. If desired, sprinkle with additional paprika.

PER SERVING: 285 cal., 9 g total fat (2 g sat. fat), 82 mg chol., 234 mg sodium, 24 g carb. (5 g fiber, 6 g sugars), 28 g pro.

BEEF and BEAN LINGUINE
with MINT-WALNUT
GREMOLATA

recipe on *page 294*

Beef and Bean Linguine with Mint-Walnut Gremolata

photo on *page 293*
SERVINGS 2 (1½ cups pasta mixture and 2 tablespoons gremolata each)
CARB. PER SERVING 33 g
PREP 15 minutes   COOK 16 minutes

    2 tablespoons snipped fresh mint or basil
    1 tablespoon chopped toasted walnuts
    1 tablespoon snipped fresh Italian
       (flat-leaf) parsley
    1 teaspoon finely shredded lemon peel
    2 ounces dry whole grain linguine
    6 ounces fresh green beans, trimmed
       (1½ cups)
    2 teaspoons olive oil
    6 ounces beef top loin steak (strip steak) or
       beef sirloin steak, trimmed of fat and cut
       into thin bite-size strips
    ⅛ teaspoon salt
    ⅛ teaspoon black pepper
       Olive oil nonstick cooking spray
    ½ cup thin bite-size red sweet pepper strips
    ¼ cup chopped onion
    1 large clove garlic, thinly sliced
    2 tablespoons coarsely shredded
       Parmesan cheese
       Crushed red pepper (optional)

1. For gremolata, in a small bowl combine mint, walnuts, parsley, and lemon peel. Set aside.
2. Cook linguine according to package directions, adding the green beans for the entire cooking time. Drain and return to the pot. Add olive oil and toss to coat. Cover to keep warm.
3. Meanwhile, in a small bowl toss steak strips with the salt and black pepper. Coat an unheated medium nonstick skillet with cooking spray; heat skillet over medium-high heat. Add steak strips, sweet pepper strips, onion, and garlic. Cook 3 to 4 minutes or until steak is pink only in center of strips, stirring occasionally.
4. Add steak mixture and cheese to pasta mixture. Toss to combine. Divide pasta mixture between two plates. If desired, sprinkle with crushed red pepper. Top with gremolata.

PER SERVING: 354 cal., 13 g total fat (3 g sat. fat), 45 mg chol., 291 mg sodium, 33 g carb. (7 g fiber, 6 g sugars), 28 g pro.

Zesty Meat Sauce with Spaghetti Squash

SERVINGS 6 (¾ cup meat mixture and ¾ cup squash mixture each)
CARB. PER SERVING 21 g
PREP 50 minutes   BAKE 45 minutes

    1 medium spaghetti squash (about
       2½ pounds), halved and seeded
    1 medium red and/or green sweet pepper,
       stemmed, seeded, and cut into thin strips
    4 ounces fresh mushrooms, quartered
    1 small onion, cut into thin wedges
       Nonstick cooking spray
   12 ounces 95% lean ground beef
    ½ cup chopped onion (1 medium)
    ½ cup chopped carrot (1 medium)
    ½ cup chopped celery (1 stalk)
    2 cloves garlic, minced
    2 8-ounce cans no-salt-added
       tomato sauce
    1 cup salsa
    1 cup water
    1 tablespoon dried Italian seasoning,
       crushed
    ¼ teaspoon black pepper
    ⅛ to ¼ teaspoon crushed red pepper
    ¼ cup finely shredded Parmesan cheese

1. Preheat oven to 350°F. Line a 15x10x1-inch baking pan with foil. Place squash, cut sides down, in prepared pan. Prick the skin all over. Arrange sweet pepper, mushrooms, and onion wedges around squash; coat with cooking spray. Bake 45 to 55 minutes or until squash is tender.
2. Meanwhile, for meat sauce, in a large skillet combine beef, chopped onion, carrot, celery, and garlic. Cook until meat is browned; drain. Stir in tomato sauce, salsa, the water, Italian seasoning, black pepper, and crushed red pepper. Bring to boiling; reduce heat. Simmer, uncovered, 10 to 15 minutes or until desired consistency, stirring occasionally.
3. Using a fork, remove the squash pulp from the shells. In a large bowl toss 4 cups of the squash pulp with the sweet pepper, mushrooms, and onion wedges. Serve meat sauce over squash-vegetable mixture. Sprinkle with cheese.

PER SERVING: 181 cal., 4 g total fat (2 g sat. fat), 37 mg chol., 236 mg sodium, 21 g carb. (6 g fiber, 11 g sugars), 16 g pro.

ZESTY MEAT SAUCE
with SPAGHETTI SQUASH

Fish with White Wine, Lemon, and Capers

SERVINGS 4 (1 fish fillet and ³/₄ cup pasta mixture each)

CARB. PER SERVING 25 g

PREP 10 minutes   BAKE 10 minutes

- 4 4- to 5-ounce fresh or frozen whitefish fillets, such as tilapia, cod, or flounder
- ¼ teaspoon salt
- ⅛ teaspoon black pepper
- 4 ounces dried whole wheat linguine
- 1 tablespoon olive oil
- ¼ cup finely chopped shallots (2 medium)
- 2 tablespoons drained capers
- 2 teaspoons finely shredded lemon peel
- ½ cup dry white wine or reduced-sodium chicken broth
- 1 tablespoon snipped fresh oregano
- 3 cups torn fresh arugula
  Lemon wedges (optional)

1. Thaw fish, if frozen. Preheat oven to 450°F. Line a shallow baking pan with foil; set aside. Rinse fish; pat dry with paper towels. Arrange fish in a single layer in the prepared baking pan. Sprinkle with the salt and pepper. Bake 10 to 12 minutes or until fish flakes easily when tested with a fork. Meanwhile, cook linguine according to package directions; drain.

2. In a large skillet heat oil over medium-high heat. Add shallots; cook and stir about 3 minutes or until tender. Stir in capers and 1 teaspoon of the lemon peel. Add wine. Cook, uncovered, 2 to 3 minutes or until wine is reduced by half. Remove from heat. Stir in oregano.

3. To serve, toss hot pasta with arugula; divide among four plates. Top with fish and caper mixture. Sprinkle with the remaining 1 teaspoon lemon peel. If desired, serve with lemon wedges.

PER SERVING: 274 cal., 6 g total fat (1 g sat. fat), 56 mg chol., 333 mg sodium, 25 g carb. (3 g fiber, 2 g sugars), 28 g pro.

EGGPLANT and GOAT CHEESE PANINI SANDWICHES

SERVINGS 4 (1 filled pita bread half each)
CARB. PER SERVING 23 g
START TO FINISH 20 minutes

- 1 tablespoon olive oil
- 1½ cups coarsely chopped unpeeled eggplant
- 1 cup red sweet pepper strips
- 2 cloves garlic, minced
- 2 tablespoons chopped bottled pepperoncini salad peppers
- 1 tablespoon snipped fresh oregano or 1 teaspoon dried oregano, crushed
- ¼ cup soft goat cheese (chèvre), softened
- ¼ cup light cream cheese spread, softened
- 2 large whole wheat pita bread rounds, halved crosswise

Nonstick cooking spray

1. In a large skillet heat oil over medium heat. Add eggplant and sweet peppers; cook about 5 minutes or just until vegetables are tender, stirring often. Add garlic; cook and stir 30 seconds. Remove from heat. Stir in pepperoncini peppers and oregano; set aside.

2. In a small bowl stir together goat cheese and cream cheese spread. Carefully open pita halves to make pockets. Spread cheese mixture inside pockets; fill with eggplant mixture. Lightly coat outsides of sandwiches with cooking spray.

3. Heat a nonstick grill pan or large nonstick skillet over medium heat. Place sandwiches on grill pan; cook until browned on both sides, turning once halfway through cooking time. (If desired, weight down sandwiches by putting a large heavy skillet on top of sandwiches; cook until browned on bottoms, then remove top skillet, turn sandwiches, and replace top skillet. Cook until browned on second sides.)

PER SERVING: 210 cal., 10 g total fat (4 g sat. fat), 17 mg chol., 305 mg sodium, 23 g carb. (4 g fiber, 4 g sugars), 8 g pro.

Asian flavors give you a lot of bang for your buck. Fresh ginger and garlic, soy sauce, rice vinegar, and toasted sesame oil each lend a unique flavor to an assertive and harmonious combination.

ASPARAGUS-SNAP PEA
STIR-FRY

flavor-punched
SIDE DISHES

Just a bit of an intensely flavored spice, vinegar,
juice, or condiment makes vegetables shout out.
These side dishes kick ho-hum
steamed veggies up a notch.

Asparagus-Snap Pea Stir-Fry

SERVINGS 6 (²/₃ cup)
CARB. PER SERVING 10 g
START TO FINISH 25 minutes

- 1 pound fresh asparagus spears
- 1 tablespoon vegetable oil
- 2 teaspoons grated fresh ginger
- 2 cloves garlic, minced
- 1 medium red onion, cut into thin wedges
- 1 medium red sweet pepper, stemmed, seeded, and cut into 1-inch pieces
- 2 cups fresh sugar snap pea pods or frozen sugar snap pea pods
- 1 tablespoon sesame seeds
- 2 tablespoons reduced-sodium soy sauce
- 2 tablespoons rice vinegar
- 1 tablespoon packed brown sugar
- 1 teaspoon toasted sesame oil

1. Snap off and discard woody bases from asparagus. If desired, scrape off scales. Bias-slice asparagus into 2-inch pieces (you should have about 3 cups).

2. In a wok or large skillet heat vegetable oil over medium-high heat. Add ginger and garlic; cook and stir 15 seconds. Add asparagus, onion, and sweet pepper; cook and stir 3 minutes. Add pea pods and sesame seeds; cook and stir 3 to 4 minutes more or until vegetables are crisp-tender.

3. Add soy sauce, rice vinegar, brown sugar, and sesame oil to vegetable mixture; toss to coat. If desired, serve with a slotted spoon.

PER SERVING: 83 cal., 4 g total fat (1 g sat. fat), 0 mg chol., 196 mg sodium, 10 g carb. (2 g fiber, 6 g sugars), 3 g pro.

SPICED SWEET POTATO
WEDGES

a PUNCH of CURRY

Curry paste is available in jars in
the Asian food section of your
supermarket. Yellow curry paste
is spicier than red curry paste, so
choose your heat level.

ROASTED CAULIFLOWER with
CURRIED PEPITA GREMOLATA

Spiced Sweet Potato Wedges

SERVINGS 4 (4 wedges each)
CARB. PER SERVING 22 g or 21 g
PREP 10 minutes   **ROAST** 25 minutes

- 2 sweet potatoes (about 10 ounces each)
- 1 tablespoon olive oil
- 1 teaspoon packed brown sugar*
- ¼ teaspoon kosher salt
- ¼ teaspoon smoked paprika
- ¼ teaspoon black pepper
- ¼ teaspoon pumpkin pie spice
- ¼ teaspoon hot chili powder

1. Preheat oven to 425°F. Place a baking sheet in the oven to preheat.
2. Scrub sweet potatoes; cut each potato lengthwise into 8 wedges (16 wedges total). In a large bowl drizzle potato wedges with olive oil; toss to coat. In a small bowl combine brown sugar, kosher salt, smoked paprika, pepper, pumpkin pie spice, and chili powder. Sprinkle spice mixture over sweet potato wedges; toss to coat.
3. Arrange wedges in a single layer on the hot baking sheet. Roast 25 to 30 minutes or until potatoes are tender and browned, turning wedges once halfway through roasting time.
*SUGAR SUBSTITUTES: Choose from Splenda Brown Sugar Blend or Sugar Twin Granulated Brown. Follow package directions to use product amount equivalent to 1 teaspoon brown sugar.

PER SERVING: 124 cal., 3 g total fat (0 g sat. fat), 0 mg chol., 182 mg sodium, 22 g carb. (3 g fiber, 5 g sugars), 2 g pro.
PER SERVING WITH SUBSTITUTE: Same as above, except 123 cal., 21 g carb.

a PUNCH of SPICE

Dried spices provide flavor without fat. In this recipe, smoked paprika, pepper, pumpkin pie spice, and chili powder do the work. Fresh spices provide stronger flavors.

Roasted Cauliflower with Curried Pepita Gremolata

SERVINGS 4 (³/₄ cup cauliflower and 1 tablespoon gremolata each)
CARB. PER SERVING 6 g
PREP 10 minutes   **ROAST** 15 minutes

- 3 cups cauliflower florets
- 1 teaspoon olive oil
- 2 tablespoons lemon juice
- 1 teaspoon red or yellow curry paste
- 2 clove garlic, minced
- ¼ cup snipped fresh cilantro
- 2 tablespoons roasted salted pumpkin seeds (pepitas)

1. Preheat oven to 425°F. Line a 15×10×1-inch baking pan with foil. Toss together cauliflower and oil in pan. Roast 15 to 20 minutes or until just crisp-tender.
2. For gremolata, in a small bowl combine lemon juice, curry paste, and garlic. Add cilantro and pepitas; toss to combine.
3. To serve, transfer roasted cauliflower to a serving bowl. Sprinkle with gremolata.

PER SERVING: 75 cal., 5 g total fat (1 g sat. fat), 0 mg chol., 71 mg sodium, 6 g carb. (2 g fiber, 2 g sugars), 4 g pro.

Mustard-Chive Mashed Potatoes

SERVINGS 8 ($^1/_2$ cup each)
CARB. PER SERVING 15 g
PREP 15 minutes **COOK** 20 minutes

- 1$^1/_2$ pounds round red potatoes, scrubbed and cut into 2-inch pieces
- $^1/_3$ cup fat-free milk
- $^1/_3$ cup light sour cream
- 2 tablespoons Dijon-style mustard
- $^1/_8$ teaspoon salt
- $^1/_4$ cup snipped fresh chives or green onion tops

1. In a large saucepan cook potatoes, covered, in enough boiling water to cover 20 to 25 minutes or until tender. Drain potatoes in a colander. Add milk to the same saucepan; heat just to boiling over medium heat. Add drained potatoes, sour cream, mustard, and salt. Remove from heat. Coarsely mash mixture with a potato masher. Stir in chives.

PER SERVING: 78 cal., 1 g total fat (1 g sat. fat), 3 mg chol., 141 mg sodium, 15 g carb. (1 g fiber, 1 g sugars), 2 g pro.

a PUNCH of GARLIC

Fresh garlic has a sharp, pungent flavor. Mellow the flavor and make it sweet by roasting the garlic first. Find it in jars in the produce section or roast your own.

Asparagus with Creamy Herb-Garlic Topper

SERVINGS 4 (4 ounces asparagus and 1$^1/_2$ tablespoons topper each)
CARB. PER SERVING 4 g
START TO FINISH 15 minutes

- 1 pound fresh asparagus spears
- $^1/_4$ cup tub-style light cream cheese, softened
- 4 teaspoons light butter or tub-style vegetable oil spread, softened
- 2 teaspoons snipped fresh chives
- 2 teaspoons snipped fresh oregano and/or thyme
- 2 teaspoons bottled roasted minced garlic*

1. Snap off and discard woody bases from asparagus. Cook asparagus in boiling water about 5 minutes or until just crisp tender. Drain.
2. Meanwhile, in a small bowl stir together cream cheese and butter until smooth. Stir in chives, oregano, and garlic.
3. To serve, arrange asparagus on a platter. Spoon cream cheese mixture over top.

*TEST KITCHEN TIP: If you can't find bottled roasted garlic, roast your own. Peel away the dry outer layers of skin from 1 head of garlic, leaving skins and cloves intact. Cut off the pointed top portion (about $^1/_4$ inch), leaving bulb intact but exposing the individual cloves. Place the garlic head, cut side up, in a custard cup. Drizzle with a little olive oil. Cover with foil and bake in a 425°F oven 25 to 35 minutes or until the cloves feel soft when pressed. Set aside just until cool enough to handle. Squeeze out the garlic paste from individual cloves. Use $^1/_2$ teaspoon in the topper. Store the remaining roasted garlic in an airtight container in the refrigerator up to 5 days.

PER SERVING: 64 cal., 5 g total fat (3 g sat. fat), 15 mg chol., 105 mg sodium, 4 g carb. (1 g fiber, 2 g sugars), 2 g pro.

a PUNCH of MUSTARD

Mustard is a great low-fat option for giving food a bit of a bite. Dijon-style mustards can vary in strength; some are particularly assertive. Be sure to use a brand you like.

MUSTARD-CHIVE
MASHED POTATOES

ASPARAGUS with CREAMY
HERB-GARLIC TOPPER

303

SKILLET SQUASH

SWEET and SPICED
DRIZZLED CARROTS

a PUNCH of SWEET

Molasses, orange juice, ginger,
nutmeg, and cinnamon have flavors
you might expect in gingerbread.
The combo adds some spice
to already-sweet carrots.

a PUNCH of CHILE

Canned green chiles are not really spicy, but they have a special flavor all their own. They add an unexpected zing to this Mediterranean-style dish.

Sweet and Spiced Drizzled Carrots

SERVINGS 4 ($^3/_4$ cup vegetables and 1 tablespoon drizzle each)
CARB. PER SERVING 17 g
START TO FINISH 15 minutes

- 1   pound baby carrots with tops, trimmed
- 2   tablespoons orange juice
- 4   teaspoons molasses or honey
- 2   teaspoons canola oil
- $^1/_8$ teaspoon salt
- $^1/_8$ teaspoon ground ginger
- $^1/_8$ teaspoon ground nutmeg
- $^1/_8$ teaspoon ground cinnamon

1. Scrub carrots; peel if desired. Halve any large carrots lengthwise. Cook carrots, covered, in a small amount of boiling water 7 to 9 minutes or until just crisp-tender. Drain.

2. In a small microwave-safe bowl combine orange juice, molasses, oil, salt, ginger, nutmeg, and cinnamon. Cover with vented plastic wrap. Microwave on 50 percent power (medium) 20 to 30 seconds or just until warm. Stir until combined.

3. Transfer carrots to a serving bowl or platter. Drizzle with spice mixture.

PER SERVING: 90 cal., 3 g total fat (0 g sat. fat), 0 mg chol., 153 mg sodium, 17 g carb. (3 g fiber, 11 g sugars), 1 g pro.

Skillet Squash

SERVINGS 6 ($^2/_3$ cup each)
CARB. PER SERVING 8 g
PREP 20 minutes   **COOK** 12 minutes

- 2   teaspoons olive oil
- 2   zucchini, halved lengthwise and sliced
- 2   yellow summer squash, halved lengthwise and sliced
- 1   onion, thinly sliced
- 1   4-ounce can diced green chiles, undrained
- 2   tomatoes, chopped
- 2   teaspoons snipped fresh oregano or $^1/_2$ teaspoon dried oregano, crushed
- $^1/_4$ teaspoon black pepper
- $^1/_8$ teaspoon salt

1. In a large nonstick skillet heat oil over medium heat. Add zucchini, yellow squash, and onion. Cook 8 to 10 minutes or until onion is just tender, stirring occasionally.

2. Add green chiles, tomatoes, and dried oregano (if using). Heat through, stirring occasionally. Stir in fresh oregano (if using), black pepper, and salt. Serve immediately.

PER SERVING: 49 cal., 2 g total fat (0 g sat. fat), 0 mg chol., 112 mg sodium, 8 g carb. (2 g fiber, 4 g sugars), 2 g pro.

a PUNCH of CAPERS

Capers are intensely flavored little pickles. They add tang and some saltiness to dishes.

Brussels Sprouts with Spicy Ginger-Soy Almonds

SERVINGS 4 ($^3/_4$ cup Brussels sprouts and 1 tablespoon nuts each)
CARB. PER SERVING 12 g
PREP 10 minutes **ROAST** 20 minutes

    1   pound Brussels sprouts
    2   teaspoons olive oil
  $^1/_4$ cup slivered almonds
    4   teaspoons reduced-sodium soy sauce
  $^1/_4$ teaspoon ground ginger
  $^1/_4$ teaspoon crushed red pepper
  $^1/_8$ teaspoon garlic powder

1. Preheat oven to 425°F. Line a 15×10×1-inch roasting pan with foil. Trim stems and remove any wilted outer leaves from Brussels sprouts; wash. Halve Brussels sprouts; spread in a single later in pan. Drizzle oil over Brussels sprouts. Roast 20 to 25 minutes or until crisp-tender, stirring once or twice.
2. Meanwhile, in a small skillet heat almonds over medium heat 4 to 6 minutes or until fragrant and toasted. Add soy sauce, ginger, crushed red pepper, and garlic powder. Toss to coat. Heat 1 minute more or until soy sauce is nearly evaporated.
3. Transfer roasted Brussels sprouts to a serving bowl. Sprinkle with almond mixture.

PER SERVING: 113 cal., 6 g total fat (1 g sat. fat), 0 mg chol., 212 mg sodium, 12 g carb. (5 g fiber, 3 g sugars), 6 g pro.

Green Beans with Tomato-Pepper Salsa

SERVINGS 4 ($^3/_4$ cup beans and 2$^1/_2$ tablespoons salsa each)
CARB. PER SERVING 8 g
PREP 10 minutes **COOK** 10 minutes

   12   ounces fresh green and/or wax beans
  $^1/_4$ cup chopped yellow sweet pepper
    2   clove garlic, minced
    4   teaspoons olive oil
  $^1/_2$ cup quartered red grape or cherry tomatoes
    2   tablespoons thinly sliced green onion tops
    2   teaspoons capers, drained
  $^1/_8$ teaspoon salt
  $^1/_8$ teaspoon black pepper

1. Remove ends and strings from beans; leave whole. Cook beans, covered, in a small amount of boiling salted water about 10 minutes or until crisp-tender; drain.
2. In a large skillet cook sweet pepper and garlic in hot oil over medium heat 3 to 4 minutes or until pepper is crisp-tender, stirring occasionally. Add tomatoes, green onion tops, capers, salt, and black pepper. Cook and stir 1 to 2 minutes more or until heated through.
3. Transfer beans to a serving bowl. Top with salsa mixture.

PER SERVING: 77 cal., 5 g total fat (1 g sat. fat), 0 mg chol., 114 mg sodium, 8 g carb. (3 g fiber, 4 g sugars), 2 g pro.

GREEN BEANS with
TOMATO-PEPPER SALSA

BRUSSELS SPROUTS with
SPICY GINGER-SOY ALMONDS

a PUNCH of PEPPER

Crushed red pepper has a bold
bite that black pepper lacks.
Combining it with soy sauce
enhances the flavors, adding more
than just a spicy kick.

roast YOUR VEGGIES

Preheat oven to 425°F. Line a 15x10x1-inch baking pan with foil; coat it with nonstick cooking spray. Toss 1 pound of vegetables with 1½ teaspoons olive oil, ¼ teaspoon salt, and ⅛ teaspoon black pepper; arrange in a single layer in the pan. Roast as directed until vegetables are browned and crispy, turning once halfway through roasting time. If desired, toss veggies with the suggested flavor kickers just before serving.

SMALL POTATOES

Halve larger potatoes. Roast 25 to 30 minutes. Toss with ¼ tsp. ground chipotle chile pepper.

SUMMER SQUASH

Halve lengthwise; slice. Roast 10 to 15 minutes. Toss with ¼ tsp. Italian seasoning and 2 Tbsp. shredded Parmesan.

CARROTS

Halve and/or quarter. Roast 20 to 25 minutes. Toss with ¼ cup walnuts, 1 tsp. honey, and ½ tsp. pumpkin pie spice.

BRUSSELS SPROUTS

Trim and halve. Roast 15 to 20 minutes. Toss with 1 Tbsp. lime juice and 1½ Tbsp. snipped cilantro.

BROCCOLI

Cut into stalks. Roast 15 to 18 minutes. Toss with 1½ tsp. lemon juice, 2 Tbsp. reduced-fat feta, and 1 Tbsp. parsley.

SWEET POTATOES

Cut unpeeled potatoes into 1-inch cubes. Roast 20 to 25 minutes. Toss with 2 tsp. snipped fresh thyme.

SWEET PEPPERS

Cut into 2-inch pieces. Roast 20 to 25 minutes. Sprinkle with 2 Tbsp. snipped fresh basil.

ONIONS

Cut into ½-inch wedges. Roast 20 to 25 minutes. Toss with 2 Tbsp. balsamic vinegar and 1 Tbsp. crumbled Gorgonzola.

ASPARAGUS

Cut into 3-inch pieces. Add 1½ tsp. minced garlic with oil. Roast 10 to 15 minutes. Toss with lemon juice.

HEALTHY HABIT:
PLAN YOUR MEALS

Eating on a meal-by-meal basis can lead you to shop in convenience stores, dine at restaurants, order from to-go eateries, or piece together bites from here and there. Planning your meals in advance makes you less susceptible to poor food choices and more successful at eating healthfully and losing weight.

MY MEAL-PLANNING GOAL

One night this week I will write out the next five days' worth of meals, as well as my grocery list—and I'll stick to the plan.

> " It wasn't a shocker that I got type 2 diabetes since it runs in my family. I just didn't expect to get it in my 40s. "

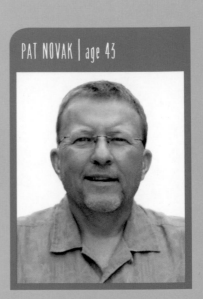

PAT NOVAK | age 43

After his type 2 diabetes diagnosis, Pat wasted no time starting medications and making some changes. Pat has also taken advantage of some of the health programs offered in his community of New Ulm, Minnesota. He took healthy-cooking classes, attended the diabetes education classes at his local hospital, started walking, and even ran his first 5K race. Pat lost 40 pounds, and his blood sugar, blood pressure, and cholesterol are all under control now. "It's helpful living in a community that supports exercise and healthy eating."

Kick-start into action: "Initially I was angry at myself for getting so out of shape and feeling like I screwed up my health and my future." But Pat views his diagnosis as a wake-up call and blessing.

Words of wisdom: "It helped when I realized a lot of people have diabetes. I learned to accept that diabetes takes vigilance, but I balance that with the things I like and want to do in life."

YOUR ONE-WEEK meal plan

Kick-start your healthy eating by following this one-week food plan. This plan is appropriate for an overweight or moderate-size woman who wants to lose weight.

	monday	tuesday	wednesday
breakfast	• 1 **Chocolate-Strawberry Breakfast Parfait** *(page 39)* • 1 hard-cooked egg • 8 oz. coffee or unsweetened tea with 2 Tbsp. fat-free half-and-half and 0-calorie sweetener	• 1 serving **Cranberry-Almond Cereal** *(page 30; prepare mix night before)* • 8 oz. coffee or unsweetened tea with 2 Tbsp. fat-free half-and-half and 0-calorie sweetener	• 1 serving **Maple Berry-Topped Waffles** *(page 39)* • 1 2% milk cheese stick twist, such as Kraft Twists • 8 oz. coffee or unsweetened tea with 2 Tbsp. fat-free half-and-half and 0-calorie sweetener
snack	• 1 2% milk cheese stick twist, such as Kraft Twists • 1 small apple (2¾-inch diameter)	• 1 frozen 7-grain waffle, such as Kashi, toasted, with 1 Tbsp. nut butter and ¼ cup berries	• 2 chocolate breakfast biscuits, such as belVita *(half package)* • ¼ cup light whipped dessert topping
lunch	• 2 slices whole grain bread with 1 slice thin sharp cheddar, 2 oz. deli-sliced turkey breast, ¼ avocado, ¼ cup spinach, and 2 tsp. whole grain mustard • 1 small cluster grapes *(15)*	• 1 serving **Hummus and Avocado Sandwiches** *(page 272)* • 1 hard-cooked egg • ¼ cup almonds	• **Meatless Taco Salad** *(page 135)* • ¾ cup pineapple chunks • 8 oz. fat-free milk
snack	• 1 large stalk celery • 1 Tbsp. nut butter	• ½ cup low-fat cottage cheese • ½ cup sliced carrot	• ½ cup sweet pepper strips • 3 Tbsp. hummus
dinner	• 1 serving **Farro-Stuffed Chicken with Sweet and Spicy Squash** *(page 322)* • 1½ cups spinach with 2 Tbsp. reduced-fat Italian dressing • 1 Tootsie Roll lollipop	• 1 serving **Honey Asian Tuna and Pineapple Pasta** *(page 323)* • 8 oz. fat-free milk • 1 cup broccoli, steamed, with lemon juice and dash salt • 1 small cluster frozen grapes	• 1 serving **Chicken and Farro Salad** *(page 321)* • 1½ cups spinach with 2 Tbsp. reduced-fat Italian dressing • 3 cups air-popped popcorn with 1 Tbsp. butter, melted
total	1,419 cal., 43 g total fat (11 g sat. fat), 331 mg chol., 2,041 mg sodium, 155 g carb. (24 g fiber, 88 g sugars), 94 g pro.	1,431 cal., 53 g total fat (11 g sat. fat), 229 mg chol., 1,973 mg sodium, 176 g carb. (39 g fiber, 67 g sugars), 79 g pro.	1,400 cal., 50 g total fat (16 g sat. fat), 108 mg chol., 2,361 mg sodium, 177 g carb. (31 g fiber, 68 g sugars), 70 g pro.

thursday	friday	saturday	sunday
• **Yogurt Breakfast Pudding** (page 30; prep night before) • 8 oz. coffee or unsweetened tea with 2 Tbsp. fat-free half-and-half and 0-calorie sweetener sweetener	• **Quick Cornmeal Sausage Pancake** (page 35) • 8 oz. coffee or unsweetened tea with 2 Tbsp. fat-free half-and-half and 0-calorie sweetener	• 1 serving **Cranberry-Almond Cereal** (page 30) and 1 egg • 8 oz. coffee or unsweetened tea with 2 Tbsp. fat-free half-and-half and 0-calorie sweetener	• 1 serving **Turkey-Sweet Pepper Strata** (page 24) • 8 oz. coffee or unsweetened tea
• 1 hard-cooked egg • 1 slice whole grain bread • 1 Tbsp. nut butter	• $^3/_4$ cup pineapple chunks • $^1/_2$ cup low-fat cottage cheese	• 2 Tbsp. golden raisins • $^1/_4$ cup pecans • $^1/_2$ small orange	• $^1/_2$ cup berries • $^1/_2$ cup low-fat cottage cheese
• 2 slices whole grain bread, 1 slice thin sharp cheddar, 2 oz. deli turkey breast, $^1/_4$ avocado, $^1/_4$ cup spinach, 2 tsp. whole grain mustard • 1 small cluster grapes	• **Shrimp and Broccoli Noodle Bowl** (page 135) • $^1/_2$ small orange • 8 oz. fat-free milk	• 1 serving **Shrimp and Edamame Salad with Ginger Dressing** (page 154) • 6 whole grain crackers, such as Triscuit • 8 oz. fat-free milk	• 1 serving **BBQ Chicken and Roasted Corn Salad** (page 157) • 1 slice whole grain bread, toasted • 8 oz. fat-free milk
• 1 2% milk cheese stick twist, such as Kraft Twists • 1 small apple	• 6 whole grain crackers, such as Triscuit • 1 oz. deli-sliced turkey • 3 Tbsp. hummus	• $^1/_2$ cup grape tomatoes • 2 Tbsp. light salad dressing • $^1/_4$ cup berries	• 1 large stalk celery • 1 Tbsp. nut butter
• 1 serving **Squash and Spinach Lasagna Roll-Ups** (page 323) • 8 oz. fat-free milk • $^1/_2$ cup sugar-free gelatin • $^1/_4$ cup light whipped topping	• 1 serving **Fish Amandine** (page 274) with $^3/_4$ cup broccoli slaw mixed with $^1/_4$ cup plain fat-free yogurt • 2 chocolate breakfast biscuits, such as belVita • $^1/_4$ cup light whipped topping	• 1 serving **Creamy Spinach and Artichoke Chicken** (page 178) • $^1/_2$ cup snow pea pods, steamed, with lemon juice and dash salt	• 1 serving **Falafel and Vegetable Pitas** (page 183) • $^1/_4$ cup almonds • 5 oz. red wine or 12 oz. light beer
1,440 cal., 51 g total fat (16 g sat. fat), 281 mg chol., 1,906 mg sodium, 166 g carb. (31 g fiber, 78 g sugars), 79 g pro.	1,417 cal., 41 g total fat (13 g sat. fat), 412 mg chol., 2,313 mg sodium, 161 g carb. (22 g fiber, 71 g sugars), 108 g pro.	1,384 cal., 47 g total fat (9 g sat. fat), 339 mg chol., 1,650 mg sodium, 175 g carb. (30 g fiber, 69 g sugars), 74 g pro.	1,437 cal., 48 g total fat (9 g sat. fat), 229 mg chol., 2,164 mg sodium, 132 g carb. (32 g fiber, 31 g sugars), 103 g pro.

SHOP SMART
cook smart

Make weeknights easier by streamlining your grocery trip. You will find two short shopping lists— each helps you build four fresh, flavorful, and unique dinners. The eight recipes for them ensure you're eating healthful, satisfying meals during the week.

Cheesy Chicken and Kale Roll-Ups
recipe, *page 316*

Open-Face French Onion Soup Burgers
recipe, *page 317*

Bolognese-Sauced Potatoes
recipe, *page 318*

Chicken Paprikash Soup
recipe, *page 319*

4 FRESH MEALS WITH ONLY 1 TRIP TO THE STORE!

SHOPPING LIST

- ☐ 5 russet potatoes
- ☐ 5 onions
- ☐ 1 bunch green onions
- ☐ 5 cups torn fresh kale
- ☐ $1\frac{1}{2}$ pounds extra-lean ground beef (95% lean)
- ☐ Four 8-ounce skinless, boneless chicken breast halves
- ☐ $3\frac{1}{2}$ ounces Fontina cheese
- ☐ One 8-ounce carton light sour cream
- ☐ Two 14.5-ounce cans crushed tomatoes
- ☐ 50%-less-sodium beef broth
- ☐ Reduced-sodium chicken broth
- ☐ 2 whole wheat reduced-calorie hamburger buns

FROM YOUR PANTRY

Keep these items on hand at all times.

- Salt
- Black pepper
- Salt-free garlic and herb seasoning blend
- Italian seasoning
- Dried thyme
- Paprika
- Garlic cloves
- Olive oil
- Nonstick cooking spray
- All-purpose flour

1 Cheesy Chicken and Kale Roll-Ups

SERVINGS 4 (1 roll-up and 3 tablespoons sauce each)

CARB. PER SERVING 8 g

PREP 45 minutes   BAKE 15 minutes

Nonstick cooking spray
- 4 teaspoons olive oil
- 3 cups torn fresh kale
- ½ cup chopped onion
- ¼ teaspoon salt
- 2 8-ounce skinless, boneless chicken breast halves, halved horizontally
- 1 teaspoon salt-free garlic and herb seasoning blend
- 2 teaspoons all-purpose flour
- 6 tablespoons reduced-sodium chicken broth
- ⅛ teaspoon salt
- 1½ ounces Fontina cheese, shredded (about ⅓ cup)
- ¼ cup light sour cream

1. Preheat oven to 400°F. Line baking sheet with foil. Lightly coat foil with cooking spray; set aside.

2. In a large nonstick skillet heat 1 teaspoon of the olive oil over medium heat. Add kale, onion, and ¼ teaspoon salt. Cook and stir about 5 minutes or until kale is wilted and onion is tender (if mixture appears dry during cooking, add 2 tablespoons water). Set aside.

3. Place chicken pieces between two sheets of plastic wrap. Using the flat side of a meat mallet, flatten chicken to a ¼-inch thickness. Season chicken with the garlic and herb seasoning.

4. Spread kale mixture evenly over chicken. Starting from a narrow end, roll up each chicken piece. Secure with wooden toothpicks.

5. Using paper towels, wipe out the skillet. Heat 1 teaspoon of the olive oil over medium-high heat. Add chicken rolls. Cook 2 minutes per side or until browned on all sides. Transfer to the prepared baking sheet; bake 15 to 20 minutes or until internal temperature of rolls reaches 165°F.

6. Meanwhile, in a small saucepan heat the remaining 2 teaspoons oil over medium heat. Whisk in the flour. Cook and stir 1 minute. Whisk in 4 tablespoons of the broth and the ⅛ teaspoon salt. Cook and stir until thickened and bubbly. Cook and stir 1 minute more. Add the cheese. Cook and stir until cheese is melted. Remove from heat and stir in the sour cream. Add the remaining 2 tablespoons broth; whisk until smooth. Return to heat and cook just until heated through. Remove toothpicks from chicken. Slice chicken crosswise and drizzle sauce over slices. Serve immediately.

PER SERVING: 268 cal., 13 g total fat (4 g sat. fat), 89 mg chol., 482 mg sodium, 8 g carb. (1 g fiber, 2 g sugars), 30 g pro.

② Open-Face French Onion Soup Burgers

SERVINGS 4 (1 burger each)
CARB. PER SERVING 15 g
PREP 15 minutes   COOK 18 minutes
GRILL 8 minutes

2   teaspoons olive oil
2   large onions, thinly sliced
½   teaspoon salt
¼   cup 50%-less-sodium beef broth
12   ounces extra-lean ground beef
     (95% lean)
1   teaspoon dried thyme, crushed
1   teaspoon cracked black pepper
Nonstick cooking spray
2   ounces Fontina cheese, shredded
2   whole wheat reduced-calorie
     hamburger buns, toasted

1. For caramelized onions, in a medium skillet heat oil over medium-low heat. Add onions and ¼ teaspoon of the salt . Cook, covered, 13 to 15 minutes or until onions are tender, stirring occasionally. Uncover; cook and stir over medium-high heat 3 to 5 minutes or until golden. Add beef broth, stirring to scrape up any browned bits from the bottom of the pan. Cook about 2 minutes more or until liquid is nearly evaporated. Set aside.

2. Meanwhile, in a medium bowl combine beef, thyme, pepper, and remaining salt. Shape meat mixture into four patties. Grill patties on the rack of an uncovered grill or grill pan directly over medium heat 8 to 10 minutes or until a thermometer insterted in side of patty registers 160°F, turning once. During last 1 to 2 minutes of grilling, top burgers with shredded cheese.

3. Serve burgers on toasted bun halves; top with caramelized onions.

PER SERVING: 265 cal., 11 g total fat (5 g sat. fat), 69 mg chol., 524 mg sodium, 15 g carb. (5 g fiber, 5 g sugars), 25 g pro.

3 Bolognese-Sauced Potatoes

SERVINGS 4 (1 potato, 1¼ cups sauce, 1½ teaspoons sour cream, and 1½ teaspoons green onions each)

CARB. PER SERVING 41 g

PREP 15 minutes   **BAKE** 50 minutes
COOK 12 minutes   **COOL** 5 minutes

- 4 medium russett potatoes (about 5 ounces each)
- 1 tablespoon olive oil
- 1 cup chopped onion
- 5 cloves garlic, minced
- 1 teaspoon Italian seasoning, crushed
- ½ teaspoon salt
- ¼ teaspoon black pepper
- 12 ounces extra-lean ground beef (95% lean)
- 1 14.5-ounce can crushed tomatoes
- 2 cups chopped fresh kale
- 2 tablespoons light sour cream
- 2 green onions, chopped

1. Preheat oven to 425°F. Scrub potatoes thoroughly with a brush; pat dry. Prick potatoes with a fork. Bake 50 to 60 minutes or until tender. Cool slightly.

2. Meanwhile, in a medium saucepan heat olive oil over medium heat. Add onion and garlic; cook 6 to 8 minutes or until tender. Add Italian seasoning, salt, and pepper; cook 1 to 2 minutes more. Add ground beef; cook 5 minutes or until browned, stirring to break up meat as it cooks. Add tomatoes and kale. Bring to boiling, stirring frequently; reduce heat. Cover and keep warm until potatoes are done, stirring occasionally.

3. Remove potatoes from oven; let cool 5 minutes. Make a lengthwise slit down the tops of potatoes and scoop out about 3 tablespoons flesh from each; discard or save for another use.

4. Top potatoes with sauce, sour cream, and green onions.

PER SERVING: 363 cal., 12 g total fat (4 g sat. fat), 56 mg chol., 467 mg sodium, 41 g carb. (7 g fiber, 4 g sugars), 24 g pro.

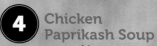

4 Chicken
Paprikash Soup

SERVINGS 4 (1¼ cups each)
CARB. PER SERVING 20 g
PREP 10 minutes   COOK 40 minutes

- 1 tablespoon olive oil
- 1 cup chopped onion
- 2 cloves garlic, minced
- 1 tablespoon all-purpose flour
- 1 tablespoon paprika
- ¼ teaspoon salt
- 1 cup canned crushed tomatoes
- 2 cups reduced-sodium chicken broth
- ¼ teaspoon freshly cracked black pepper
- 1 pound skinless, boneless chicken breast halves, cut into 2-inch pieces
- 1 8-ounce potato, peeled and cut into ½ inch cubes
- 6 tablespoons light sour cream
- Freshly cracked black pepper (optional)

1. In a medium saucepan heat oil over medium heat. Add onions and garlic; cook and stir 3 to 4 minutes or until tender. Stir in the flour, paprika, and salt; cook and stir 1 minute more. Add the tomatoes; stirring to scrape up any browned bits from the bottom of the saucepan. Simmer 3 to 4 minutes or until thickened. Add the broth; bring to boiling.

2. Sprinkle ¼ teaspoon pepper on chicken. Add the chicken to broth mixture. Return to boiling; reduce heat . Simmer, covered, 20 minutes or until chicken is no longer pink.

3. Remove chicken from the broth and place on a cutting board. When chicken is cool enough to handle, use two forks to pull meat apart into shreds; set aside.

4. Meanwhile, add the potatoes to the broth. Simmer, uncovered, 8 to 10 minutes or until tender. Stir in the shredded chicken. Heat through.

5. Remove soup from heat and stir in 4 tablespoons of the sour cream. Garnish with remaining sour cream and, if desired, freshly cracked pepper.

PER SERVING: 271 cal., 9 g total fat (2 g sat. fat), 79 mg chol., 386 mg sodium, 20 g carb. (3 g fiber, 2 g sugars), 29 g pro.

1

Chicken and Farro Salad

recipe,
page 321

2

Farro-Stuffed Chicken with Sweet and Spicy Squash

recipe,
page 322

3

Honey Asian Tuna and Pineapple Pasta

recipe,
page 323

4

Squash and Spinach Lasagna Roll-Ups

recipe,
page 323

USE THIS LIST FOR 4 MORE DINNERS

SHOPPING LIST

- ☐ Two 10-ounce packages frozen chopped spinach
- ☐ Three 12-ounce packages frozen cooked winter squash
- ☐ 1 cup semipearled farro
- ☐ Two 8-ounce cans pineapple chunks packed in 100 percent fruit juice
- ☐ Reduced-sodium soy sauce
- ☐ Two 14.5-ounce cans no-salt-added diced tomatoes with basil, garlic, and oregano
- ☐ 1½ cups shredded part-skim mozzarella cheese
- ☐ One 6.4-ounce pouch white albacore tuna packed in water
- ☐ 2 ounces walnut pieces
- ☐ Two 8-ounce packages frozen chopped green peppers and onions
- ☐ 12 dried whole grain lasagna noodles
- ☐ 36 ounces skinless, boneless chicken breast halves (6 breast halves)

FROM YOUR PANTRY

Keep these items on hand at all times.

- Salt
- Black pepper
- Red wine vinegar
- Honey
- Olive oil
- Canola oil
- Nonstick cooking spray
- Cornstarch
- Chili powder
- Egg
- Brown sugar

① Chicken and Farro Salad

SERVINGS 4 (1 cup each)
CARB. PER SERVING 32 g
PREP 20 minutes **COOK** 30 minutes
CHILL 1 to 8 hours

1	8-ounce can pineapple chunks (juice pack)
3	tablespoons red wine vinegar
4	teaspoons olive oil
1¼	cups water
⅔	cup semipearled farro, rinsed and drained
1	10-ounce package frozen chopped spinach, thawed and squeezed dry
12	ounces skinless, boneless chicken breast halves, cut into bite-size pieces

1. For dressing, drain pineapple, reserving juice. Set pineapple aside. In a small screw-top jar combine 2 tablespoons of the reserved pineapple juice, the red wine vinegar, oil, ½ teaspoon *salt*, and ¼ teaspoon *black pepper*. Cover and shake well to combine; set aside.

2. In a medium saucepan combine the water and farro. Bring to boiling; reduce heat. Simmer, covered, about 30 minutes or until farro is tender and water is absorbed. Stir in spinach. Let cool.

3. Meanwhile, sprinkle chicken with ⅛ teaspoon *salt* and ⅛ teaspoon *black pepper*. Coat a large nonstick skillet with *nonstick cooking spray*. Heat skillet over medium-high heat. Add chicken; cook until no longer pink, stirring occasionally. Remove from heat; let cool.

4. In a large bowl combine the farro mixture, chicken, and pineapple chunks. Add dressing.* Toss to combine. Cover and chill at least 1 hour or up to 8 hours before serving. If desired, sprinkle with *freshly ground black pepper*.

*TEST KITCHEN TIP: If you prefer, chill dressing and salad separately up to 24 hours before serving. Toss salad with the dressing just before serving.

PER SERVING: 300 cal., 7 g total fat (1 g sat. fat), 54 mg chol., 539 mg sodium, 32 g carb. (4 g fiber, 6 g sugars), 25 g pro.

2 Farro-Stuffed Chicken with Sweet and Spicy Squash

SERVINGS 4 (1 chicken breast half, ¼ cup stuffing, and ⅔ cup squash mixture each)
CARB. PER SERVING 33 g or 29 g **PREP** 25 minutes
COOK 29 minutes **BAKE** 18 minutes

- ½ cup canned no-salt-added diced tomatoes with basil, garlic, and oregano, drained
- ¼ cup semipearled farro, rinsed and drained
- ½ cup frozen chopped green peppers and onions
- 4 6-ounce skinless, boneless chicken breast halves
- 4 teaspoons olive oil
- 2 12-ounce packages frozen cooked winter squash, thawed
- 2 tablespoons packed brown sugar*
- 1 to 2 teaspoons chili powder

1. Preheat oven to 400°F. In a small saucepan combine ¾ cup *water*, the tomatoes, farro, ¼ teaspoon *salt*, and ¼ teaspoon *black pepper*. Bring to boiling; reduce heat. Simmer, covered, 20 to 25 minutes or until liquid is absorbed and farro is just tender. Add green peppers and onions. Cover and cook 1 minute more. Remove from heat; cool slightly.

2. Cut a pocket in each chicken breast half by cutting horizontally through the thickest portion to, but not through, the opposite side. Spoon farro mixture into pockets. If needed, secure pockets with wooden toothpicks. Sprinkle with ⅛ teaspoon *salt* and ⅛ teaspoon *black pepper*.
3. In an extra-large oven-going skillet heat oil over medium-high heat. Add chicken; cook about 8 minutes or until browned, turning to brown evenly. Transfer skillet to oven. Bake about 18 minutes or until chicken is no longer pink and an instant-read thermometer inserted in chicken (not in stuffing) registers 165°F.
4. Meanwhile, in a medium saucepan combine squash, brown sugar, chili powder, ⅛ teaspoon *salt*, and ⅛ teaspoon *black pepper*. Cook over medium heat until heated, stirring occasionally.
5. To serve, divide squash mixture among four plates; top squash mixture with stuffed chicken breasts.

*****SUGAR SUBSTITUTE:** Choose Splenda Brown Sugar Blend. Follow package directions to use product amount equivalent to 2 tablespoons brown sugar.

PER SERVING: 399 cal., 9 g total fat (2 g sat. fat), 109 mg chol., 484 mg sodium, 33 g carb. (4 g fiber, 15 g sugars), 39 g pro.
PER SERVING WITH SUBSTITUTE: Same as above, except 387 cal., 29 g carb. (11 g sugars).

3 Honey Asian Tuna and Pineapple Pasta

SERVINGS 4 (1¼ cups each)
CARB. PER SERVING 40 g
START TO FINISH 25 minutes

- 6 dried whole grain lasagna noodles
- 1 8-ounce can pineapple chunks (juice pack)
- 2 tablespoons reduced-sodium soy sauce
- 2 teaspoons honey
- 1 teaspoon cornstarch
- 2 teaspoons canola oil
- 1 8-ounce package frozen chopped green peppers and onions
- 1 6.4-ounce pouch white albacore tuna in water

1. Cook lasagna noodles according to package directions. Drain; let cool. Cut each lasagna noodle in half crosswise, then cut each half into long thin strips.

2. Drain pineapple, reserving juice. Set pineapple aside. In a small bowl whisk together the pineapple juice, soy sauce, honey, and cornstarch.

3. In a large nonstick skillet heat oil over medium-high heat. Add green peppers and onions. Cook 2 minutes. Stir in pineapple juice mixture. Cook and stir until thickened and bubbly. Stir in lasagna noodle strips, pineapple chunks, and tuna. Cook and gently stir until heated through. If desired, sprinkle with *freshly ground black pepper.*

PER SERVING: 248 cal., 4 g total fat (1 g sat. fat), 16 mg chol., 427 mg sodium, 40 g carb. (5 g fiber, 13 g sugars), 15 g pro.

4 Squash and Spinach Lasagna Roll-Ups

SERVINGS 6 (1 roll-up each)
CARB. PER SERVING 25 g
PREP 25 minutes BAKE 50 minutes

- 6 dried whole grain lasagna noodles
- 1 egg, lightly beaten
- ½ of a 12-ounce package frozen cooked winter squash, thawed
- ½ of a 10-ounce package frozen chopped spinach, thawed and squeezed dry
- 1½ cups shredded part-skim mozzarella cheese
- 6 tablespoons walnut pieces, chopped and toasted
- 1 14.5-ounce can no-salt-added diced tomatoes with basil, garlic, and oregano, undrained

1. Lightly coat a piece of foil with *nonstick cooking spray;* set aside. Cook lasagna noodles according to package directions, except cook 2 minutes less than suggested time; drain. Place noodles in a single layer on the prepared foil.

2. Preheat oven to 350°F. In a bowl combine egg, squash, spinach, ¼ teaspoon *salt,* and ¼ teaspoon *black pepper.* Stir in ¾ cup of the cheese. Spread mixture evenly on noodles; sprinkle with walnuts. Roll up noodles. Arrange roll-ups in a 1½-quart baking dish. Set aside.

3. In a food processor combine tomatoes, ¼ teaspoon *salt,* and ¼ teaspoon *black pepper.* Cover; process until smooth. Pour over roll-ups.

4. Cover and bake 40 minutes. Sprinkle with the remaining ¾ cup cheese. Bake, uncovered, about 10 minutes or until cheese is melted.

PER SERVING: 248 cal., 11 g total fat (4 g sat. fat), 49 mg chol., 426 mg sodium, 25 g carb. (8 g fiber, 6 g sugars), 14 g pro.

WHAT ABOUT
snacks?

You may have heard that people with type 2 diabetes need to snack in order to avoid low blood sugar. But with current medications, including insulin, snacking is no longer a must—and it might even make it harder to reach your weight or blood glucose goal. Follow these tips for fitting snacks into your day the smart way.

DON'T SNACK just to prevent low blood sugars. Years ago, when few types of medications were available, snacks were necessary to prevent blood glucose from dropping too low between meals. That's not the case with many of today's blood glucose-lowering medications. If you regularly experience lows, talk to your health care provider about decreasing or changing medications.

DO SNACK if it helps you meet nutrition needs and fit in the food groups you need for the day, such as fruits, vegetables, whole grains, and nuts.

DO SNACK on healthful foods if such a snack helps you stop out-of-control eating. A piece of fruit in the afternoon might tame your hunger enough to hold you over until dinner.

DON'T SNACK if it leads to overeating. Even an extra 50 calories twice a day can stand between you and a tighter notch on your belt.

CHOOSE THIS, not that

CHOOSE	NOT	WHY?
thin pretzels	thick sourdough pretzels	Enjoy 11 thin crispy pretzels for every one big sourdough hard pretzel.
Tootsie Roll lollipop	$\frac{1}{4}$ cup of M&M's	Go for a sweet lollipop with a chocolate center to save 22 grams of carb.
light string cheese stick	cheese-flavor crackers	Eat real cheese, cut 19 grams of carb., and get 15% daily calcium in one stick.
a chocolate rice cake	a chocolate snack cake	Take in 14 fewer grams of carb. and still enjoy a chocolaty treat.
frozen low-fat Greek yogurt	gourmet ice cream	Cut 110 calories; gain high-protein and probiotics not found in ice cream.
a mini bagel with reduced-fat strawberry cream cheese	a cream-filled doughnut	Eat a sweet, chewy bagel snack that's a good source of fiber and protein and save 165 calories.

light & easy SNACKS

Eating a portion-controlled, nutritionally-balanced snack between meals can help keep your blood glucose stabilized, stave off hunger, and give you an energy boost.

CHOCOLATE PEANUT BUTTER GRANOLA BARS

SERVINGS 18 (1 granola bar each)
CARB. PER SERVING 23 g
PREP 20 minutes BAKE 22 minutes

Nonstick cooking spray
1 cup regular rolled oats
¼ cup light-color corn syrup
¼ cup peanut butter
3 tablespoons packed brown sugar
2 tablespoons butter
2 tablespoons honey
1 tablespoon vanilla
½ teaspoon salt
2 cups crisp rice cereal
¾ cup coarsely broken pretzel sticks
¼ cup toasted wheat germ
2 tablespoons chia seeds
¼ cup miniature semisweet chocolate pieces

1. Preheat oven to 350°F. Line a 13×9×2-inch baking pan with foil. Coat foil with cooking spray; set aside. Spread oats in a 15×10×1-inch baking pan. Bake 10 to 15 minutes or until toasted, stirring twice. Remove from oven; let cool. Reduce oven temperature to 300°F.
2. Meanwhile, in a small saucepan combine the corn syrup, peanut butter, brown sugar, butter, and honey. Heat and stir over medium heat just until peanut butter and brown sugar are melted. Remove from heat. Stir in vanilla and salt.
3. In a bowl combine the toasted oats, rice cereal, pretzels, wheat germ, and chia seeds. Pour syrup mixture over oat mixture; mix well.
4. Press mixture into the prepared pan. Sprinkle chocolate over top; press into oat mixture. Bake 12 to 15 minutes or until firm. Cool completely.

PER SERVING: 148 cal., 5 g total fat (2 g sat. fat), 3 mg chol., 147 mg sodium, 23 g carb. (2 g fiber, 11 g sugars), 4 g pro.

HONEY-SESAME SNACK MIX

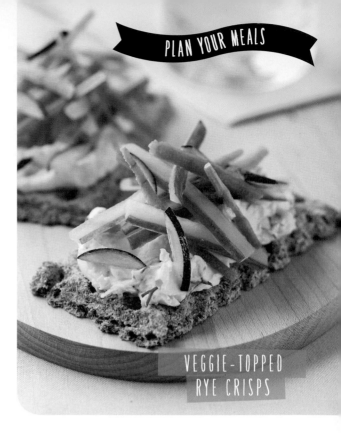

Honey-Sesame Snack Mix

SERVINGS 16 ($\frac{1}{2}$ cup each)
CARB. PER SERVING 13 g
PREP 15 minutes BAKE 20 minutes

- 2 cups rice square cereal
- 2 cups puffed wheat cereal
- $1\frac{1}{2}$ cups lightly salted brown rice crisps or chips
- $1\frac{1}{2}$ cups sea salt-flavored thin almond crackers or sea salt-flavored baked almond chips
- $\frac{1}{2}$ cup pumpkin seeds (pepitas) or wasabi-flavor dried peas
- $\frac{1}{2}$ cup unsalted soy nuts
- 2 tablespoons toasted sesame oil
- 2 tablespoons honey
- 2 tablespoons lemon juice
- 2 tablespoons reduced-sodium soy sauce
- 1 tablespoon sesame seeds
- 2 teaspoons prepared horseradish (optional)

1. Preheat oven to 300°F. In a shallow baking pan combine rice cereal, wheat cereal, rice crackers, almond crackers, pumpkin seeds, and soy nuts. In a small saucepan stir together oil, honey, lemon juice, soy sauce, sesame seeds, and, if desired, horseradish. Cook and stir just until boiling. Remove from heat. Pour over cereal mixture, tossing just until coated. Spread cereal mixture in an even layer.

2. Bake, uncovered, 20 to 25 minutes or until mixture is lightly toasted and crisp, stirring twice. Remove from oven. Immediately turn out onto a large piece of foil; cool completely.

TO STORE: Place mix in an airtight container. Store at room temperature up to 2 days or freeze up to 2 weeks.

PER SERVING: 117 cal., 6 g total fat (1 g sat. fat), 0 mg chol., 109 mg sodium, 13 g carb. (1 g fiber, 3 g sugars), 4 g pro.

VEGGIE-TOPPED RYE CRISPS

Veggie-Topped Rye Crisps

SERVINGS 4 (2 topped crackers each)
CARB. PER SERVING 21 g
START TO FINISH 20 minutes

- $\frac{1}{2}$ cup light cream cheese spread, softened
- $\frac{1}{2}$ teaspoon finely shredded lemon peel
- $\frac{1}{2}$ teaspoon snipped fresh dill weed or $\frac{1}{4}$ teaspoon dried dill weed
- 1 small clove garlic, minced
- 8 $3\frac{1}{2}$x$1\frac{1}{2}$-inch crisp rye crackers
- $\frac{1}{2}$ cup bite-size English cucumber strips
- $\frac{1}{2}$ cup coarsely shredded carrot (1 medium)
- $\frac{1}{4}$ cup thin bite-size radish strips

1. In a small bowl stir together cream cheese, lemon peel, dill weed, and garlic. Spread on crackers. Top with vegetables.

MAKE-AHEAD DIRECTIONS: Prepare cream cheese mixture as directed. Transfer to an airtight container; cover. Store in the refrigerator up to 2 days. Within 4 hours of assembling the crisps, cut up the vegetables and store, covered, in the refrigerator.

PER SERVING: 144 cal., 5 g total fat (3 g sat. fat), 15 mg chol., 246 mg sodium, 21 g carb. (4 g fiber, 3 g sugars), 5 g pro.

Creamy Avocado-Horseradish Dip

SERVINGS 6 (2 tablespoons dip with 2 leaves endive and ⅓ cup other vegetables each)
CARB. PER SERVING 6 g
PREP 15 minutes

- 1 medium ripe avocado, halved, seeded, and peeled
- ¼ cup light mayonnaise
- 2 tablespoons finely chopped green onion
- 2 teaspoons lemon juice
- 1 to 2 teaspoons prepared horseradish
- ⅛ teaspoon salt
- 1 head Belgian endive
- 2 cups carrot sticks, sweet pepper strips, and/or broccoli florets

1. In a medium bowl use a fork or potato masher to finely mash avocado. Stir in mayonnaise, green onion, lemon juice, horseradish, and salt until well combined.
2. Trim endive. Separate into leaves. Serve dip with endive leaves and carrot sticks, pepper strips, and/or broccoli florets.

MAKE-AHEAD DIRECTIONS: Prepare as directed in Step 1. Cover surface of dip completely with plastic wrap. Chill up to 8 hours. Serve as directed.

PER SERVING: 87 cal., 7 g total fat (1 g sat. fat), 4 mg chol., 131 mg sodium, 6 g carb. (3 g fiber, 2 g sugars), 1 g pro.

CREAMY AVOCADO-HORSERADISH DIP

BARBECUE-SPICED ROASTED CHICKPEAS

SERVINGS 12 (¼ cup each)
CARB. PER SERVING 10 g
PREP 5 minutes   **ROAST** 30 minutes

2 15-ounce cans no-salt-added garbanzo beans (chickpeas), rinsed and drained
¼ cup olive oil
1 teaspoon barbecue spice
1 teaspoon paprika
1 teaspoon chili powder
¼ teaspoon garlic salt
¼ teaspoon celery salt
¼ teaspoon onion powder

1. Preheat oven to 450°F. In a medium bowl combine garbanzo beans, oil, barbecue spice, paprika, chili powder, garlic salt, celery salt, and onion powder. Spread in an even layer in a 15×10×1-inch baking pan. Roast about 30 minutes or until browned and crisp, stirring once halfway through roasting. Cool completely.

MAKE-AHEAD DIRECTIONS: Place cooled chickpeas in an airtight container; cover. Store at room temperature up to 1 week.

PER SERVING: 101 cal., 5 g total fat (1 g sat. fat), 0 mg chol., 122 mg sodium, 10 g carb. (3 g fiber, 0 g sugars), 4 g pro.

TOMATO-LENTIL SALSA with CUMIN-SPICED CHIPS

Tomato-Lentil Salsa with Cumin-Spiced Chips

SERVINGS 6 ($^1/_3$ cup salsa and $^3/_4$ ounce Cumin-Spiced Chips each)
CARB. PER SERVING 19 g
PREP 20 minutes CHILL 8 hours

- 1 large tomato, cored and chopped
- $^1/_2$ cup refrigerated steamed lentils
- $^1/_4$ cup chopped fresh mango
- $^1/_4$ cup finely chopped radishes
- $^1/_4$ cup thinly sliced green onions
- 1 small fresh serrano chile pepper, seeded if desired and finely chopped (tip, *page 252*)
- 1 tablespoon snipped fresh cilantro
- 1 tablespoon snipped fresh mint
- 1 tablespoon lemon juice
- 1 recipe Cumin-Spiced Chips

1. In a medium bowl stir together tomato, lentils, mango, radishes, green onions, chile pepper, cilantro, mint, and lemon juice. Cover and chill up to 8 hours. Serve with Cumin-Spiced Chips.

CUMIN-SPICED CHIPS: Preheat oven to 375°F. Lightly coat a large baking sheet with nonstick cooking spray; set aside. Place 4 ounces plain pita chips in a bowl; lightly coat chips with cooking spray. In a small bowl combine 1 teaspoon paprika, $^1/_2$ teaspoon garlic powder, $^1/_4$ teaspoon ground coriander, $^1/_4$ teaspoon ground cumin, and a pinch salt. Sprinkle chips with spices while alternately tossing gently to coat. Spread chips on the prepared baking sheet. Bake 4 to 5 minutes or until lightly browned.

PER SERVING: 123 cal., 4 g total fat (0 g sat. fat), 0 mg chol., 247 mg sodium, 19 g carb. (3 g fiber, 3 g sugars), 4 g pro.

Ham-Wrapped Stuffed Celery Sticks

SERVINGS 6 (2 sticks each)
CARB. PER SERVING 5 g
PREP 15 minutes

- 3 ounces goat cheese (chèvre), softened
- $^1/_4$ cup light cream cheese spread, softened
- 1 tablespoon snipped fresh chives
- 1 tablespoon honey
- $^1/_4$ teaspoon black pepper
- 6 stalks celery
- $1^1/_2$ ounces thinly sliced lower-sodium ham

1. In a small bowl stir together goat cheese, cream cheese, chives, honey, and pepper until well combined. Set aside.
2. Trim celery stalks. Cut stalks in half crosswise. Spread cheese mixture evenly into celery sticks. Cut the ham slices lengthwise into 12 strips total. Wrap strips evenly around the center of each celery stick.

PER SERVING: 104 cal., 7 g total fat (4 g sat. fat), 22 mg chol., 221 mg sodium, 5 g carb. (1 g fiber, 4 g sugars), 6 g pro.

HAM-WRAPPED STUFFED CELERY STICKS

Caprese-Stuffed Cherry Tomatoes

SERVINGS 4 (6 stuffed tomatoes each)
CARB. PER SERVING 7 g
START TO FINISH 15 minutes

24 cherry tomatoes
4 ounces part-skim mozzarella cheese
2 tablespoons snipped fresh basil
1 tablespoon white balsamic vinegar
¼ teaspoon black pepper

1. Using a sharp knife, cut off the top third of each cherry tomato on the stem end. Hollow out the cherry tomatoes; invert on paper towels to drain. Set aside.

2. Cut the mozzarella into 24 cubes. In a medium bowl combine the cheese cubes, basil, vinegar, and pepper. Stuff each tomato with a coated cheese cube.

PER SERVING: 112 cal., 6 g total fat (3 g sat. fat), 15 mg chol., 190 mg sodium, 7 g carb. (1 g fiber, 5 g sugars), 8 g pro.

CAPRESE-STUFFED CHERRY TOMATOES

7-LAYER FRUIT DIP

SERVINGS 8 (2 tablespoons dip and 6 nut thins each)
CARB. PER SERVING 17 g
PREP 15 minutes   **CHILL** 12 hours

½ of an 8-ounce package reduced-fat cream cheese (Neufchâtel), softened
1 tablespoon honey
¼ teaspoon ground cinnamon
¼ teaspoon ground ginger
⅓ cup plain fat-free Greek-style yogurt
3 clementines, peeled and segmented
2 tablespoons snipped pitted dates or golden raisins
2 tablespoons unsweetened shredded coconut, toasted
2 tablespoons chopped dry-roasted salted pistachio nuts
2 tablespoons snipped fresh mint
48 almond nut thins

1. In a small bowl stir together cream cheese, honey, cinnamon, and ginger until well combined. Spread mixture into an 8-inch circle on a serving plate. Spread yogurt over cream cheese mixture, leaving about a ½-inch border around the edge. Arrange orange segments in a single layer on yogurt.

2. Sprinkle dates, coconut, pistachio nuts, and mint on orange segments. Serve with nut thins for scooping.

MAKE-AHEAD DIRECTIONS: Cover with plastic wrap and chill up to 12 hours.

PER SERVING: 133 cal., 6 g total fat (2 g sat. fat), 10 mg chol., 104 mg sodium, 17 g carb. (1 g fiber, 7 g sugars), 4 g pro.

FRUITY APPLESAUCE POPS

SERVINGS 16 (1 pop each)
CARB. PER SERVING 8 g
PREP 25 minutes   FREEZE overnight

1 32-ounce jar unsweetened applesauce
2 cups assorted fresh berries, such as raspberries, blackberries, blueberries, and/or sliced strawberries, and halved sweet cherries

1. In a large bowl stir together the applesauce and berries. Spoon into 16 freezer pop containers. Cover and freeze overnight. (Or spoon into sixteen 5-ounce paper cups. Cover cups with plastic wrap; secure wrap with tape or a rubber band. Insert a pop sticks through the plastic wrap into applesauce mixture. Freeze overnight.)

PER SERVING: 32 cal., 0 g total fat, 0 mg chol., 1 mg sodium, 8 g carb. (1 g fiber, 6 g sugars), 0 g pro.

HEALTHY HABIT:
MOVE MORE | STRESS LESS

Being active and managing your stress are among the most powerful ways to beat back diabetes. Get moving for at least 30 minutes five days each week and learn how to organize your thoughts, let go, and rethink the things that cause you stress. Those actions can help you see your diagnosis in a new light. Maybe it's just the motivation you need to adopt new and better habits.

MY MOVE-MORE GOAL

Three times this week I will go for a walk around my neighborhood after dinner.

SUCCESS STORY

> " **I'm conscious of the consequences of my behavior. Now when I'm stressed, I turn to exercise.** "

JUAN RAIDI | age 39

By the time he was 22 years old, Juan had reached 400 pounds. Though he had shed 180 pounds prior to his type 2 diabetes diagnosis, his blood glucose was still elevated— as high as 400 mg/dl at times. Juan moved to the U.S. from Venezuela in 2013 and was amazed by the scarcity of accurate diabetes information for Spanish-speaking people. Juan's sister introduced him to a Spanish language diabetes online community, EsTuDiabetes, which was a gateway of information, motivation, and support from others facing similar challenges. Juan no longer felt alone.

Kick-start into action: "Realizing I was killing myself with food was my wake-up call," says Juan, who manages his diabetes with regular exercise, better eating, and two blood glucose-lowering medications, Januvia and metformin.

Words of wisdom: "It's up to you, and no one is going to do it for you. But you are not alone in this—seek out a few diabetes comrades for support."

6 EASY WAYS TO MOVE MORE

No time to exercise? No problem! Sneak movement into your everyday routines. Little movements add up to big benefits.

If you're like a lot of people, you don't move as much as you should. The average American spends at least 10 hours a day doing sedentary activities: watching TV, surfing the Internet, talking on the phone, and reading. All of this sitting can make diabetes harder to control. According to the *Journal of Preventive Medicine*, women who sit for prolonged periods of time are more likely to have increased insulin resistance and chronic inflammation. And the more you sit, the worse it gets.

Another study found that adults who sit for 11 hours or more on a daily basis have a 40 percent greater risk of dying in the next three years than people who spend less than four hours a day in a chair.

Use these tips to incorporate more movement into the activities you're already doing.

1

START YOUR DAY WITH A QUICK WALK AROUND THE BLOCK

Nothing intense, nothing long—just a brisk walk to get you going. Leave your walking shoes by the door before bed so you'll be ready. Listen to your favorite morning news program on the go.

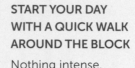

2

HOOK A PEDOMETER TO YOUR BODY

Studies show that when people are keeping track of their steps, they tend to walk more. You can even get into a friendly competition with your spouse or a coworker to see who can rack up the most steps in a day or a week. Reliable pedometers are available for less than $20.

3

DON'T WASTE COMMERCIAL TIME

While watching TV, get up and do a minute of jumping jacks or a minute of knee raises every time a commercial comes on. Research shows that people who step in place during commercials burn an average of 148 calories in about 25 minutes.

4

PARK AWAY

Drive to the farthest part of the lot to park your car instead of wasting time circling for a close spot. It's an easy way to add some extra steps to your daily routine, and it helps avoid door dings, too!

5

PASS THE CART FOR QUICK TRIPS

If you need just a handful of items at the grocery store, take two reusable bags and throw them over your shoulders. Put your food in the bags as you shop. While you wait to pay, hold the bags by your sides and do shoulder shrugs.

6 BE INEFFICIENT

Do you have loads of laundry to haul upstairs
or downstairs? Take one basket or one handful
of clothes at a time. Do you have groceries to
carry in from the car? Don't tote them all at once.
Deliberately break up daily tasks so you make
multiple, frequent trips.

DOWN TO THE core

You will benefit from low-impact exercises that increase the strength of your body core using your own body weight as resistance. Having a strong core determines how well you do any physical movement, including staying on your feet as you age and living independently.

By Sheri R. Colberg, Ph.D.

When you have diabetes, you are likely to lose twice as much of your muscle mass as you age as everyone else due to insulin resistance, and you can't afford to let that happen. Your muscle mass is especially critical to living long and well and remaining independent. Simple tasks like getting up out of a chair and carrying groceries require muscle strength, which you will be losing as time goes on if you're not doing any resistance exercises.

Luckily, you can keep and build your muscles by doing low-impact core exercises that don't require any special equipment or a gym membership. Having a strong core allows you to do more for yourself, avoid falling down, protect your joints from injury by strengthening the muscles around them, improve your posture, and prevent low back pain. Having more muscle will also help manage your blood glucose and help you lose weight and keep it off.

PLANKS

Planks are one of the best exercises you can do with or without diabetes to keep your upper body and core strong, but do them on a floor mat, rug, carpet, or softer floor surface to prevent injuries. *If this exercise is too hard for you, try a modified plank by bending your knees and resting on them instead.*

- Bend your elbows and rest on your forearms. Your elbows should be directly beneath your shoulders, and your body should form a straight line to your feet.

- Try to hold this position for 30 seconds (or as long as you can to start) and work up to holding for longer times.

- Repeat as many times as you can (at least 3 to 5 reps) for as long as possible each time, working up to 10 to 15 reps.

TAKE THE FLOOR

Working on your abdominal strength is a critical part of preventing diabetes-induced muscle loss and preventing low back pain related to carrying extra weight around your middle. Keep your core engaged throughout these floor exercises.

CRUNCHES

- Lie down on your back with your knees bent.

- Place your hands on your head behind your ears.

- While breathing out, contract your abdominal muscles to lift your head, neck, and shoulders off the floor and curl forward no more than 45 degrees.

- Hold for a moment before returning to the starting position. Do as many crunches as you can, working up to 15 or more.

WAIST WORKER

- Lie on your back with your legs bent, your feet flat on the floor, and your left hand behind your head.

- Stretch your right hand across your body toward your opposite (left) knee and circle your hand three times around that knee in a counterclockwise direction; your right shoulder blade will lift off the mat.

- Switch sides and repeat the stretch and circular movement around the right knee using your left arm, this time in a clockwise motion.

- Keep your head in a neutral position and relax your neck to contract your abdomen only.

- Work up to 15 reps on each side of your body.

BRIDGING

- Slowly raise your buttocks from the floor, keeping your stomach tight.
- Hold for 3 to 5 seconds before gently lowering your back to the floor.
- Repeat 15 times.

BRIDGING WITH STRAIGHT LEG RAISES

- With your legs bent, lift your buttocks off the floor. Slowly extend your right knee, keeping your stomach tight. Hold for a few seconds.
- Bend your knee and set your foot back down, then lower your buttocks to the ground.
- Repeat 15 times with each leg straight (all on one side at a time or alternating sides).

GRAB A CHAIR

If getting on the floor is difficult, work on arm and core strength with the help of a chair. Use a sturdy chair with a firm seat as you build strength.

CHAIR SIT-UPS

- Sit up straight with your feet on the floor and hands on seat edge for support.

- Bend forward, keeping your lower back straight, moving your chest down toward your thighs.

- Slowly straighten back up, using your lower back muscles to raise your torso.

- Repeat 15 times or more.

- For added resistance, put a resistance band under both feet and hold one end in each hand.

CHAIR PUSH-UPS

- Using your hands, grasp the arms of a sturdy chair.

- Slowly push your body as far as you can up off the chair. (Use your arms, not your legs.) Hold your weight for as long as you can (aim for 15 to 30 seconds), then slowly lower yourself back down. Don't drop into the chair.

- Work up to 15 reps.

- To vary the workout, lean slightly forward while doing the push-ups or sit on a phone book or cushion.

SIT-TO-STAND

- Sit toward the front of a sturdy chair and fold your arms across your chest.

- Keeping your back and shoulders straight, lean forward slightly. Stand up and sit back down slowly using only your legs.

- To assist you initially, place pillows on the chair behind your lower back.

- Repeat as many times as you can throughout the day.

BEND YOUR KNEES

People with diabetes are more prone to low back pain and can lose strength and flexibility faster than normal as they age. These exercises work on proper lifting techniques and help improve lower-body strength and flexibility.

SUITCASE LIFTS

- Place two items (hand weights, water bottles, or cans) slightly forward and between your feet on the floor. Stand up with your back straight.

- Keep your arms and back straight with your hands in front of your abdomen. Bend only your knees and reach down to pick up the items.

- Pick up the items in both hands, then push up with your legs and stand up, keeping your back straight. Repeat 15 times.

KNEE DIPS

- Get into a sprinter's stance as though you were at the starting line of a race— one leg forward and one behind and your hands on the floor in front of you.

- Bend both legs as much as is comfortable, bringing your knees as close to the floor as possible without touching.

- Push your body upward until your legs are almost straight without locking your knees.

- Switch the position of your legs and repeat with each leg forward 15 times.

SOOTHE YOUR
stress

Are you working hard on getting
healthier but still having trouble
controlling your blood sugar?
The problem could be runaway stress.

By Linda Wasmer Andrews

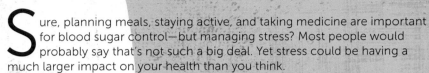

Sure, planning meals, staying active, and taking medicine are important for blood sugar control—but managing stress? Most people would probably say that's not such a big deal. Yet stress could be having a much larger impact on your health than you think.

"Stress management doesn't get the attention it deserves," says Joseph Napora, Ph.D., an instructor at the Johns Hopkins Comprehensive Diabetes Center and author of *Stress-Free Diabetes* (American Diabetes Association, 2010). "It's really the fourth dimension of diabetes control."

Luckily, there are a number of proven, practical strategies you can use to bring more serenity into your life. The first step is to understand how stress may be affecting your blood sugar levels.

UNDER STRAIN FROM STRESS

When you feel threatened, your brain tells your body to mobilize for fast action—a physiological reaction called the fight-or-flight response. As part of the response, the hormone cortisol is released. "This stimulates your liver to secrete more glucose to power your muscles," Napora says.

That's a good thing if you're preparing to fight or flee. But if you have diabetes, insulin may not be able to get all the extra glucose into your cells for energy, so the glucose builds up in your blood. Although people respond differently, Napora says that those with type 2 diabetes often notice that their glucose levels shoot up in stressful situations. (In people with type 1 diabetes, the effects of stress are more variable—glucose levels rise for most people but fall for others.)

Meanwhile, the stress response also triggers other physiological changes designed to help you, say, escape from a wild animal. "For example, your heart pumps faster and harder to get more blood to your arm and leg muscles," Napora says. Body functions that are less critical for immediate survival, such as immune function, slow down.

The problem is that your body reacts this way whether the threat is real or imagined, physical or psychological. In today's world, you're more likely to be faced with long work hours or high hospital bills than an attacking animal, and wrestling or running isn't much help in those situations. Plus, the stress may drag on for months or years, and living in a constant state of high alert takes a toll on your mind and body. "Prolonged, excessive stress can be a factor in depression, heart disease, impaired immune function, and other health problems," Napora says.

DISTRESSED AND DISTRACTED

Stressing out also harms your health in a stealthier way: It uses up much of the time and energy that might otherwise go into taking care of yourself.

"Stress throws people off their reliable routines," says Ann Goebel-Fabbri, Ph.D., a psychologist at the Joslin Diabetes Center and assistant professor of psychiatry at Harvard Medical School. "This means that they may take their medicines less reliably, do fewer glucose checks, eat differently, or allot less time for exercise."

When your attention is distracted by conflicts or worries, it's easy to slip back unthinkingly into old, unhealthy habits, such as overindulging in comfort foods or alcohol. "It's crucial to have some healthy, go-to strategies ready for managing stress so you don't fall back on these knee-jerk reactions," says Amy Walters, Ph.D., a psychologist at St. Luke's Humphreys Diabetes Center in Boise and the mom of a child with diabetes.

TAKE CHARGE OF THE CLOCK

When you have diabetes, it can be a major challenge to squeeze everything into your day, from checking your blood sugar to shopping for fresh veggies. Without a plan, you can easily end up feeling frazzled and frustrated. Try these tips to take control of your time:

TRIM THE TIME WASTERS. Keep a time diary for a couple of weeks, suggests Walters. Break each day into half-hour increments and write down what you do during each of these time blocks. Then look back through your diary for nonessential activities you can cut to make room for more important things. For example, by cutting out an hour of watching TV, you can find 60 minutes for taking a walk and cooking a nutritious meal.

PENCIL YOURSELF IN. To make sure you use the allotted time for this health-smart purpose, put it on your calendar. Then keep the appointment with yourself, just as you would an appointment with a friend or your doctor.

MAKE DE-STRESSING A PRIORITY. Remember that managing stress is essential for your health, too. Be sure to allocate some time for fun, relaxing activities, such as pursuing a hobby or visiting with friends.

STREAMLINE YOUR CARE. Work with your diabetes care team to simplify your treatment routine as much as possible, says Goebel-Fabbri. For example, your doctor might be able to switch you from taking multiple doses of medicine each day to taking a single dose of an extended-release preparation.

Hope Warshaw, RD, CDE   Jessie Shafer, RD

READY, SET, go!

When you make the decision to improve your health, it can sometimes feel like the start of a footrace—a dead sprint toward weight loss and better numbers. But that's just the type of approach that sends people off track, resulting in exhaustion and disappointment.

You've likely heard that the best way to manage your diabetes, lose weight, and improve your health is to make some lifestyle changes. That's true. But how do you go about changing your lifestyle? For starters, understand that it won't happen overnight. But rest assured, it can and will happen! The key is to start adopting healthy habits and shedding the bad ones.

Habits build up and break down over time until your little steps and positive choices snowball into results you can see and feel.

So where do you start? I've been working closely with diabetes expert Hope Warshaw, RD, CDE, to outline the top 10 healthy habits that are research-driven, evidence-based ways you can beat diabetes and prediabetes. I've also enlisted the help of the nation's top nutrition and diabetes professionals and the recipe creators in the Better Homes and Gardens® Test Kitchen to bring you dozens of expert tips and delicious, healthful recipes. Put them to work for you and soon you'll have adopted some new healthy habits.

Gain motivation from others, like Darlene Maalo *(page 42)*, who turned her health around by deciding that now is the time to act. You can't change your lifestyle overnight, but you can take the first step. Keep heading down that track to health. Even if you take a step backward now and then, you'll be amazed at how far you've traveled a week, a month, and a year from now. A healthy future is waiting. So off you go!

Jessie

Jessie Shafer, RD, has served as the food and nutrition editor at *Diabetic Living*®

CONTENTS

BEAT DIABETES

10 HABITS TO EAT YOUR WAY HEALTHY

MEET OUR advisers

The following health, food, and fitness professionals review articles that appear in *Diabetic Living*® publications.

Nicolas B. Argento, M.D., PWD type 1, is the diabetes technology and electronic medical records director at Maryland Endocrine, PA. He is also the diabetes program medical adviser for Howard County General Hospital.

Connie Crawley, M.S., RD, LD, is a nutrition and health specialist for the University of Georgia Cooperative Extension Service, specializing in diabetes and weight loss. She is a member of the Academy of Nutrition and Dietetics Diabetes Care and Education (DCE) practice group.

Marjorie Cypress, Ph.D., CNP, CDE, is a diabetes nurse practitioner in the department of endocrinology at ABQ Health Partners in Albuquerque. She is the president for Health Care and Education for the American Diabetes Association.

Marion J. Franz, M.S., RD, LD, CDE, has authored more than 200 publications on diabetes and nutrition, including core-curriculum materials for diabetes educators. She is a member of the Academy of Nutrition and Dietetics DCE practice group.

Joanne Gallivan, M.S., RD, is executive director of the National Diabetes Education Program at the National Institutes of Health. She is a member of the Academy of Nutrition and Dietetics DCE practice group.

Frank L. Greenway, M.D., is head of outpatient research at Pennington Biomedical Research Center of the Louisiana State University System. He is a fellow of the Obesity Society.

Sharonne Hayes, M.D., FACC, FAHA, is a cardiologist and founder of the Women's Heart Clinic at Mayo Clinic in Rochester, Minnesota. She maintains an active medical practice focusing on preventive cardiology and heart disease in women.

Marty Irons, R.Ph., CDE, practices at a community pharmacy and also served in industry and the military. He presents at diabetes education classes and is an author.

Irene B. Lewis-McCormick, M.S.,CSCS, is a fitness presenter and is certified by leading fitness organizations. She is an author, educator, and faculty member of the American Council on Exercise.

Chef Art Smith, star of Bravo's *Top Chef Masters* and former personal chef for Oprah Winfrey, has type 2 diabetes. He's the winner of two James Beard Awards and founder of Common Threads, which teaches healthful cooking to low-income kids.

Hope S. Warshaw, M.S., RD, CDE, BC-ADM, is a writer specializing in diabetes care. She has authored several American Diabetes Association books and is the 2015 president-elect of the American Association of Diabetes Educators.

John Zrebiec, M.S.W., CDE, is director of Behavioral Health Services at the Joslin Diabetes Center in Boston and a lecturer in the department of psychiatry at Harvard Medical School.

BEAT DIABETES

Your doctor just told you that you have prediabetes or diabetes. Now what? Don't panic. Both are conditions you can do something about. Take the diagnosis seriously and figure out what you're facing in terms of overall health—diet, exercise, and other lifestyle changes. Then take control. Adopt some new habits that will help you lose weight and improve your health.

MY NUMBER ONE GOAL

Take charge of my health and well-being.

> " Diabetes runs in my family. I've seen its damage. I had gestational diabetes with my fourth pregnancy and was well aware of my risks. "

KAREN BIRKENHOLZ | age 50

Karen, a medical technologist, enrolled in a yearlong diabetes prevention program offered at the hospital where she works. Goal one was to lose weight and her begrudging attitude about regular exercise and healthy eating. That she did. Karen lost 40 pounds, which she's keeping off. She takes no diabetes-related medications.

Kick-start into action: "I don't know what I dreaded more, dieting or walking. To fit exercise in, I ate lunch, then went directly to the hospital gym and the treadmill with my Kindle in hand. I've grown to like exercise and find it relaxing." Plotting her weight in class and seeing the steady decline was encouraging. And she learned realistic weight control strategies, like enjoying a few bites of dessert rather than just saying no.

Words of wisdom: "Planning is paramount. I do much better if I plan. Change how you define dieting. For me it had a start and an end. Now I'm choosing to eat healthfully, which includes eating more fruits and vegetables. Assemble your cheerleaders and keep them close by."

NOW IS THE TIME

To slow the progression of prediabetes and type 2 diabetes, don't wait or hesitate. **Act now.** There's good reason to start taking your prediabetes or type 2 diabetes more seriously and to make changes today. The research behind this urgent call to action is snowballing based on findings from lengthy diabetes research studies conducted around the globe.

FOR PEOPLE WITH PREDIABETES

Prediabetes means your blood sugar is higher than normal but not high enough to be classified as type 2 diabetes. You can significantly slow your progression to type 2 diabetes. The 15-year results of the Diabetes Prevention Program Outcome Study (DPPOS) conducted with people at high risk for or with prediabetes showed the group that made intensive lifestyle changes had a 27 percent lower rate of progression to type 2 diabetes compared with people who received just basic education. The intensive group was encouraged to eat less fat and calories, exercise at least 150 minutes each week, lose at least 5 percent of their initial weight, and get regular assistance from behavioral counselors. Comparatively, participants who took the insulin-sensitizing medication metformin and were provided with basic education decreased their risk of type 2 diabetes by 17 percent.

Additionally, participants in the intensive lifestyle group continue to have lower average glucose, lower blood pressure, and improved blood lipids, all while taking fewer medications.

"These studies show us it's never too early in prediabetes and type 2 diabetes to start living a healthy lifestyle and to practice it for the long haul," says Sam Dagogo-Jack, M.D., professor and chief of the diabetes division at the University of Tennessee Health Sciences Center in Memphis. "The Diabetes Prevention Program Outcome Study also proved that people of all races benefit the same," he says.

> "These studies show us it's never too early in prediabetes and type 2 diabetes to **start living a healthy lifestyle** and to practice it for the long haul."
>
> — Sam Dagogo-Jack, M.D. and professor

STRESS-BUSTING strategies

Need some help calming your mind and taming your tension? As you get better at managing stress, you may notice a happy side effect. Napora says, "You'll have greater confidence and self-esteem just knowing that you're prepared to face any situation more calmly." These strategies can help you stress less with diabetes:

TAKE A CLASS

Take a diabetes education class. "This is a disease that may require multiple lifestyle changes and a complex medication regimen," Goebel-Fabbri says. If you develop a complication, such as heart disease or foot problems, that only adds to the challenges. Gaining knowledge and skills to manage your condition helps you feel more in control and less overwhelmed.

MOVE A MUSCLE

Get moving. Take a walk, ride your bike, practice yoga, or hit the gym. "Exercise has a dual benefit," Walters says. "It helps reduce your emotional stress while it helps lower your blood sugar."

MAKE TIME EVERY DAY

Make time every day for R&R. Listen to music, call a friend, play with your pet, or lose yourself in a good book. "Doing something healthy and relaxing helps take your mind off a stressful situation," Walters says.

JOIN A SUPPORT GROUP

Participate in a diabetes support group. Or check out the American Diabetes Association's online message boards at *community.diabetes.org*. "It can be very comforting to know that you're not the only one with a particular problem and then to hear how someone else solved it," Napora says.

LIVE IN THE MOMENT

Mindfulness involves focusing on your experiences as they unfold. The idea is to become fully aware of what you're feeling, thinking, or doing in the present moment—and then to move on to the next moment. This helps you avoid getting stuck on a discouraging thought or reaching automatically for a doughnut after a bad day. In one study, people with diabetes who participated in a mindfulness group for eight weeks were less stressed, depressed, and anxious than those who didn't take part.

MIND YOUR THOUGHTS

If you have an upsetting thought about diabetes, ask yourself whether it's completely accurate—if not, try restating it in more accurate terms. For example, Walters says that some people jump straight from the fact that they have diabetes to the thought that they will go blind or lose a leg. A more accurate restatement is "Yes, these are possible long-term complications, but I can take care of myself to prevent them."

TAKE DEEP BREATHS

"Imagine yourself blowing bubbles," Walters says. "Take a big deep breath in through your nose. Then let it out slowly through your mouth like you would when using a bubble wand."

PUT IT IN PERSPECTIVE

Walters' advice: "Ask yourself, 'How big of a deal is this event that has me feeling so stressed? Does it really warrant my reaction?'" She suggests rating both the size of the threat and the amount of your stress on a scale from 1 (the least) to 10 (the most) and then comparing the numbers. For example, imagine that you're driving home from shopping or work. If getting home a few minutes later won't make a big difference (threat rating 2), but you still find yourself fuming at the slow traffic (stress rating 7), noting the discrepancy may help you dial back your response to a more appropriate level.

VISUALIZE TRANQUILTY

When you can, take a 5- to 10-minute mental vacation from everyday life. "Imagine yourself in a place you find very calming," Walters says. "Engage all your senses, imagining the sights, sounds, smells, tastes, and textures of the experience." Kick back and enjoy!

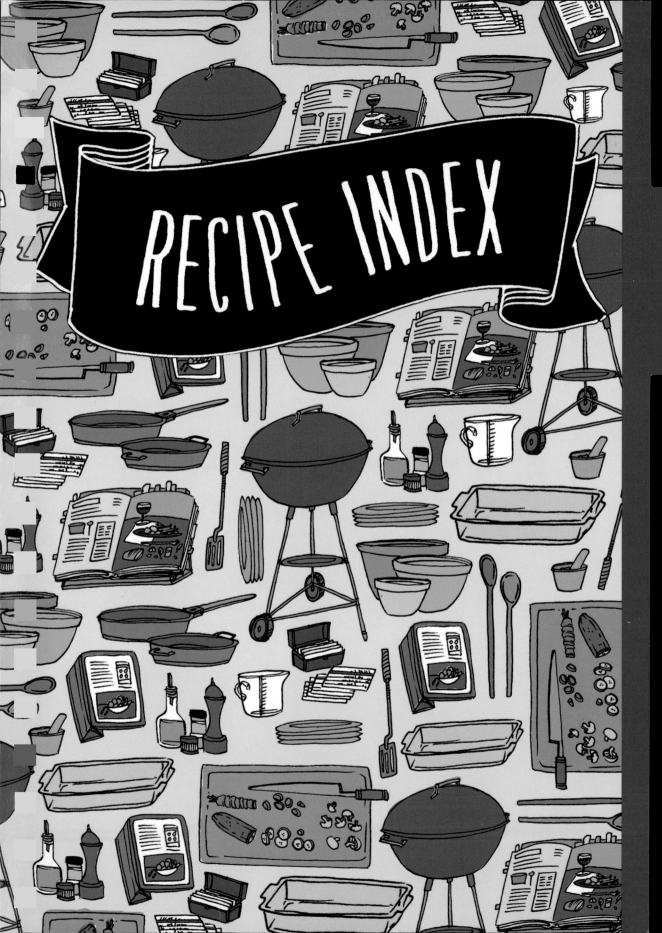

RECIPE INDEX

> " My husband bought me a high-end food scale. I weigh and measure everything to keep me honest. "

TRISH MYERS | age 75

Trish remembers being duly warned about diabetes by her physician, but she didn't take action. "The pounds crept on over the years, especially during a very trying time in my life when I went through a messy divorce. I used food, baked sweets, and bread for comfort." Trish gained 50 pounds and her A1C hit 6.6% before she was diagnosed with type 2 diabetes.

Kick-start into action: The lightbulb went off for Trish when her physician showed her on his computer how her A1C numbers had escalated. Happily remarried and active again, Trish got to work losing weight and changing her eating and exercise habits. She and her husband began dining out less, walking more, and giving Segway tours at a tourist park in her hometown.

Words of wisdom: "Discover what motivates you. For me, it's my six beautiful grandchildren. I want to watch them grow up and be a positive role model for them."

A

Alfredo-Sauced Chicken, 228
Almonds
Almond-Chocolate Banana
Smoothie, 129 GF
Brussels Sprouts with Spicy
Ginger-Soy Almonds, 306
Cocoa-Almond French Toast, 40
Cranberry-Almond Cereal
Mix, 30
Fish Amandine, 274
Moroccan Vegetable Quinoa
with Golden Raisins and
Almonds, 184 GF
Amaranth
Curried Sweet Potato and
Amaranth Soup, 114
Pork Stew with Amaranth Biscuit
Topper, 112 GF
Apples
Barley Waldorf Salad, 119
Curried Chicken Salad, 232
Ham and Double Swiss
Salad, 142
Lean & Green Smoothie, 127 GF
Pretzel-Pistachio-Crusted Tofu
Salad, 156
Seared Tuna with Fennel-Apple
Slaw, 155
Warm Pear-Apple Cider, 51 GF
Applesauce Pops, Fruity, 336, GF
Apricot-Chipotle Grilled Pork
Tenderloin and Zucchini, 218
Artichokes
Artichoke Flatbreads with
Spinach, Parmesan, and
Lemon, 187
Chicken and Artichoke Spinach
Salad, 143 GF
Creamy Spinach and Artichoke
Chicken, 178
Arugula
Fish with White Wine, Lemon,
and Capers, 296
Skewered Shrimp and Tomato
Linguine, 174
Asparagus
Asparagus-Snap Pea Stir-Fry,
299
Asparagus with Creamy Herb-
Garlic Topper, 302 GF
Cauliflower-Watercress Salad
with Dill-Shallot Dressing,
158 GF
Roasted Asparagus, 308 GF
Vegetarian Fried Rice, 287
Avocados
Chicken-Avocado BLT Wrap, 140
Creamy Avocado-Horseradish
Dip, 330 GF
Creamy Green Smoothies,
131 GF
Hummus and Avocado Salad
Sandwiches, 272

Shrimp Tacos with Avocado
Topper, 238 GF
Skinny Guacamole, 239 GF

B

Bacon
Bacon-Orange Breakfast
Toasts, 27
Bacon-Wrapped Turkey Meatball
and Cabbage Salad, 158
BLT Salad, 63
Chicken Avocado BLT Wrap, 140
Crispy Chicken Bacon
Sandwiches, 102
Vegetable, Bacon, and Quinoa
Quiche, 96 GF
Baked Cavatelli, 228
Balsamic Roasted Chicken and
Squash, 68
Bananas
Almond-Chocolate Banana
Smoothies, 129 GF
Cherry-Berry Banana
Smoothies, 127 GF
Coconut-Orange Banana Blast
Smoothies, 131 GF
Peanut Butter Banana Breakfast
Sandwich, 37
Barbecue-Sauced Pork
Sandwiches, 291
Barbecue-Spiced Roasted
Chickpeas, 331 GF
Barley
Barley Waldorf Salad, 119
Cranberry-Almond Cereal
Mix, 30
Curried Chicken, Barley, and
Vegetables, 118
Italian Beef and Barley Cups, 117
Basil
Creamy Basil-Rosemary Chicken
and Rice, 111
Pizza Margherita, 225
Quinoa Salad, 99 GF
BBQ Chicken and Roasted Corn
Salad, 157
Beans. *See also* Edamame; Green
beans; Lentils
Barbecue-Spiced Roasted
Chickpeas, 331 GF
Basil Quinoa Salad, 99 GF
BBQ Chicken and Roasted Corn
Salad, 157
Beef and Bean Linguine with
Mint-Walnut Gremolata, 294
Chili-Lime Chicken Tostada with
Pico de Gallo and Chipotle
Crema, 240
Chili Verde with White Beans,
261 GF

Curried Sweet Potato and
Amaranth Soup, 115
Falafel and Vegetable Pitas, 183
Meatless Taco Salad, 135 GF
Mexican Rice and Bean
Patties, 109
Potato and Brussels Sprouts
Salad with Lemon-Honey
Vinaigrette, 159 GF
Pumpkin-Chicken Enchiladas,
236
Salad Tacos, 198 GF
Slow-Cooked Refried Beans,
262 GF
Southwest Breakfast
Quesadilla, 35
Spicy Sweet Potato and Pork
Salad, 157 GF
Beef
Beef and Bean Linguine with
Mint-Walnut Gremolata, 294
Beef and Blue Wrap, 140
Beef and Broccoli Noodles, 221
Beef-and-Vegetable Stir-Fry, 212
Beef Burgundy, 226
Beef Rigatoni Stew, 248
Beer-Braised Pot Roast with
Parsnips and Carrots, 248
Bolognese-Sauced Potatoes,
318 GF
Classic Beef Stroganoff, 251
Dijon Beef Stew, 174
Grilled Flank Steak and Romaine
Salad with Beets, 170
Italian Beef and Barley Cups, 117
Korean-Style Beef Tacos, 252
Loaded Nachos, 237
Open-Face French Onion Soup
Burgers, 317
Open-Face Reubens, 235
Porter and Roasted Red Pepper
Sloppy Joes, 255
Southwest Meat Loaf, 211 GF
Spicy Beef Cabbage Rolls, 279
Steak and Chimichurri Salad, 155
Steak and Mushroom Pizzas, 169
Steak and Mushrooms with
Parsley Mashed Potatoes, 60
Steak with Watercress
Pesto, 75 GF
Vietnamese-Style Beef and
Noodle Bowls, 222
Zesty Meat Sauce with Spaghetti
Squash, 294 GF
Beer-Braised Pot Roast with
Parsnips and Carrots, 248
Beets
Fresh Slaw, 75 GF
Goat Cheese and Beet
Flatbread, 272
Grilled Flank Steak and Romaine
Salad with Beets, 170

continued

P

V

W – Z

METRIC INFORMATION

PRODUCT DIFFERENCES

Most of the ingredients called for in the recipes in this book are available in most countries. However, some are known by different names. Here are some common American ingredients and their possible counterparts:

* Sugar (white) is granulated, fine granulated, or castor sugar.
* Powdered sugar is icing sugar.
* All-purpose flour is enriched, bleached or unbleached white household flour. When self-rising flour is used in place of all-purpose flour in a recipe that calls for leavening, omit the leavening agent (baking soda or baking powder) and salt.
* Light-color corn syrup is golden syrup.
* Cornstarch is cornflour.
* Baking soda is bicarbonate of soda.
* Vanilla or vanilla extract is vanilla essence.
* Green, red, or yellow sweet peppers are capsicums or bell peppers.
* Golden raisins are sultanas.

VOLUME and WEIGHT

The United States traditionally uses cup measures for liquid and solid ingredients. The chart below shows the approximate imperial and metric equivalents. If you are accustomed to weighing solid ingredients, the following approximate equivalents will be helpful.

* 1 cup butter, castor sugar, or rice = 8 ounces = ½ pound = 250 grams
* 1 cup flour = 4 ounces = ¼ pound = 125 grams
* 1 cup icing sugar = 5 ounces = 150 grams
* Canadian and U.S. volume for a cup measure is 8 fluid ounces (237 ml), but the standard metric equivalent is 250 ml.
* 1 British imperial cup is 10 fluid ounces.
* In Australia, 1 tablespoon equals 20 ml, and there are 4 teaspoons in the Australian tablespoon.
* Spoon measures are used for smaller amounts of ingredients. Although the size of the tablespoon varies slightly in different countries, for practical purposes and for recipes in this book, a straight substitution is all that's necessary. Measurements made using cups or spoons always should be level unless stated otherwise.

Common Weight Range Replacements

Imperial / U.S.	Metric
½ ounce	15 g
1 ounce	25 g or 30 g
4 ounces (¼ pound)	115 g or 125 g
8 ounces (½ pound)	225 g or 250 g
16 ounces (1 pound)	450 g or 500 g
1¼ pounds	625 g
1½ pounds	750 g
2 pounds or 2¼ pounds	1,000 g or 1 Kg

Oven Temperature Equivalents

Fahrenheit Setting		Gas Setting
300°F	150°C	Gas Mark 2 (very low)
325°F	160°C	Gas Mark 3 (low)
350°F	180°C	Gas Mark 4 (moderate)
375°F	190°C	Gas Mark 5 (moderate)
400°F	200°C	Gas Mark 6 (hot)
425°F	220°C	Gas Mark 7 (hot)
450°F	230°C	Gas Mark 8 (very hot)
475°F	240°C	Gas Mark 9 (very hot)
500°F	260°C	Gas Mark 10 (extremely hot)
Broil	Broil	Grill

Electric and gas ovens may be calibrated using celsius. However, for an electric oven, increase celsius setting 10 to 20 degrees when cooking above 160°C. For convection or forced air ovens (gas or electric), lower the temperature setting 25°F/10°C when cooking at all heat levels.

Baking Pan Sizes

Imperial / U.S.	Metric
9×1½-inch round cake pan	22- or 23×4-cm (1.5 L)
9×1½-inch pie plate	22- or 23×4-cm (1 L)
8×8×2-inch square cake pan	20×5-cm (2 L)
9×9×2-inch square cake pan	22- or 23×4.5-cm (2.5 L)
11×7×1½-inch baking pan	28×17×4-cm (2 L)
2-quart rectangular baking pan	30×19×4.5-cm (3 L)
13×9×2-inch baking pan	34×22×4.5-cm (3.5 L)
15×10×1-inch jelly roll pan	40×25×2-cm
9×5×3-inch loaf pan	23×13×8-cm (2 L)
2-quart casserole	2 L

U.S. / Standard Metric Equivalents

⅛ teaspoon = 0.5 ml	
¼ teaspoon = 1 ml	
½ teaspoon = 2 ml	
1 teaspoon = 5 ml	
1 tablespoon = 15 ml	
2 tablespoons = 25 ml	
¼ cup = 2 fluid ounces = 50 ml	
⅓ cup = 3 fluid ounces = 75 ml	
½ cup = 4 fluid ounces = 125 ml	
⅔ cup = 5 fluid ounces = 150 ml	
¾ cup = 6 fluid ounces = 175 ml	
1 cup = 8 fluid ounces = 250 ml	
2 cups = 1 pint = 500 ml	
1 quart = 1 litre	